SIR CHARLES ARDEN-CLARKE

Sir Charles Arden-Clarke

DAVID ROONEY

1982
REX COLLINGS
LONDON

First published in Great Britain by
Rex Collings Ltd
6 Paddington Street, London W1

© David Rooney 1982

ISBN 086036   157   8

Typesetting by Malvern Printers
Printed by Grijelmo, S. A. Spain

Contents

Contents

To
Mike Graves

Introduction

I wish to acknowledge with gratitude the help and encouragement I have received from many people; Dorothy Wilkinson, who first put me in touch with Lady Arden-Clarke and suggested that I write this book; to Lady Arden-Clarke and her family who allowed me to use the Arden-Clarke Papers; to Sir George Sinclair who backed my project so enthusiastically; to Richard Rathbone whose excellent historical work on this period was generously put at my disposal; to the British Academy for an Overseas Travelling Fellowship which made it possible for me to visit Ghana and conduct my research there; to George and Dorothy Amuah, and Jimmy and Rachel Phillips for their hospitality and generosity during my visit to Ghana; to my wife whose links with Achimota since 1946 made all this possible.

My own links with Ghana started in Bombay in 1945 when I volunteered to serve with the Gold Coast regiment. Shortly after, I arrived at Takoradi, and I had the good fortune to serve in Tamale, Wa and then Accra 1946–7. After demobilization I read History at Oxford and specialized in Colonial History under Professor Vincent Harlow and Freddie Madden. At this time—the early 1950s—Arden-Clarke appeared to me to be the giant on the Colonial stage with his brilliant achievements in Ghana. After teaching in Ulster I re-established my Ghanaian contacts when, on the staff at the RMA Sandhurst, I ran a Special African Course, and this included many Ghanaian cadets. In 1975, again through our Achimota links, I was given the opportunity to write the biography of Sir Charles Arden-Clarke—a challenge I felt both proud and delighted to undertake.

Finally I am grateful to Sir George Sinclair, John Codrington and George Levack—former colleagues of Arden-Clarke—who kindly gave their time to read the manuscript and gave invaluable advice; to Mrs Eileen Cole of Swavesey for her patient and accurate typing; but, after all the help I have received, the responsibility for any mistakes is solely mine.

DAVID ROONEY

NIGERIA

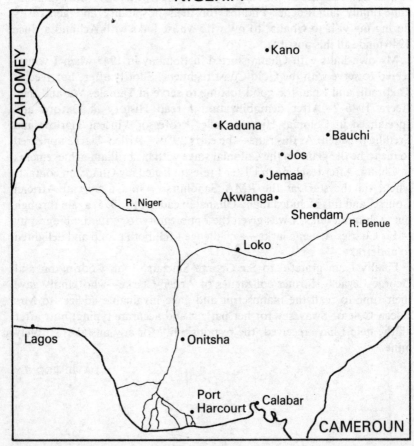

BECHUANALAND

Caprivi Strip

RHODESIA

SOUTH
WEST
AFRICA

Okavango
Swamp

• Maun

L. Ngami

Bosoli •
Francistown •

L. Dow

• Khanzi

Serowe
•

• Kalkfontein

Palapye•

Kalahari
Desert

BECHUANALAND

Molepolole
•

S. AFRICA

Gaberones •

Pretoria
•

• Mafeking

SOUTH AFRICA

Johannesburg
•

• Kuruman

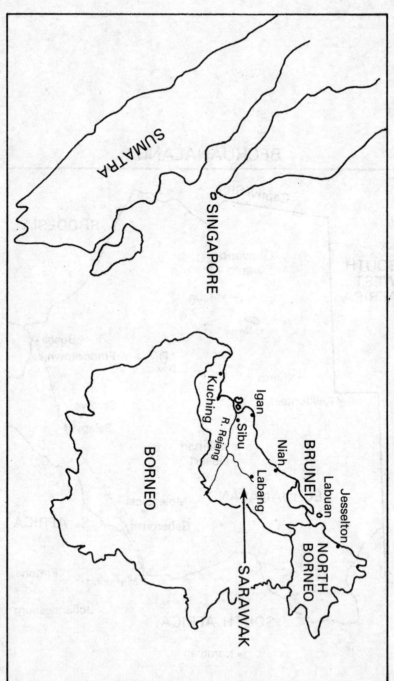

SARAWAK AND BORNEO

SUMATRA

SINGAPORE

BORNEO

Kuching
R. Rejang
Sibu
Igan
Niah
Labang
BRUNEI
Labuan
Jesselton
NORTH BORNEO
SARAWAK

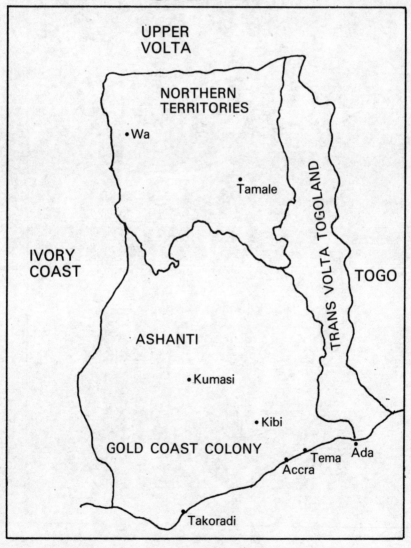

GHANA 1950

UPPER VOLTA

NORTHERN TERRITORIES

•Wa

•Tamale

IVORY COAST

TRANS VOLTA TOGOLAND

TOGO

ASHANTI

•Kumasi

•Kibi

GOLD COAST COLONY

•Tema

•Ada

•Accra

•Takoradi

CHAPTER ONE
Colonial Cadet: Nigeria

After his retirement as Governor-General of the newly independent Ghana in 1957, Sir Charles Arden-Clarke collected together his papers for a book which was never written. He planned to start his memoirs with a quotation from Lord Hailey, who spoke at the Royal African Society on the occasion of his ninetieth birthday.

> I am convinced that we should never apologize for the past of the Colonial Empire. I would no sooner think of apologizing to posterity in that connection than of apologizing when I meet my Maker (as soon I must) for having spent some of the best years of my life in India and, afterwards, those equally enjoyable years trying to describe the work of that gallant company, who sought to plant civilization in Africa.[1]

As Governor of the Gold Coast, from 1949 until it gained independence, Arden-Clarke filled with great distinction one of the most critical roles in the post-war history of Africa. The world had witnessed the upheavals and independence of India, Pakistan and Ceylon, but few saw this as having any immediate relevance to Africa. Few realized the latent excitement and the power of the nationalism, sparked off by the example of India, which fermented below the apparent calm of West Africa. Arden-Clarke, posted against his strong protests, from Sarawak, where he had re-established the country after the Japanese withdrawal, arrived in Accra in August 1949. Here for the next eight years he held to his difficult and lonely path, resisting the pressures of the wilder elements of the Convention Peoples Party, resisting the old guard of Gold Coast lawyers like Danquah, who signally failed to play the new political game, resisting his fellow Governors, who thought they had 20 years to play with, and resisting Whitehall and the Tory Colonial Office which looked askance at the pace of his policies. With massive integrity, he held to his aim with bluff and realistic good humour, recognizing, as few did, the reality of African power, and through this, creating a respect and confidence without which the whole noble project could easily have failed.

His early experience as a District Officer in Nigeria was not perhaps

[1] *African Affairs* 1962.

the ideal training for guiding the first African colony to political independence. Of his pre-war service he later wrote:

> The ultimate object of our policy was clear enough: to achieve the transfer of our power to the indigenous people, and the independence of the country, but there were few, if any, of us who believed that this objective would be achieved in our own time. Certainly if anyone had told me at any time before World War II that I would see in my working lifetime, one of our African British Colonies achieving its independence and standing on its own feet as a recognized national entity in the comity of nations, I would have scoffed . . . We felt we had all the time in the world in which to work towards our objective, and that there would still be work of this kind to be done by our successors in office long after we had retired.[2]

On the other hand a young District Officer had to face the unexpected, to take serious responsibilities and critical decisions, usually on his own, often isolated and under extreme pressure, and always in the knowledge that if it was the wrong decision he, alone, would be there to face the consequences.

Born in 1898, the second of four sons of a CMS Missionary, who had retired from India in 1914, Arden-Clarke had attended Rossall School. He left school in April 1917, enlisted in the Army and received a commission in the Machine Gun Corps. Posted to France early in 1918 he took part in the fighting in France and Flanders, and was wounded and gassed when his battalion was in action near Wimereux. After convalescence he joined the Army of occupation at Bad Godesberg on the Rhine. During this period he was billetted on a German family. The daughter of the family, Else, suffered from an appallingly unhappy marriage, and Arden-Clarke in a romantic and chivalrous gesture had even offered to take her to England. Soon after he had made this offer, he heard a senior officer in the regimental mess, making extremely derogatory remarks about the lady, so Arden-Clarke, who had been his Divisional heavy weight boxing champion, took the major by the scruff of his neck, bundled him outside the Mess and beat him up. For this he could clearly have been court-martialled, although among his fellow officers—probably familiar with the sentiments of the song 'When a ladies name is mentioned in the Mess'—there was considerable sympathy for him. Fortunately for him the Colonel handled the matter wisely. Arden-Clarke received the biggest dressing down of his life and was posted to Russia the next day. There he was attached to the British Military Mission serving with the White Russian Commander General Denikin, and helped to train the Don Cossacks as machine gunners.

---

[2] Unpublished MS, p. 137—page refs given elsewhere

Sir Charles Arden-Clarke

Sir Charles with a Dyak Chief in Sarawak

A Chief greeting the Governor at a Durbar in the Gold Coast

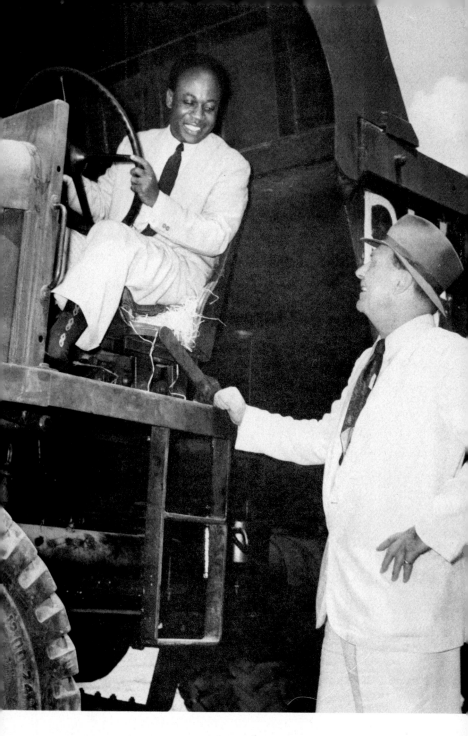

Dr Kwame Nkrumah, then Prime Minister, with the Governor at the initiation of Tema Harbour Construction Works in February 1955

Demobilized in 1920, he faced a grim prospect. At Rossall he had intended to read medicine, but at the age of 22 he felt he could hardly ask his father to keep him for a further five or six years. He had been born in India, but his family all advised him against the Indian Civil Service as a career. He wrote:

At the end of my gratuity, I could always fall back, as a temporary modus vivendi, on the Black and Tans, then anxiously seeking trained machine gunners, and I also had a pressing offer from my former Army Boxing Instructor, recently demobilized, to join the ranks of professional boxers. Fortunately, I was accepted for the Colonial Service shortly before my gratuity ran out and there was no need for me to consider the rather depressing alternative with which I had faced myself.[3]

His school, Rossall, played an important part in this decision. As a boy Arden-Clarke had admired the career and achievements of an old Rossallian, Lord Lugard, the great pioneer of Indirect Rule in Africa, who had established British control over the whole of Northern Nigeria with a staff of less than one hundred. His imagination fired by this example, and attracted by the possibility of carrying out real pioneer work in West Africa, he rejected ideas of a career in the Church,[4] or of taking up the offer of a scholarship in classics at Emmanuel College Cambridge, and decided on the Colonial Service.

After a perfunctory interview, in which the interviewing officer, who had to hurry off to another meeting, merely handed over a batch of forms to be filled in, Arden-Clarke accepted a place on the three month African Tropical Service Course in London. The cadets received what they considered the totally inadequate allowance of £20 per month, and, after the course, with considerable relief Arden-Clarke set sail for Nigeria, arriving in Lagos on 29 December 1920.

Having landed at Lagos he took the train to Zaria with a friend, Thompstone.[5] Sitting in the train at Zaria he wrote his first letter home:

My Darlings, There will just be time for this to catch the home mail. I am sitting in the boat train . . . waiting at Zaria. I sleep the night in the train and tomorrow there is a train down the branch line to Bukuru. My plans are to get off at Jos, where some forty carriers will be waiting for me, and trek with Thompstone to Jemaa. Jemaa is the capital of the Nassarawa province and the Residents HQ are there. I'll

---

[3] Unpublished MS, p. 6.
[4] In a final school report the Headmaster of Rossall suggested that the boy might well go into the Church—a remark which later caused some surprise among the Arden-Clarke family.
[5] Later Sir Eric Thompstone, Lt Governor of Northern Nigeria 1951–2.

probably be stuck in an office and told to work there.[6]

He went on to describe his arrival in Lagos with his friend Thompstone:

He is easy going, is a pukka sahib, and has a sense of humour. The result is that both of us spend most of our time laughing at all the accidents that occur, much to the annoyance of those people who are everlastingly getting flustered and losing their tempers.

At Lagos he had been initiated into another aspect of the Colonial Service. He and Thompstone had been invited to lunch at Government House.

We had lunch with Sir Hugh and Lady Clifford. They are delightful people—very kind and homely and immediately put one at one's ease. Government House itself is a palatial residence and delightfully cool and comfortable. I wouldn't mind having a five year tour out here if I lived in a place like that and fed as they do . . . It was awfully kind of the Governor to think of having us up for meals with him and for putting a car at our disposal. Apparently he always does that with young officials who are going north. Both he and Lady Clifford were kindness itself and made you feel absolutely at home. All the same I should think he would be a nasty fellow when he was annoyed. I am not hankering to be told off by him about anything.

He left the train after Jos and trekked to Jemaa with 40 carriers and his 'boy', called Sugar. Jemaa, though a Provincial Headquarters, was really just a bush station, with no motor roads, and three days trek from Jos. Jos on the 4,000 ft Bauchi plateau, which he compared to the Russian steppe, was both a mining and railway centre, but the route to Jemaa led down from the treeless plateau by a precipitous track to uneven savannah or orchard bush, interspersed with stretches of thick tropical forest along the water courses.

The trek to Jemaa went through the territory of the Bauchi Highland pagans, who wore a bunch of leaves on their bottom, painted their legs a bright red, and had tribal marks on their faces. The area also contained settlements of the Hausa people and also the fairer skinned Fulani who were great cattle traders and had been notorious for their slaving activities until, some 20 years before, Lugard put a stop to their worst depredations. Arden-Clarke described the trek:

We got started about 8 a.m. having had brekker and packed up. We had an enormous cavalcade. There were 98 carriers, two government Messengers who act as N.C.O.'s to the carriers, three policemen, three

[6] Letter to Family 19.1.21. Arden-Clarke wrote regular letters home, and throughout all his service his mother preserved them meticulously. They are an invaluable source of information on his early years in Nigeria, and give a vivid and colourful description of the life of a young district officer.

servants, two grooms, three horses and our two selves. The way we trekked was to send the carriers along ahead of us and follow behind at any distance we liked. T. had his horse and a horse had been sent up for me but I did not ride as we could only go at a walk the whole time and I hate lolling about on a horse's back doing nothing. At each village the village Chief or King comes out and bows down and pays his respects. They are awfully meticulous about saluting. Every native one meets kicks off his sandals, if he happens to be wearing any, gets off the path, gets down on his haunches and touches the ground with his right hand or both hands, at the same time murmuring 'Zaiki' or 'O Lion'. If he is feeling very respectful he says 'O Lion King of the World'. Sometimes we passed through a village market place. Immediately everyone gets down and a great sigh of 'Zaiki' goes up to the heavens. Altogether it gives one a magnified idea of one's own importance in the scheme of creation,—which is however counterbalanced when one starts taking over the new job and finds one knows nothing at all about anything.

Having arrived at Jemaa, Arden-Clarke was put in charge of the Resident's Provincial Office—a fairly normal procedure to teach a cadet the basic office routine. He recorded how he was hopelessly at sea on all aspects of office routine and accounting, but was initiated into the mysteries by an African clerk from the Gold Coast, Mr Mends. Thirty years later as Governor of the Gold Coast he sought out Mr Mends and thanked him for teaching him so effectively.

To run the Provincial Office may have sounded a simple enough assignment, but the young Arden-Clarke found himself also in charge of the police and prisons, because of the absence through illness of the Police Commissioner, in charge of the district when the District Officer was on trek, in charge of the Public Works Department and responsible for the construction and maintenance of roads and bridges, as well as being a Magistrate.

Soon after arriving in Jemaa he described a typical day:

A more or less normal day will probably run something like this. From 6.30–7.30 a.m. I'll prowl about in the bush with my gun or go for a ride or take some form of exercise. Brekker at 7.30 a.m. and office hours are from 8 a.m.–2 p.m. Then comes lunch at 2 p.m. and a bit of a rest until 4 p.m. Then a cup of tea and perhaps a Hausa lesson with one of my 'boys', a game of tennis at 5.30 p.m. and after tennis we take it in turns to go to each others houses and have drinks and small chop. Dinner from 8–8.30 p.m. and after dinner bed . . .

The great thing I long for in this country is someone to look after my domestic arrangements. These African boys are the outside edge, dirty, slack, and born thieves. Running one's own house is a perpetual undercurrent of worry. They all have a wonderful knack of breaking all one's most useful possessions. My steward boy, ebon black and ugly as sin appeared rolling his eyes the other day and presented the fragments of a plate with the excuse 'I go wash him sah and he go break in pieces in my hands sah. I think this clockerly very bad sah; you go buy good set sah'. Then he grinned all over his face. I should have cursed him, but instead burst into a roar of laughter at the effrontery of the brute. It's a wonderful life.'[7]

Soon after his arrival at Jemaa and while he still had responsibility for the police and the Public Works Department, he had to build a bridge—an incident which illustrated many aspects of colonial rule. The bridge had to span a river bed which went through the station and was dry for much of the year, but a raging torrent in the wet season. No money had been allotted for the project, but he had a Hausa Sergeant Major of Police and a squad of convicts available for labour, equipped with machetes, shovels, a saw and hammer. Logs had to be cut from the bush and carried in on the heads of the convicts, as was five tons of stone.[8] The chief problem was the lack of nails and staples to secure the heavy logs, but he got a number of old pick-axes melted down by the local blacksmith. They proudly finished the bridge just before the rains, and a real engineer inspected it and even approved it for motor traffic. Since there were neither roads nor motor vehicles in the area this seemed fairly safe. They solved the final problem of how to pay the blacksmith by using convicts to collect a good crop of mangoes from the station roads, and by selling the fruit to the market women.

Soon after this the Resident and his wife returned to the station, and young Arden-Clarke took 'Mrs Resident' down to see the bridge. He was proudly showing her the girders when he felt a series of bites up his leg and realized he had been standing on a column of black soldier ants. Too shy to take off his trousers in front of her he simply rushed back to his bungalow. Shortly after, the Resident retrieved his wife and they came to commiserate with the victim, sitting in his tin bath.

The majority of his Public Works responsibilities centred on making bricks; building houses and thatching them; and farming, but most of his time and energy were concentrated on police and magistrate's duties. Purists might object to one man being police, prosecutor and magistrate, but the rough justice meted out seemed to satisfy the people and saved them from getting into the hands of lawyers demanding fat fees. As a magistrate his powers were limited to a £25 fine and three months im-

---

[7] Letter to Family 24.2.21.
[8] Lugard's system in Nigeria included both flogging and hard labour. He caused an outcry from the humanitarians but retorted that he had better things to do with his meagre revenue than to build prisons. By 1920 flogging was no longer a legal punishment.

prisonment. Even the gaol provided lighter moments—one prisoner, formerly a mason, suggested how the doors could be strengthened so that the prisoners could not all run away, and another after serving a year's hard labour asked for and received a testimonial. The District Officer had to witness when a prisoner was flogged, but Arden-Clarke felt less than happy at the idea of hanging. He wrote:

My only dread is that some silly idiot may get condemned to death for murder, in which case it will be my job to hang him. I'm hoping a proper police officer will turn up before I am let in for anything like that.

On another occasion he tried a man for possessing stolen property including a large bunch of keys. The man explained that he used the keys when he went to steal from a white man, but added 'No Sir, I no be thief man, I be good man'.

Lugard established as an essential part of his whole system, close cooperation in both administration and law, between the authority of the Resident or District Officer on the one hand and the Chief's or Emir's court on the other, and, many cases, especially those involving matrimonial affairs were handed to the Emir's court.

Like many District Officers at that time, Arden-Clarke had to build his own accommodation. This consisted of two circular huts, diameter 22 feet, with conical thatched roofs, and a covered passage-way between the huts. There were open rectangles for door and windows, with guinea corn blinds for use in storms. The huts were built of sun dried bricks and the beaten earth floor was treated with egg-plant and had a smooth and pleasant black surface. One served as bedroom and bathroom, the other as the living room, furnished with camp table, chairs, bed and boxes, with a few local rugs. While building his house he heard from home of some financial difficulties, and wrote to apologize for not being able to help, because of the expense of moving into his house. He added 'I hate having vast masses of debts everlastingly hanging over my head. However, they will grow less in time I hope'; eloquent testimony to the modest salary paid to the dedicated young men who administered Britain's African possessions.[9]

In the 1920s the town of Jos developed fairly rapidly as a rail centre, and, because of the development which the railway created, as a mining centre. The building of the railway with its heavy demands for unskilled labour, created further problems for the local District Officers, who had to collect and deliver the money to pay the labourers. The expedition from Jemaa to collect money from Jos consisted of some 300 carriers with a police escort. On the three day journey back to Jemaa the huge

---

[9] Letter to Family 6.3.21.

expedition travelled along narrow bush and jungle paths, the mass of undisciplined carriers a constant problem for the police and the District Officer. At night he slept in the rest house with the boxes of money stacked beside him and a police guard outside.

Arden-Clarke was destined to spend many years with the backward Mama and Mada people, and one of his early expeditions from Jemaa took him into their territory and also taught him a valuable lesson. He had reported that two Mada men who had refused to pay taxes were 'caught tried and suitably dealt with before the assembled villagers'. The Lieutenant Governor had commented 'I hope this punishment was legal.' In fact the culprits had publicly been given 12 strokes with the cane, in best public school tradition, as a spectacular and effective punishment. By that time this type of punishment was illegal, though still widely used. His mistake was to report it officially.

In isolated stations like Jemaa, the incidence of sickness and disease among Europeans remained high, but the local people seemed to respond well to the relatively untutored attentions of the District Officer. Arden-Clarke wrote:

> I've been having quite an amusing time lately posing as a doctor. Quite a number of the prisoners have been getting ill, due to the arrival of the rains and the change of weather I suppose. Anyhow the complaints vary from opthalmia and guinea worm to fever and small pox. There are only two medicines in store—a bottle of liquid quinine and some cough mixture. I raked up out of my own kit a bottle of mouldy aspirin pills and some very ancient cough lozenges. So every morning you may see me wandering round with these four medicines, solemnly feeling the pulses of my patients, making them stick their tongues out, and taking their temperatures by laying my hand on their foreheads. I then prescribe a mouldy pill or cough lozenge to those that don't seem to be very bad; the worse cases get cough mixture or quinine or sometimes a mixture. One fellow, suffering from some complaint I couldn't diagnose, got a dose of quinine and cough mixture with half a mouldy aspirin powdered up inside it. He was better next day and my reputation as a doctor is now pretty considerable.[10]

The opportunity to carry out real pioneering work, in the tradition of Lugard, had been a major factor in Arden-Clarke's decision to seek a career in the Colonial Service, and when he arrived in Jemaa and heard of the Mada and Mama people, he was immediately attracted to the idea of taking charge of their district. The Madas, who were to be his first contact, lived in isolated hilly country, to which they had retreated during the worst days of slaving. They fought among themselves and

[10] Letter to Family 1.7.21.

with anyone from outside. In 1914 a prospector and a missionary who had entered their district had both been murdered and since then no European had been allowed in. During the war nothing had been done and even after 1918 a couple of perfunctory military patrols had achieved little. Now the railway to Jos had to pass through the area and it became increasingly urgent that these recalcitrant people were brought under control.

To his delight, Arden-Clarke, after six months in the country and at the age of 22, was posted to Akwanga to deal with the Madas and Mamas.[11] The Resident gave him sound advice: to use resource and initiative rather than frequent reference to higher authority; not to put too much down on paper; to enforce law and order because without that nothing else could be achieved; once order had been established to teach the people to run their own affairs and stand on their own feet. Finally, the resident said 'And remember this young man, if you go and get yourself killed, I shall never never forgive you'. Most young Colonial Service officers received frequent postings and were rarely able to identify with one particular area or people, and in this respect Arden-Clarke was fortunate in spending five years with the Mada and Mama people.

He set off for Akwanga, a huge retinue of carriers transporting all his possessions, and with a sum of 10 pounds to build his house and office when he arrived. Once again convict labour came to the rescue, together with some tax dodgers who commuted their taxes by a fortnight's work. Soon after his arrival at Akwanga, he had to set off again with a retinue of 80 local men, because the Lieutenant Governor had expressed the wish to see the Mada and Mama dancers on his visit to Loko on the Benue River. Arden-Clarke made severe criticism of this whole venture which took 80 men on a journey of 16 days to entertain the Lieutenant Governor for less than half an hour. During the journey both Madas and Mamas practised their full dress Ju Ju dances in front of Arden-Clarke, and he also described vividly how, when travelling through tsetse fly country, where he had to leave his horse behind, his bearers helped him across rivers.

One man carries me on his back; two more on either side lift up my legs when they hang too close to the water, one man goes in front as a guide looking out for holes; two more follow behind with a tight grip on my shirt ready to catch me if I happen to fall backwards. The rest of one's people stand on the banks and solemnly intone 'Hunkali, Hunkali Zaiki' meaning 'Carefully, Carefully O Lion'—the lion

[11] In a letter home he commented 'This looks to me to be a great chance. The thing is to make the most of it'.

meanwhile being quite helpless in the grip of six stalwart natives, unable to move hand or foot for himself.[12]

On the journey back from Loko he had to make a detour with his retinue to subdue, if possible without force, a village which had flouted all authority and had become a hideout for lawbreakers. He approached the village by canoe, arriving at dawn, with three armed Hausa police, an interpreter, and four local men to paddle. He found the local Ju Ju man in the centre of the village brewing some potion, surrounded by a tough looking bunch of supporters, and chanting a spell against the 'Juji' or Whiteman.[13]

He asked for the headman and two other ringleaders, but was told they were away hunting. He demanded that they should report within two hours, and then sat down to take his breakfast. The Ju Ju man continued his incantations, encouraging the people to attack the Whiteman and throw his body in the river. Arden-Clarke sensing a growing truculence among the people, got up, strode down and kicked over the pot of Ju Ju medicine. This proved a rash thing to do as the mob which outnumbered his party by 50 to one was also armed with guns, cutlasses and spears, but, in fact, the Ju Ju man slunk away. Shortly the village head and the ringleaders appeared and were arrested. Arden-Clarke explained that they would be taken away, and gave dire warnings to future law breakers. To a cacophony of hoots and yells he embarked on the canoe with the prisoners and police. At this critical moment the canoe stuck fast, the crowd edged noisily nearer and the Ju Ju man re-appeared demanding vengeance. The crowd on the bank grew more and more menacing and the police fixed bayonets. Then Arden-Clarke, remembering a story of how someone had quelled a mob by suddenly roaring with laughter, tried this trick. He gave a roar of apparently uncontrollable laughter, the mob drew back, and with a final heave the canoe shot out into the river and they paddled peacefully away. He reflected that orders to quell hostile villages without using force were more easily given than obeyed.

After the unnecessary interruption of the visit to Loko, he returned to Akwanga to take up the challenging task of pacifying the Madas. Their villages, perched on high hills, in ideal defensive positions, could only be approached on foot because the rough bush tracks were so steep. The Madas numbered about 200,000 and had a rudimentary clan organization with village Councils and headmen.

Reports of increasing violence and crime made it imperative to take some action. Recalling his brief from the Resident, he decided to make

---

[12] Letter to Family 6.8.21.
[13] A corruption of Judge—meaning the District Officer.

an initial friendly contact. He set out with four armed Hausa police for the first village. Before the group reached the village they discovered a wanted criminal, so one of the police was despatched to take him back to Akwanga. On the way the criminal tried to run off but the policeman shot and wounded him and eventually got him home. Arden-Clarke, now with only three police, a dangerously depleted group, went on to the village. They were accompanied by a Government Messenger who a few weeks before had been set upon in the village and crucified, only being rescued after dark by one or two friendly natives. When they reached the village most people had fled, so, there being no Rest House, they occupied an empty compound which could be easily defended. Eventually some old men approached. They were told to assemble the villagers and were promised that no arrests or punishment would be carried out. The old men said that their young men were drunk and truculent, and begged the party to leave. Arden-Clarke said he was determined to stay until the villagers returned. After dark the men appeared, drinking vast quantities of beer, but keeping their distance. They lacked the courage to attack, but shot a few poisoned arrows and also tried to burn down the compound by setting fire to the roof. The defenders deterred them by firing an occasional round, but no serious clash took place. In the morning some elders appeared and a further stiff warning was given to the village before the party left.

The next village, which had a feud with the first, gave the party a friendly welcome and gave details of the malefactors in the first village. The party spent four further days making friendly contacts with villages and their headmen, finding many that were peacefully inclined. The trek finished with another hostile village, which put in an attack while the party came down a precipitous slope, and Arden-Clarke, slipping down on his bottom, was sped on his way by a volley of poisoned arrows.

Soon after this relatively successful initial reconnaissance he wrote:

> I had to try and decide how best I could make decent citizens of these lawless and truculent people.[14]

He decided to build on the friendly contacts in the villages and to use, with patience and persistence, the technique of a friendly but firm approach with a small police patrol. This policy, approved from above, would be followed by the assessment and collection of taxes, by the building of Rest Houses at strategic points, and by opening up the area with improved communications. When the construction of the railway reached the area, the District Officer had the responsibility for providing a regular supply of labour.

[14] Unpublished MS p. 35.

The completion of assessment reports for the three Mada sub-districts gave a remarkable insight into the whole social and economic life of the people. The social structure depended on the family and clan, and it was often discovered that the wrong person had been suggested as Headman, in order to deceive the authorities. The assessment also included an estimate of the value of all livestock and crops, as well as the value of the products of the bush like wild honey, thatching grass and timber, and it showed that there was little variation in the overall poverty. These reports give invaluable information. Later, as Governor of the Gold Coast, Arden-Clarke regretted that similar reports, which gave information not only about the people but also about junior administrative staff, were not available, but, at the time, with all the wrath of the man in the field he wrote:

This report writing is a wicked shame. All headquarters really require to know are the figures of the tax and a few particulars as to how they were arrived at. Instead of this one is expected to write a beautiful screed of umpteen pages of foolscap, then some bloated Secretariat official sitting in a comfortable office surrounded by official clerks makes caustic comments about it, never remembering it was probably written by some poor wretch sitting in a filthy mud hovel after a tiring day trekking.[15]

After the assessment each male had to pay an annual tax of two shillings and each female one shilling. Lugard, who had set up the whole system of Indirect Rule in Nigeria, believed that taxation taught respect for authority, taught useful social lessons and prevented idleness. His views expressed largely in his Political Memoranda, were accepted as gospel, and certainly proved effective in the Mada country. Although the collection of taxes was, naturally, unpopular, it created an effective link between the District Officer and the village headman, who had to collect the money. Later, as the benefits of taxation appeared, with better roads and bridges, new dispensaries and improved market facilities, this helped to bolster up the position and authority of the Headman. Arden-Clarke dealt severely with those who refused to pay tax or encouraged others to refuse. Once he had three elders caned in public, making it a big and impressive ceremonial occasion. He added in a letter home:

I wonder what they would think if they knew that the white judge who was meting out such awesome punishment, was, less than ten years before being given six of the best for pillow fighting in the dormitory after lights out.[16]

---

[15] Unpublished MS 37.
[16] Letter to Family 4.6.21.

His tax collecting certainly proved effective and within a short time he had £1,000 in the local Treasury. Unfortunately there had been a bureaucratic hitch and the tax assessment had not been officially approved. He fumed at the rebuke of a visiting official.

Soon after this imposition of taxes, railway construction started in the area, and this solved most problems. Although reluctant, at first, to work on the railway, the Madas found that they could quickly acquire what to them was untold wealth. They earned ninepence per day, and after two week's work, with substantial meals available, they had enough to pay their own and their wives' taxes and could, in addition buy a cotton robe—a considerable status symbol—and enough hoops of iron to provide hoes, knives and arrow heads for their farming work.

Before his first tour of duty with the Madas ended Arden-Clarke had to deal with trouble in the same village that he had first visited. Threats to murder him and his escort had been reported from friendly sources. He therefore went to the village and arranged for three additional police to meet him there. He wanted to catch about six ringleaders and therefore since they were not present when he arrived, without arousing their suspicions, went on to another village. He intended to return with a larger number of police disguised as bearers, and had his plans carefully laid, when the whole project was nearly ruined. His District Officer had received a garbled message about the murder plot and sent for a company of troops and a machine gun, and Arden-Clarke received a frantic message to hold on until reinforcements arrived. He therefore had to postpone his plans while he rushed off back to Akwanga to prevent the troops marching in and ruining all his work. This he managed to do, and was able to return to the village with nine extra police acting as bearers. The meeting had been called ostensibly to discuss the new taxes, and all the wanted men were present, together with the whole population of the village. The 'bearers' had been told to wait in a neighbouring hut, where they put on uniform and prepared their rifles and bayonets. Arden-Clarke spoke to the people, warned them to remain still, and then gave a blast on his whistle. Twelve police with fixed bayonets quickly appeared, surrounded the gathering, and arrested the malefactors. They were taken off to court in Akwanga, a new headman appointed, and thereafter Arden-Clarke enjoyed cordial relations with the whole area.

Before the end of his first tour he had clearly emerged from being the fledgling District Officer, albeit with a mind of his own, into a character who had obviously made his mark in the local area and with his superiors. His views develop a confidence and maturity which show a highly professional approach, linked with the bubbling enthusiasm and gusto which occasionally break out in a young man carrying very heavy responsibilities.

On Empire Day 1921 he was at Jemaa with his colleague Bulger, and they decided to organize a parade. They erected a flagpole in the centre of the market place and, at the appointed time, drew up the parade, with the police in full dress on one side and the native police, Messengers and Emir's bodyguard on the other.

> We halted in front of the flag. I gave the order 'fix bayonets', 'slope arms'; then we had the salute. The police presented arms while the bugler blew the general salute. Bulger and I stood at the salute and all the messengers and people got down on their faces and kow towed. Then Bulger gave three cheers for the King and everyone yelled at the top of their voices . . . The office clerks all turned out in European dress with their wives, and dazzled the eyes of the Jemaa proletariat with their sartorial resplendency.

Arden-Clarke added a green cummerbund and war medals to his usual khaki drill with riding breeches and puttees, telling Bulger that he was too hidebound with conventionality and dress-regulations.[17]

Soon afterwards, Bulger's replacement arrived from England, 'and brought his wife with him. By Jove, it was topping seeing a white woman again. She is plump and chubby with a gorgeous English bloom on her face.'[18] In the same letter he described how he had to put a woman in prison, and what a fuss she and others made. 'The women cause all the trouble in this country. Brrr!!'

All officers had to pass examinations in a native language, and Arden-Clarke was concerned that he had devoted so little time to studying Hausa. In spite of a scholarship in Classics to Emmanuel College Cambridge he realized he was no linguist, making the point in a light-hearted letter home 'Mes chers vieux haricots. (That's French for dear old beans).'

In bush stations, the rainy season directly and dramatically affected people's lives. In September 1921 a tornado hit Akwanga damaging most of the houses; it reminded him vividly of a night when, having just come out of the line in France, the Germans had shelled the rest camp.

> I remember the absolute terror I was in and how I crawled under the bedclothes stuffed up both ears and tightly closed my eyes . . . When a tornado comes when I am in bed I always remember that night.[19]

His friend Thompstone joined him for Christmas at Akwanga, which he described movingly:

> Of course we had nothing like an English Christmas; no church or

[17] Letter to Family 29.5.21.
[18] Letter to Family 18.6.21.
[19] Letter to Family 27.9.21.

carols or home, but we managed thoroughly to enjoy ourselves. We had a great dinner at Clarke's house with plum pudding, with the best turkey I have ever seen in England or in any other country, beautifully cooked, though the cooks only had an old kerosene tin as an oven. After dinner we drank a toast or two—first the King, then Home, then 'wives and sweethearts may they never meet' then a silent toast. Then we talked and sang and were very cheery. All the same it wasn't really Christmas—it can't be away from home.[20]

He was also able to spend the occasional weekend with Thompstone, and admired his bungalow 'a real one with doors and windows and such like modern luxuries'.

Even though he was just setting out on his career, Arden-Clarke took a heavy load of responsibility for his parents and family. During 1921 he encouraged them to take a holiday in Florence—which they eventually did—largely because his father, after retiring from the CMS in India had suffered a prolonged period of nervous ill health. Arden-Clarke, whose salary was now £500 per annum plus allowances, which in a bush station covered most of his expenses, twice sent cheques of £20 to help with the cost of the trip to Florence. He constantly insisted that his father should take things easy for at least a period of six months. They had an interesting relationship, on occasion the role of parent and son being almost reversed. Early in 1922 he wrote:

Now, look here, Doodles old boy, you need talking to in a pretty straight fashion. No sooner did you get well than you plunged head foremost into work and made yourself bad again.

He went on to emphasize that his father was not playing the game with the rest of the family, and even added:

If you go on doing this sort of thing, I'll have to chuck up this job and find some work to do at home.

The letter concluded on another issue which obviously meant a great deal to the family:

I'm awfully pleased about Sherry (his younger brother) deciding to become a missionary. I know it will buck you up no end, because I'm sure you were very disappointed about me.[20]

His pleasure that his parents had gone for a prolonged stay in Florence was tempered to some extent by the problems this posed for his leave due in July or August 1922. As a devoted son he clearly wanted to be with his parents but he also wanted to spend his leave with Gina Reid. They had had a very early attachment at the age of seven in India, knew each other

[20] Letter to Family 1.1.22.

in their teens in Scarborough, and then had met again just before he left for Nigeria. His letters contain heavy hints that the family are not keeping sufficient contact with the Reids. When he does not hear from Gina he says he would prefer her to have 'flu than an attractive male. How deep his feelings were may have been hidden in a semi-jocular note to the family:

We'll have to advertise 'Wanted—a keeper for young and woolly bachelor of extravagant ideas, untidy habits and uncouth appearance. Must be feminine, petite, charming, tidy but not too much so, not fussy, eyes greenish grey with golden flecks, fond of poetry, intelligent, economical but able to enjoy a good bust every now and then, pretty, well dressed and a good sort.' I've only met one who will fill the bill so far, but she is not keen on the job. It's a pretty mouldy world—sometimes.[21]

He fairly frequently complained about the tedium of office work and especially of the assessment reports—'The difficult part has been done— the boring part (the ink splashing) remains', but he realized that as these went directly to the Lt Governor they played an important part in moulding a junior officer's reputation. He was delighted when two came back highly commended by the Governor as 'a very interesting excellent and useful report by an officer in his first tour'. He felt equally pleased that his plan to reorganize the administration of the Mada area had been approved by the Resident and forwarded to Lagos.

Early in 1922 he makes frequent mention of the Mama people, among whom he was later to do such impressive work. He showed acute powers of observation and a genuine and sincere interest, not only in their ways and customs, but also in the role of the District Officer in pacifying them.

The Mamas aren't half such a woolly crowd as they are made out to be. They are absolute savages of course and don't wear a stitch of clothing but they are not half as truculent as were some of the hill Madas. The Mamas build excellent strong houses with plenty of stones. But no real progress will be made in administering them until someone is posted here, whose main job is to look after the Mamas and spend most of his time among them. With any luck I might get the job, if the Mada Scheme is adopted and proves a success.

This rough, more or less pioneer work appeals to me intensely. I think it suits me rather well. I never was and never will be much of a success in an office or a drawing room.

Practically every complaint one receives here is one of child stealing, a tremendous trade in children goes on, the usual price for one child being an Ox.

[21] Letter to Family 28.1.22.

Trekking among the hills could be difficult and dangerous but had its more enjoyable moments. With a colleague he went to see the Sha Falls where the Rua River tumbles off the 4,000 ft Bauchi plateau. They set off at 7 am with the local chief as guide, with three carriers, his boy, cook, and orderlies with the breakfast loads. After looking at the falls they spotted some baboons and, to the delight of the local village, shot one. He described their picnic breakfast beside the falls:

Quaker oats, tinned milk, and golden syrup, followed by some excellent tinned sausages and some eggs, toast, marmalade and coffee.[22]

Arden-Clarke's humorous and unstuffy attitudes show clearly in his description of a bathe after the picnic.

J.C.O. (his colleague) thought it would be undignified to take our shirts off and bathe in front of our orderlies and the four pagans. (You see our position out here is something like judge, emperor and pope rolled into one). After fooling about like two children in bare feet for so long, this belated snatch at our long vanished dignity struck me as being very amusing. Old J.C.O. standing there in a battered old khaki topee, unshaven, clad only in an ancient bush shirt open at the neck, and a pair of disreputable khaki shorts, talking about our dignity set me off into screams of laughter.

We hadn't any bathing dresses or towels but that didn't matter. We simply took off our shirts, emptied our trouser pockets, and swam about in shorts and our hats. The sun was too hot to allow of us taking off our hats. It was absolutely topping.

During one of his initial treks into the rugged and hilly Mama country, he described how the hamlets clung to the tops of the hills in ideal defensive positions.

We climbed to the top . . . and walked slap into the middle of the Ungwa and found it stripped for action: bows, newly poisoned arrows, knives etc., were hanging at the doors of the houses. The men were all sitting down, their only articles of clothing being necklaces, straws in their noses and lips, and knives tied to their waists by pieces of string. There were no women to be seen. Both J.C.O. and I felt a bit uncomfortable . . . We were both packing our guns in our trouser pockets and I was very glad to feel a comfortable revolver butt nestling into the palm of my hand as we walked through them—each of us with our right hands in our trouser pockets.[23]

Later they watched a Ju Ju dance. First the women danced, but then they were sent away because no woman was permitted to see the male Ju Ju dance.

[22] Letter to Family 17.2.22.
[23] Letter to Family 21.2.22.

The pagan Ju-Ju superstition is not an entirely bad thing by any means—it imposes a high standard of sexual morality and is rarely infringed. By far the most moral people sexually I have ever seen are the Madas and Mamas—they are infinitely more so than any European nation. Venereal disease is practically unknown among them while the Mohammedan Hausas and Fulani are rotten with it . . .

All the young men gathered round the big Ju-Ju stone, then the drums began and the whole lot started leaping around to the mad rhythm. It was wonderful—lithe naked figures leaping in and out of the patches of light, the beat of the tom toms, the crash of the sacred rattles, the palm trees and native huts dimly showing up in the starlight, the play of the dancers' muscles under their skins glistening with sweat, the weird booming of the buffalo horn and sudden cat calls made a scene as savage as one could find . . . it seemed to strip off the veneer of civilization and rouse all one's latent savagery. It made me long to pitch off my clothes and join in the dance. [24]

At the same time, clearly prompted by his father, he was giving thought to the missionary question. He wrote to his father and explained his views. The government were not keen on missionaries because of the bad effect on a native's moral character when he is converted to Christianity.

He becomes undisciplined and a general nuisance to the community. [25]

He felt that often the wrong type of person was sent out, and gave an example of how four missionaries had set up a stall in the village market and started telling the story of the Cross, in English, with the result that the natives all thought they were quite mad. He suggested that instead of sending out 20 poorly paid and unsuitable missionaries, they should select a few really good men, train them in simple medicine for 12 months and then equip them properly before they left. Too much stress should not be laid on monogamy because the Mahommedan emphasized a heaven where seven dusky beauties awaited a man. He added a significant warning that unless the missionary approach improved:

Christianity will be knocked out by Mahommedanism. [26]

His involvement in every aspect of the lives of the Mada and Mama people is shown by his plan to reorganize their administration. He planned to divide the Madas into two well defined districts each with a District Head and both responsible to a strong character called Bashai. He would head the new small independent emirate, and be equal in rank to the Amir of Lafia who was already well established. After describing various gruesome aspects of local customs he concludes,

[24] Letter to Family 21.2.22.
[25] Letter to Family 15.5.22.
[26] Letter to Family 15.5.22.

The first thing to be done is to show that murder, assaulting people on the roads and highway robbery of all kinds, and the trading of children must stop.[27]

However dramatic or serious his letters, humour was never far away. One day a bicycle got a puncture and a Mada pagan was sent to fetch it:

The poor fellow couldn't manage it at all. He tried carrying it on his head but couldn't manage that at all. Eventually he festooned the machine round his neck in some weird and impossible way and started to bring the bike in. Before he had gone five yards his fingers had been scraped by the spokes of one wheel and a pedal had caught him a crack under the chin. He tried shifting the position of the bike but only got his fingers pinched. Then he sang softly to it to soothe the evil spirit in it—and got another bang from the pedal. Eventually he laid it down by the side of the road and got down and prayed to it, firmly convinced it was an evil Ju Ju of the white man.[28]

In the final months before going on leave in August 1922, he received congratulations from the Lieutenant Governor on his Mada Scheme, he had an energetic final trek 'climbing beastly hills and burning down the houses of the bad men' (they had murdered two people by gwasha poison), and gave a brief philosophical comment about Parliament:

The powers that be are so frightened of questions in Parliament when some idiot gets up and says he has heard of brutal treatment meted out to some poor helpless native—the 'poor helpless native' being a bunch of Mada with sheaves of poisoned arrows and bristling with swords and spears, spending his energies in getting his fellow 'helpless natives' to drive out the white man.[29]

He had clearly had a successful first tour and had made his mark as a tough, reliable and efficient young man, well able to accept responsibility, and who had the ability to plan and think clearly. His detailed and well thought out plans for reorganizing the administration of the Madas and Mamas were to give him, in his next tours, great opportunities of which he took full advantage.

[27] Letter to Family 5.3.22.
[28] Letter to Family 5.3.22.
[29] Letter to Family 6.6.22.

CHAPTER TWO
The Madas and Mamas

In early 1923 Arden-Clarke returned from home leave having become engaged to Gina Reid. The march of progress was soon apparent, for instead of a three day trek to Jemaa from Bukuru, he took a lorry, piled his kit and his boys on the back, and driving up the new motor road arrived within seven hours. At the end of the road, just short of Jemaa, 75 carriers awaited him.

After a few days at Jemaa, he left for Kagoro. Although only 14 miles distant it was nearly a thousand feet higher and had been chosen as the new headquarters because it lay on a high plateau, and enjoyed a healthier climate than Jemaa, which suffered from a high incidence of sleeping sickness. He had to check the tax assessment figures for three districts because his predecessor had made a complete hash of them, and then to site and design a completely new station HQ, with offices and two European's houses. For this project he received £70 and the help of 300 unskilled pagan labourers.

Throughout most of his service Arden-Clarke, a tough and robust character, enjoyed good health even in the most unsalubrious stations, but soon after his return he suffered from either fever or sunstroke and spent four agonizing days nursed only by his faithful boy. He made little of this, trying now to reassure both mother and fiancee, and was soon back in his routine work seeing the amusing side of most incidents. After assessing tax for the district, he called in all the family heads and gave them cowrie shells to remind them how much tax to pay.

There was one dear old idiot there, about 90 years old he looked, with a long white beard. I gave him his cowries and beans and he thanked me profusely and put them away in a little leather bag he was carrying. When he got up to go, I noticed cowries and beans dropping on the ground behind him out of a hole in his wretched bag. So I called him back and asked him how much tax he had to pay. He scratched his head for a bit and then opened his bag and had a hunt inside for his cowries. After pulling out bits of tobacco, an old pipe, a couple of arrow heads and a few other oddments he eventually found two cowries (I had originally given him twenty five). He looked a bit puzzled but gravely informed me his tax was £2. After a little talk I showed him the hole in his bag and gave him a new lot of cowries and beans. The very first thing the old ass did was solemnly to pour them into his bag again . . . He kept me in fits of laughter. [1]

In sharp contrast he was soon to face the repellent responsibility of a public hanging.

Elford the policeman is here and this afternoon or tomorrow morning we will publicly hang a murderer; then I have to hold an inquest on the body. I've just been preparing rough drafts of the form of inquisition and making a rough draft of the evidence I'll require in the formal proceedings. It is all stereotyped kind of stuff. It's a beastly job; I'll be glad when it is over. It is all so cold blooded; that is the rotten part of it. I've killed men before but there has always been plenty of excitement about it and plenty of men being killed round about. Also I'm afraid I've become less callous in the last three years since leaving Russia where one saw dead bodies and plenty of them practically every day. However it's necessary, right and part of one's duty so there's an end of it. [2]

The following day he wrote a short note that the hanging had been carried out; adding that he wanted to forget the whole thing as quickly as possible.

Although he enjoyed robust good health himself, his letters give evidence enough of the harsh effect of service in bush stations. Concerned about two colleagues being unusually depressed he laid on a special dinner to cheer them up, helped by a parcel of tinned goods from Gina.

The menu was rather a good effort for Akwanga. Thick soup; salmon kedgeree; a leg of mutton with mashed yam and green peas; boiled corn cob with melted butter; peaches and cream; almonds and raisins and preserved figs; and coffee.

Some three weeks later while out on trek he was called back to Akwanga because the man who had been so depressed finally went off his head, and Arden-Clarke and the doctor, Burnie, spent three hours holding him down. The following day the other Europeans escorted the patient to hospital in Enugu, leaving Arden-Clarke to investigate a £100 embezzlement from the treasury, two murders, and revolts over tax payments. He also had his law examinations in two weeks.

Most District Officers preferred the danger and excitement of being on trek to the dull routine of office work—Lord Twining then a young DO in Uganda at about the same time gave a remarkably similar view. [3] At one outlying station Arden-Clarke, after a long day's trek was about to

[1] Letter to Family 8.4.23.
[2] Letter to Family 18.4.23.
[3] See D. Bates *A Gust of Plumes*, London, 1975.

get into bed when Hook, a visitor in the Rest House about 40 yards away, rushed in, saying a leopard had jumped into his house and snatched his dog. They followed the spoor for some distance but without success. They went back to bed, but almost at once a violent storm blew up. The boys helped to collect things into boxes and to cover the bed with ground-sheets. At that moment the wall of Arden-Clarke's hut blew in and the roof started creaking, so he dashed through the driving rain to the Rest House. Here Hook fitted him out with dry clothes and they chatted till 2 a.m., by which time the storm had abated. He then returned to his hut and finding that the bed was dry, settled down again. A moment later all his goats, probably frightened by the leopard, charged into his hut knocking over his dog, which cowered under his bed. His African boy then rushed in and chased off all the goats except for a young kid which hid under the table. Shortly it howled for its mother.

> The boy arrived on the scene, deposited his lamp on the floor, and bent down to get a good aim with his stick. At this moment the mother arrived at the gallop; there was a crash as mother's horns landed with a thud on the place where the seat of the boy's trousers would have been if he had been wearing any, a howl from the boy, a crash as the lamp overturned and went out, a yelp from the dog whose nerves were beginning to get a bit frayed, and the sound of hooves disappearing in the distance with a loud paean of praise from the reunited mother and child. I lay back and hooted with laughter.[4]

Much of the more serious side of the District Officer's work consisted of travelling to remote towns and villages, establishing law and order, and enforcing the tax collection, often against the truculent opposition of the local Ju Ju man. In the Akwanga area two minor chiefs from the Doma area on the banks of the Benue River had been particularly troublesome, so Arden-Clarke went down to deal with them. He took a small expedition of four police, two messengers and his boy. When he arrived at Ajio the village was deserted except for a few women and children. He spoke in a friendly way to the Chief's wife and tried, without much success, to ingratiate himself with her little daughter. After his friendly overtures failed, he resorted to sternness and threatened big trouble if the husband did not appear promptly the next day. He then left with his small group for Attia, the next village. Here they had not got wind of his arrival and so everyone was there. He sent for the Chief and, hearing voices coming from a large hut, looked inside. He saw six of the leading men of the village preparing for a 'full dress Ju Ju palava', drinking from a cup of milky liquid, mumbling incantations as it passed from hand to hand. He told them to come out, but they

---

[4] Letter to Family 22.6.23.

ignored him until he spoke in Hausa to his senior policeman, when they quickly obeyed. The Chief, a scowling truculent brute, agreed that two of his men should call the village together. While they waited for the villagers to assemble, the Chief's father, a filthy old leper with only one leg and wrapped in loathsome rags, crawled about completing the Ju Ju process, stirring various pots on the fire, adding feathers to an evil-looking mixture, and accompanying each movement with vile incantations.

Eventually all the people had assembled and Arden-Clarke pointed out their wrong doings. They made some pathetic excuses and he then announced that he would take away the Chief. As he left the crowd grew truculent and threatening, and edged closer as the small party tried to heave off the canoe with their prisoner. Eventually they got away safely into the main stream, and went back to Ajio. Here they spent a dangerous night with similar excitements, but he was able to return to Akwanga with the two leading trouble makers. They were made to appear before the Native Court, which imprisoned them both for a year, and imposed heavy fines on the other tax dodgers. Arden-Clarke's final comment was 'They are all behaving like little lambs now that the ringleaders have been sat on so heavily'. [5]

He soon settled back into the routine of the District Officer. For three weeks of every month he travelled on foot from one Mada village to another, camping in the Rest Houses which, for the most part he had built, or else in empty huts in the village. At the end of each month he returned to Akwanga to replenish his stores and collect cash to pay his carriers. While he was back in the station, he had to check the Treasury accounts and do any office work, though there was very little of this and routine matters were dealt with by the African clerk.

Most District Officers enjoyed the trekking although it was a lonely life. Arden-Clarke recalled that after a day's trek he got to the Rest House and there his companions were his dog, the camp fire and books. During this period he read many of the great classics and on one occasion Gibbon's *Decline and Fall of the Roman Empire* kept him company for many weeks. He consoled himself that it was more interesting and instructive than any conversation he would have had. Each month the engineer in charge of building bridges for the new roads and railway, came back to collect money to pay his labourers. They would settle down for the evening with three weeks conversation bottled up inside them, and, neither one listening, they would talk for hours at a time.

Sometimes in the villages he had the company of a Hausa Mallam who coached him in Hausa for his language examination. Officers had to pass

[5] Letter to Family 4.11.23.

an examination before they could be confirmed in their appointments. Hausa, the lingua franca not only of Northern Nigeria but Northern Ghana and the Royal West African Frontier Force, was a relatively easy language to learn. As Arden-Clarke had identified so strongly with the Madas it had been suggested that he should take his language examination in Mada, but Mada was a tonal language and had never been written down, so, conscious again of his inadequacy as a linguist, he studied Hausa. Here fate was kind to him. He had taken a senior official who was a distinguished Hausa scholar on a tour of the Mada. The scholar, with his fluent Hausa could not communicate with the Mada at all. Some months later he turned out to be Arden-Clarke's colloquial ·Hausa examiner. He allowed him to pass, merely commenting that he had spent a week listening to him speaking the most abominable Hausa ever heard—and he could not stand any more of it—but, since it appeared to get over to the Mada, that was acceptable. Later Arden-Clarke rewarded the Mallam for getting him through the examination, but did not tell him the distinction he had gained.

The rugged pioneering work and the constant trekking kept Arden-Clarke fit, in spite of the unhealthy and insanitary conditions in which he lived. On trek, food and water became major problems. All water had to be boiled and filtered. Food tended to be dull and unpalatable, because there were no local resources. Fresh vegetables were unobtainable, and yams or cassava were a poor substitute for potatoes. Local chicken, a sinewy and athletic breed, provided most of his meat, varied with the occasional bush fowl or guinea fowl. The prevalence of mosquitoes made it necessary to take five grains of quinine a day, but, especially on trek this upset his stomach and added to his difficulties.

The Mada people among whom he lived and worked suffered from appalling tropical diseases: yaws, leprosy, dysentery, meningitis, sleeping-sickness and small-pox. In such an area medical resources were rudimentary or non existent, and if there was an epidemic, the brunt fell on the District Officer. In 1923 a small-pox epidemic swept through the Mada hills. The nearest doctor was 50 miles away and Arden-Clarke summoned him by runner. The doctor came, confirmed the disease, explained what should be done, and left again. He sent a medical orderly with a supply of vaccine and scalpels, but the orderly—a southerner and terrified of the ferocious Mada—initially proved to be of little value. It fell to Arden-Clarke to find ways of convincing the suspicious people, and to carry out the vaccination. After some failures he managed to get an influential headman to agree to his village being vaccinated. The elders, naturally demanded that Arden-Clarke was vaccinated first, so he bared his arm, rubbed it with spirit, and then the orderly scratched in the vaccine. Then the elders followed, and once they had been done, they made certain that everyone else in the village followed. This system proved effective, but Arden-Clarke suffered considerably as he had to vaccinate himself at each village. He explained each step to the assembled villagers and then, in order to get rid of accumulated layers of dirt, and to emphasize the significance of the whiteman's magic he personally rubbed each arm with spirit. He warned the patients not to scratch or touch the scab which formed, but often they ignored his advice, and he would see them again with deep septic holes in their arms. This they seemed to attribute to the whiteman's magic and as the epidemic waned they accepted their sufferings stoically.

Respect for his medicine was slowly established and this helped when a meningitis epidemic broke out. This proved more severe than the small-pox outbreak, and the Madas died in hundreds. There was no dramatic remedy like vaccination, only a slow and patient campaign against dust and dirt. Whole villages were encouraged to leave the dust of their huts, to go and camp in the open, and to gargle morning and night—another boarding-school tradition being upheld. Here, too, Arden-Clarke led the way in the collective ritual gargle. Sometimes in a particularly dirty or dusty settlement, he contrived that the thatch on the roofs of the huts would 'accidentally' catch fire thus ensuring that the huts were ef-fectively disinfected. The roofs could be fairly easily replaced with a day or two's work in the open air.

Having established himself among the Mada as a caring father-figure, Arden-Clarke frequently received messages asking for help. One village sent a deputation saying that he was their 'Father and Mother' and ought to save his children from a leopard which was killing their dogs and goats—they even added, as an unimportant afterthought, that it had killed an old woman. He went to the village, tethered a stray dog and a goat to a post and retreated to a platform in the hope of getting a shot at the leopard during the night. The dog quietly chewed through the goat's tether, and in the middle of the night the goat suddenly charged off into the nearest hut where the carriers were sleeping. This caused immediate panic and pandemonium, with black bodies and finally the goat erupting from the hut, with enough noise to frighten off any leopard for miles around. After this fiasco Arden-Clarke left on trek, but later in the day was brought the skin of a newly killed leopard. It appeared that the leopard, having killed a buck, had itself been attacked and injured by a lion. Some villagers finished it off with rocks, but attributed its death to the whiteman's magic. As an experienced administrator Arden-Clarke did nothing to curb this belief.

His strong, patient, determined and humorous approach gradually paid off. The prompt arrest and punishment of offenders engendered a respect for the law. He settled disputes between villages—in the past a frequent cause of violence—quickly and fairly. The collection of taxes and the improvements these made possible enhanced the prestige and effectiveness of the Headman and his elders, and gradually taxpayers came to be respected as good and positive citizens.

Next, to his delight, Arden-Clarke received the dangerous and challenging task of subduing the Mamas. Clearly it had been decided to give him this opportunity because of his thorough and thoughtful work with the neighbouring Mada people. He accepted the challenge with relish, and when the work had been successfully completed received the congratulations of the Governor, commendation which undoubtedly counted heavily in his future promotion.

The Mama district lay below the 2,000 foot Bauchi plateau where he had spent some of his first tour. Roughly divided by a range of hills, the bleaker northern half, where Arden-Clarke did most of his work, was a wild, rugged, bush-covered wilderness. Rivers and streams tumbled down gorges. Empty in the dry season, and raging torrents in the rains between July and September, they added substantially to the difficulty of establishing control over the area. Even game seemed to have fled from the harsh terrain. Having for generations suffered from the depredations of the Fulani slave raiders, the people had retreated from the valleys and gorges to defensive villages on the hill tops. There were no roads, and the narrow bushtracks frequently studded with deep game pits, formed the only link between villages, or from the villages to their fields of guinea corn and millet.

Socially, the Mamas menaced both themselves and their neighbours. Villages, hamlets and even families feuded with each other. They owed no loyalty to the tribe and hardly even to their family. Among a population of only 7,000 they spoke different languages and dialects. Head hunting and cannibalism were hardly suppressed. Kidnapping, murder, slave dealing, and the abduction of wives or children occurred daily; consequently no traders or outsiders ventured near. Their evil reputation was signified clearly enough in the Hausa names for the three main villages: blood—evil—death. The British administration had discouraged open warfare but in spite of this, internal law and order had broken down completely. At the approach of a British patrol, the Mamas hid their grain and other meagre possessions in the bush, and fled deep in the jungle, only emerging to snipe with poisoned arrows at any stragglers.

Arden-Clarke set out on his mission to the Mamas by staying at Arum, one of the most notorious villages. He had sent a messenger ahead to get some huts built, but the Mamas had hit him on the head with rocks. He survived this, and there were one or two miserable huts ready when Arden-Clarke arrived. From his bedroom hut he could see the stars through the roof, and he was constantly assailed by hordes of unpleasant insects. He had great difficulty in getting the Mamas to work, and only succeeded by constant vigilance and bloodcurdling threats. He described them as:

> Great bushy savages, magnificent physical specimens, bulging with muscle, stark naked all of them except for grass strings round their waist . . . on every man a knife; a great shock of woolly hair about two inches long hanging round their faces, which in some cases are painted with daubs of red; each man with a cudgel or axe in his hand. Once I've taught them that the law is to be obeyed and that murder, kidnapping, highway robbery and slave dealing are not the chief objects in life, they'll be topping fellows. But they've got to respect and obey the law as a preliminary.[6]

He went on to describe a murder case which had to be tried. It was fairly straightforward. A man believing a woman had killed his son by witchcraft shot her cold-bloodedly with a poisoned arrow. Arden-Clarke had to write up the case and added interesting comments.

> The papers are headed resoundingly 'Holden in the Provincial Court . . . at Arum'. Arum, ye gods! With a title like that, one conjures up visions of a palace of justice, majestic ritual, the periwigged potentates of the law resplendent in their robes—instead, a ramshackle grass hovel in the bush, a Union Jack tied on to a spear stuck in the ground, a white man in khaki shorts and shirt with a battered topee on his head. Still it's the justice and not the externals that count.[6]

After nearly a month of tedium and frustration, he got his headquarters and Rest House completed, and felt it was a sound base from which to operate as soon as the patrol was authorized. He had to deal with one troublesome hamlet, Gauchia. They ignored an initial warning, so he moved in in force, broke all their pots and burned the village. He added 'I always loathe this part of the job. It seems such a senseless wasteful bit of destruction.' But the results were good, and that from a village with about 80 men who had carried out three cattle raids, two murders, a gruesome bit of cannibalism and five cases of kidnapping. He explained:

> It gives you some idea of why one has to take fairly drastic measures occasionally. But I wish you could see these people—I'm getting fairly used to them now, but when I first came here, even after my experience with other pagan tribes . . . they struck me as the woolliest types of stark savagery that I should ever be likely to see.[7]

[6] Letter to Family 25.2.25.
[7] Letter to Family 9.3.25.

A member of a geological survey team, Raeburn, came to survey the Mama district, and was surprised at the way the patrols worked:

> He thought that burning a village just meant mooching up and putting a match to a few roofs. But when he saw me sweeping the bush for hidden snipers, and the posting of the sentries, and one of his own labourers receive a thrashing for attempted looting, and the scouting parties that were sent out, he began to realize a little what one was up against.[7]

During this period of preliminary contact and reconnaissance with the Mamas, he laid the foundation for much of the Mama Patrol's future success. The Mamas had no code of law, either written or spoken, so he drew up a Mama ten commandments, and made the leaders of each village learn it by heart; then the whole village had to sit round saying it after their leader.

> It's more or less a catalogue on their ten favourite offences with 'thou shalt not' stuck in front, e.g., thou shalt not murder, or steal or go in for slave dealing, or pinch your neighbour's wife, or hide criminals, or commit highway robbery etc.[7]

He visited one village, having given them due warning, and found the whole lot drunk from a wake the previous evening. He could not get any sense out of them. The chief was too drunk to interpret, and found the situation, with the owlish looking audience belching and farting, to be highly amusing. Arden-Clarke who had half killed himself getting to the village in the hot sun was less amused. He gave the chief a crack across the knuckles with his stick, and took him and two elders away to sober up and learn their ten commandments.

Again at this time he remarked on the terrible responsibility which fell on young District Officers in dealing with hanging cases; pointing out that in England a judge shared the awful responsibility with a jury. He felt that without the panoply of the law, and sitting in a grass hut with the victim squatting in front of him, it made the whole thing cold-blooded. Even though he had seen frequent hangings in Russia, it took more out of him than he had expected.

He spent the weeks of preparatory work for the main Mama Patrol, in visiting all 27 villages, establishing where possible friendly contact with chiefs and elders, and also in publicizing the names of wanted criminals, together with firm warnings to those who flouted the law. Although his reception was hostile, and hidden snipers attacked him with poisoned arrows, he did not anticipate concerted resistance. His travels enabled him to carry out a full reconnaissance, to establish strategically sited base camps, and to build bridges where necessary.

As a young bachelor just contemplating marriage, it amused him to have to deal with matrimonial problems. One morning a husky savage brought in his erring wife who had been spending all her time at beer parties.

As a social butterfly her appearance was hardly what one would expect; a hideous black woman, stark naked except for a string round her stomach, a few wooden bangles and a straw thrust through her nose, her head half shaved and her body glistening with red palm oil. Her husband's accoutrements consisted of an enormous phallic ornament and a club. I gave the good lady a terse lecture on the wifely duties of giving hubby dinner when he came home at night . . . then wagging an admonitory finger at her I told her that if I was again troubled with her matrimonial irregularities I should have her tied up and taken to Akwanga (the last thing I should ever dream of doing, really) there to meditate until such time as she came to her senses. The couple were then dismissed. Hubby seemed satisfied, but I doubt whether he'll find any improvement in his wife. Savages are remarkably like us in many ways. It amused me intensely to be called in to teach a wife her duties and I nearly spoiled my homily by laughing in the middle of it.

Matrimonial matters are so often settled by the club or poisoned arrow out here that I have to pay rather a lot of attention to them. The chief causes of trouble are the same as in England, women and beer. [8]

In his letters home—as the eldest son in a family where the father suffered from frequent and prolonged nervous illness—he played a guiding role. Assuaging his mother's worries about his two younger brothers, he gave mature and philosophical advice. Of himself he said:

The war cured me of expecting anything nice at all, with the result that life has given me more than I ever thought possible in my wildest dreams, and I've found out that the world can be a wonderfully happy place after all.

In May 1925 he had completed his preparations for the Mama Patrol. His final action in his tour of the area had been to deal with a group of men who had terrorized the neighbourhood and had stolen large numbers of cattle and goats. He sentenced three men to 18 months imprisonment and 24 lashes each. Since robbery·with violence merited life imprisonment he expected to be ticked off for being too lenient.

The main patrol with L. S. Clinton, the local Assistant Commissioner of Police, a doctor, and 40 police assembled at Arum on 6 May 1925. The patrol arrived to subdue those villages which had become hideouts for criminals, who had resisted or rejected all peaceable measures. Out of all the villages only two had surrendered their criminals, and the patrol now set out against all the others. Even at this stage every attempt was made to get hold of the criminals before punitive action was taken.

[8] Letter to Family 24.3.25.

Before the patrol arrived, the Headman received a summons with the names of the criminals to be surrendered, and, as the patrol moved into the base camp in the centre of a group of villages, a second summons was sent. If this proved ineffective—and usually it did—the patrol moved in. Even then Arden-Clarke, with a small escort, went ahead of the main patrol to give them yet another and final chance to co-operate.

Lord Lugard, who had established British rule in Northern Nigeria and, with a tiny force, had overcome the powerful emirates of Kano, Katsina and Sokoto, had drawn up detailed instructions for District Officers in his Political Memoranda. These dictated the procedures upon which the Mama Patrol now embarked. The 'Extreme Measures' laid down by Lugard were vividly described by Arden-Clarke as the patrol moved into the first village.

> We usually bring our brekker loads and all the Mada carriers come too, and then we settle down and smash to pieces all the compounds in the village except those of people I know to be really friendly and doing their best to help me. As far as I am concerned there is no such thing as neutrality; a man is either an active friend of the administration or he is an enemy. If an enemy, his compound is levelled to the ground and the grass roof burnt. It's a pretty serious punishment of course but they knew that it was going to happen and deliberately chose it rather than surrender the few men I had asked for. They know perfectly well what I want and why they are being punished. They have hidden their food supplies and at the moment they think I shall soon go away and leave them and they'll be able to go back to their evil ways after suffering a certain amount of temporary discomfort. I shall of course go on walloping them until they surrender. It's rather a piteous sight watching a village being knocked to pieces and I wish there was some other way but unfortunately there isn't.[8]

A number of notorious criminals and murderers had fled to a small hamlet Gashia, and Arden-Clarke decided to try to catch them by a surprise night attack. The doctor 'a large fat man, rather excitable, and about as nimble on his feet as a hippopotamus suffering from housemaids knee' was left behind. The wanted men were known to be hiding in some compounds on the far side of the village and on top of the hill. As the patrol advanced they realized that the pagans were sleeping outside and had sentries posted. This made their task more difficult, but the whole patrol, well trained and well disciplined, managed to pass the first sentries without being discovered. They crept on, silently, in spite of loose rocks and stones and creepers. The patrol, tense with excitement, was nearing the murderers' compounds.

Suddenly out of a patch of shadow there came the rush of feet and the dim shapes of two figures tearing away into the village. Instantly there was pandemonium, a shout, dogs barking, the wail of a baby, and the thud of running feet. I ran straight for the murderers' compound in the hopes of catching at least one of them but all I saw was a dark shape slipping into the bush, too far off and too dim to be worth a shot from my revolver. [8]

Arden-Clarke admitted, philosophically, that he had not altogether expected to succeed with a night attack, but added:

It was all rather fun and relieved the monotony of things—I like these little adventures occasionally—there is no danger but there is always the excitement and the moonlight, and then sitting by a wood fire watching the flames and waiting for the dawn. [8]

The patrol with its heavy pressures and stresses on Arden-Clarke lasted through June and July, and into August. By then he had apprehended 75 criminals, all for known crimes committed within the last two years. He realized that kid glove methods could not be used to tame people who had known nothing but murder, slavery, kidnapping and violence. Throughout this demanding period he kept his balance, his humour, his detachment and his deep concern for the long term welfare of the Mama people.

Many of their murders are due entirely to their implicit belief in witchcraft. A man sickens and dies—it may be of sleeping sickness or pneumonia or anything. They say he has been bewitched—the wizard is found—and he is made to undergo a trial by ordeal and drink a bowl of sasswood poison. If he vomits and lives he has proved his innocence—more usually he dies . . . Here they often forego the trial by-ordeal, and the relations of the dead man catch the so called wizard and hang him out of hand or put a poisoned arrow into him or cut his throat.
   Another difficulty in obtaining the arrest of these people is that their fellow villagers are frightened to catch a man I want for fear he should bewitch them and so kill them. It's no good telling them witchcraft does not exist, they *know* it does . . . Meanwhile I take a different line with them. I tell them that the whiteman as they see, excels them in knowledge, power, cunning and strength. They agree. Then I ask them why, if I excel them in all that, they should think that I do not excel them in the arts of magic and witchcraft too. Then as emphatically as I can I tell them that whosoever obeys me and helps me, comes under my protection and the protection of my magic which is good magic. And while under my protection no lesser magic can ever touch them or hurt them. It may seem strange but often they believe me. And so we go slowly on. [9]

[9] Letter to Family 4.8.25.

Having dealt with the two toughest villages the patrols set out to sweep through the bush. These sweeps proved most effective, for they drove the outlaws deeper and deeper into the bush, away from friends and supporters, and forced them to survive during the rains with no food or shelter. At the same time, friendly natives found during the patrol were brought into camp where they were put to work and paid for what they did. The camps became friendly meeting places and frequently developed as small markets for palm oil, wild honey and other local products. These friendly contacts proved to be of vital and long lasting importance in establishing sound relations with the Mama people. During one patrol a Mama man had been shot and wounded. He was taken into camp and nursed until he was fit again. Clearly, under his own code of ethics, he thought his life was forfeit, and when he was spared he brought a pot of wild honey as a touching thank offering. Thereafter he spent most of his time in the camp, proving a mine of local information and acting as guide, as interpreter, and as chief instructor in the Mama's ten commandments.

The village of Turkwan and the area round it had been one of the most difficult to subdue, partly because of the appalling terrain. As more and more sweeps were made, the outlaws retreated into wilder and more daunting country, and into a maze of deep and treacherous caves. Patrolling such an area in the rains was a nightmare. The patrols, too, adapted to the conditions and made overnight stops in the caves. They often identified the outlaws' hideouts by sighting a rifle on a tripod on to the light of fires at night, and simply followed the direction the next morning. Two days after the main patrol in the Turkwan area, all the outlaws surrendered and subsequently fourteen were convicted of armed robbery.

The same patrol had to subdue a remote village in the Nungu district, which had been notorious as the main centre for selling Mama children into slavery. Arden-Clarke was most heartened when, shortly afterwards, the village Headman supported by all the village delivered to him a Fulani slave trader, together with a large herd of cows and goats, which he had brought with him to exchange for Mama slave children.

The Hausa police, including some ex-servicemen, played a key role in the whole of this exercise, and Arden-Clarke paid handsome tribute to them and their steadfastness in trying or dangerous conditions. On one occasion a sudden downpour caught his patrol in a precipitous gulley, while Mama snipers shot at them with poisoned arrows. The patrol came to a chasm, six foot wide, with wet slippery rocks on either side, which had to be jumped. Having a poor head for heights, he just could not jump. Realizing his difficulty, one Hausa policeman leapt across, and then with one on either side of the gap they made a human bridge, and strong arms helped him safely across.

As the vigorous patrolling proceeded, the patrols met a more friendly reception; villagers handed over the wanted criminals, and both men and women would come to the camp selling local produce or looking for work. While the women bartered or worked grinding corn, the men often had an impromptu class in the Mama's ten commandments. The patrol completed its work on 23 August 1925.

For Arden-Clarke, on whom the tensions and responsibility for the four months of patrolling had fallen, there followed several weeks of trials of all the criminals who had been caught. Charges included 21 cases of robbery with violence, eight of child stealing, 27 of slave dealing, and six of murder. One suspected murderer—a very powerful Ju Ju man who had committed revolting and inhuman crimes—so terrified the people that no one dared to come into open court to give evidence. Arden-Clarke, determined that the man would not escape justice, indulged in some histrionics. He brought the prisoner into court loaded with chains, leg irons and handcuffs. He spoke to all the people pointing out that his magic was obviously stronger than the Ju Ju man's. He assured them that they could quite safely give evidence and no harm would befall them because the whiteman's magic was strongest and would protect them. As he spoke, he suddenly felt dizzy with the onset of an attack of malaria. He realized that if he showed any sign of weakness or faintness at this critical moment, the whole effect of his histrionic performance would be ruined, so he gritted his teeth, carried on, and finally convinced enough witnesses to give the necessary evidence. In another murder case, a witness pointed to the right side where a poisoned arrow had struck the victim, whereat the accused—proud of his marksmanship—interrupted and assured the court the arrow had directly entered the heart.

Of the six convicted murderers, Arden-Clarke recommended that four should have their death sentences commuted to 18 months imprisonment—the maximum time these wild people could stand without pining away completely. The other two had committed such foul and brutal murders that he felt they could not be pardoned—a view shared by the local people as well. The Governor confirmed all the sentences, but by then Clinton, the police officer had left. Arden-Clarke pointed out that it was unreasonable for him, having caught and tried the murderers, to have to hang them as well. The authorities agreed and sent a young police officer to carry out the public execution. Unfortunately the two murderers had to be taken on a three day trek with a police escort to their own village. One accepted his fate philosophically, but for two nights the other, in spite of attempts to silence him, keened a wild, weird and fearsome death song. This so upset the young police officer that he had a nervous breakdown and had to be sent back to Akwanga, and Arden-Clarke had to face the grim final act alone.

The executions, conducted publicly and with formal ceremonial, took place on a hillside near the man's village. He addressed the assembled people, who had been brought in by their Headmen, and explained that execution was the penalty under the law for those who killed others. The Hausa police then set up the gallows and carried out the execution. When they took the body down from the gallows and removed the noose from his neck, the body gave a great sigh, and for one ghastly, panic-stricken moment Arden-Clarke thought the man was still alive. In fact the sigh was the air escaping from the lungs, and the man was dead. Then all the villagers filed past the body.

Years later Arden-Clarke wrote:

> This was a terrible business and there was no doubt that, conducted as it had been with awsome solemnity and cold blooded efficiency it had had a terrifying effect on the Mamas, cheap though they normally held human life to be. Years later, long after I had left the district, I was told that for five years after this public execution there was no more murders or killings reported in that area. [10]

Some time later he received a copy of the despatch from the Governor to the Secretary of State, which stated:

> When it is remembered that the Mamas are a people who have a fine art of passive resistance and whose tactics are favoured by every natural feature of their country, it becomes apparent that only the most skilful dispositions, executed with utmost perseverance and patience could have brought about results so complete and so satisfactory. I consider that in his conduct of the operations Captain C. N. Arden-Clarke displayed abilities of so high an order that his services deserve to be brought specially to your notice. [11]

There was to be a further postscript to his work with the Mada and Mama people. On his next tour he returned briefly to Akwanga, only to find the excellent system he had built up with so much vigour, and so successfully, in pathetic disarray. He fiercely criticized the new Resident who had unpractical and foolish ideas about the 'oppressed peasantry' and was allowing the whole area to relapse into lawlessness through weak, misguided and ineffective administration.

Having had two strenuous tours as a bachelor, roughing it in isolated bush stations, Arden-Clarke now had the joy of having his wife Gina with him, to share both the pleasures and hardships of life in the bush. They had as their first home, at Shendam, a large mud and thatched

[10] Unpublished MS.
[11] Letter to Family 17.2.26.

bungalow with holes in the walls for windows, and mud floors plagued by termites. His wife took all these discomforts in her stride—except for one thing. Because their house was bigger than most and the roof higher, the ceiling had become the home of a large colony of bats, which she could not abide. After unsuccessful attempts to remove them both by smoke and by buckshot, a false ceiling was erected which at least kept the bats out of the living quarters. Most District Officers serve tours of 18 months, followed by home leave of 18 weeks plus travelling time. Few wives came out to bush stations for the whole 18 months but usually came for a period in the middle of their husband's tour. At this time children were not allowed out on the West Coast, and wives normally returned to Britain to have their babies. Out of the first twelve years of the Arden-Clarke's married life they were apart for six.

At Shendam and again at Kagoro, his wife often accompanied him when he went on trek through his district. When they set off she would start by riding her pony, but for the heat of the day she would sit in a rhookhi chair or covered palanquin carried by four bearers. These stalwarts accepted their duty cheerfully, since this 'Missus' weighed exactly half as much as her predecessor. On one occasion she accompanied her husband and helped to take a new census—a count not only of all the people but all their livestock as well. She sometimes made slow progress on the counting because she became so absorbed with the mothers, young children and babies.

In contrast to the situation in the bush, he was amazed at the progress that had been made when he returned to Jos in 1927. A broad gauged railway now reached the town direct from the coalfields, and mining companies were rapidly developing. New bungalows seemed to spring up like mushrooms, a block of government offices had been built, there were 200 European women in the area, and he even went into a mining office and found a European typist.

In spite of the growing sophistication of places like Jos, the bush still had its element of danger. After his wife had gone back to England, Arden-Clarke set out for another expedition among the Mamas. He had two companions and at the first night stop, in primitive mud huts, he warned them of the danger of leopards. During the night he was taken violently ill and after a particularly violent paroxysm of vomiting he tried to crawl the short distance to his companions' hut. As he neared their hut, he was so weak he could not even shout for help, but just lay gasping. He thought to himself that his gasping would sound like a leopard, and how ironic it would be to be shot by his friends as a result of his own warning. The next day he felt even worse and when his urine became the colour of stout he realized he had blackwater fever. Having seen cases of blackwater before, he realized that he must keep absolutely

still and also must consume as much liquid as possible. A runner left
to fetch a doctor who came promptly, driving a motor cycle combi-
nation through the bush. The young doctor had not dealt with a case
of blackwater before, and for some time treated it as something else.
Arden-Clarke lay for three weeks in a bush hut, nursed by the wife of a
survey officer who happened to be in the area. The doctor's self-
confidence rapidly dwindled and he became more and more inept. One
day he gave Arden-Clarke a sheaf of telegrams that had come through,
including one which said that after he died his liver should be sent to the
Yellow Fever Research Institute. Having commented on the other
telegrams, he said to the doctor that he could tell the Research people
that the patient damn well refused to die. He soon realized that he was
not getting better and that he needed proper hospital treatment. The
local Headman was therefore approached and they willingly turned out
with all their people to flatten a rough road so that a Ford van could get
through to the nearest stop on the railway. More than a thousand of the
Mamas, with whom he had often dealt so severely, turned out to help
and, finally, to watch him being taken away in the lorry—a tribute he
found deeply moving. He reached Jos in a pitiable state, but with proper
medical care he soon recovered and was invalided home on sick leave. To
his delight, he was in England in 1928 with his wife when their first child
Paul was born.

Having made his mark as a really outstanding District Officer, Arden-
Clarke, when he returned from sick leave, entered the next phase of his
career in the northern Secretariat at Kaduna. Here at first he longed
again for the bush with its excitement and challenge, but as he became
more senior he experienced the fascination of seeing the wider sweep of
policy and how it was implemented under very varied conditions. His
service started at Kaduna but also included periods in the Provincial
Secretariat in Jos.

The great Lord Lugard had personally led the campaign which
brought the northern Emirates of Kano, Sokoto and Katsina under
British control in May 1903, and from his experience in this area he drew
up his monumental Political Memoranda. This gigantic work, running to
400 closely printed pages, dealt with every possible aspect of colonial
administration from matters of high policy and the whole philosophy of
colonial rule, down to such mundane matters as canoe registration on the
Niger and Benue rivers. It became the bible not only of all Nigerian
administrators, but of the whole system of Indirect Rule. This system
which Lugard set up during the dramatic campaign of 1903, emphasized
the responisiblity of the Chief or Emir, and emphasized the joint role of
the District Officer and Chief working together for the good of the
people. The system worked at its best in Northern Nigeria where the

tribal system flourished, but when it was imposed elsewhere—notably in the south among the more advanced Ibo and Yoruba peoples—it proved less successful and more open to criticism.

Naturally enough, in Kaduna, the administration tended to accept the Political Memoranda as they stood, and often demanded that every detail was followed unquestioningly. Arden-Clarke rejected this uncritical approach which led to stratification, but he admitted that working within the framework of Lugard's system was the finest possible training in Colonial administration.

Lugard, after he retired in 1919—the year before Arden-Clarke joined the Nigerian service—wrote his great philosophical work *The Dual Mandate in British Tropical Africa*, in which he expounds in detail his conviction that it was the duty of Britain to bring peace, prosperity and civilization to the African people, while at the same time increasing Britain's trade. The key to his philosophy is summed up in two telling sentences in the *Dual Mandate*:

> If there is unrest and a desire for independence as in India and Egypt, it is because we have taught the value of liberty and freedom, which for centuries these people had not known. Their very discontent is a measure of their progress. [12]

When the system of Indirect Rule was later criticized for being feudal, reactionary and paternalistic, this aspect of Lugard's policy and his amazing foresight were often overlooked or ignored. Arden-Clarke who did not go along with the uncritical acceptance of every detail of the Political Memoranda, had clearly accepted Lugard's wider philosophy. He accepted totally—and more openly than most of his contemporaries in the 1930s, or even the 1940s—that the whole purpose of their work was, while eliminating uncivilized abuses, to train the indigenous people, through their own institutions and customs, to adapt to modern conditions, to take a dignified place in the modern world, and ultimately to gain their independence. At that time whether in Kaduna or Lagos, the majority of Nigerians appeared content with paternal but beneficent and honest administration. Arden-Clarke with his wide knowledge of Northern Nigeria and his realistic and critical approach, realized that especially in the powerful northern emirates, some reactionary and backward systems were upheld, but he believed that this did not seriously detract from the positive forward looking policy of Indirect Rule as a whole.

In 1933 he received dramatic and significant promotion, when he was transferred to the Governor's Secretariat in Lagos to be in charge of Native Affairs. At 35 he was extremely young to have such a senior and

[12] *Dual Mandate* p.618. (Published 1922)

responsible post, but even so he deeply regretted leaving the North where he had been so fully involved with the people. He came to Lagos when Sir Donald Cameron, who had a reputation for being tough and autocratic, was starting to carry through his major reorganization of the Northern Emirates. His proposals included the complete banning of corporal punishment throughout Nigeria. Having just come from the North, and having vivid memories and experiences of corporal punishment being effectively used, Arden-Clarke strongly opposed its abolition. Having just arrived in his new post, as a very young head of department, he hesitated before crossing swords with a Governor of the calibre and reputation of Sir Donald Cameron. However, he wrote a detailed Minute supporting his case, went out and bought—for one shilling and sixpence—a Bulala whip, which was at the centre of some of the controversy over corporal punishment, and sent off the file containing both his Minute and the whip. Soon afterwards the Chief Secretary summoned him and cross-questioned him, both about the Minute and the whip. Two months later the new directive came out, and although it imposed certain restrictions it did not abolish corporal punishment.

. For the next three years Arden-Clarke worked in the Secretariat while the reorganization of the Northern Emirates was completed. This brought fierce clashes between Cameron and many of the senior officials in the North, but for a young man, freshly appointed to a senior and responsible post, it was an excellent training in administrative methods at a high level. Cameron, in spite of his reputation as an autocrat, showed outstanding kindness and consideration to his younger staff. He came to know Arden-Clarke very well, and said that he had first been impressed by his Minute on corporal punishment, and the way he stood up for what he thought was right.

Although he had done extremely well in Nigeria and had gained rapid promotion, the mid-1930s brought serious problems. In 1936 he suffered from acute appendicitis as well as amoebic and bacillic dysentery. This period of fairly serious illness, coupled with the long periods of separation from his wife and three young children made him decide to seek a transfer to a healthier climate. His seniors told him that the chance of such a transfer was remote. His colleagues advised him against transferring, since he had obviously been picked out for rapid promotion, and he had a good chance of taking over a Province. In spite of this encouragement he thought very seriously of retirement. Having joined the Colonial Service in 1920, he would have been able to retire in 1938, but realized the serious problem he would face in obtaining another job, since he had no academic or professional qualifications. He earnestly considered the possibility of reading for an external degree of London

University. At this low pitch in his life, when he had virtually decided to retire, he received a despatch offering him a transfer to Bechuanaland as Government Secretary and Assistant Resident Commissioner. He read the despatch a second time, and then looked up *Whitakers Almanac* to see where Bechuanaland was. At that time it had no capital and the Headquarters of the Administration worked from Mafeking in the Cape Province of South Africa. This meant that if he went there the whole family could be together. This weighed very heavily both with him and his wife and proved to be the decisive factor in their decision to accept the transfer. Thus he went, on secondment, to Bechuanaland and to the service, not of the Colonial Office, but of the Commonwealth Relations Office, and in 1936 after 16 eventful years, he left Nigeria.

CHAPTER THREE
Bechuanaland and Basutoland

When Arden-Clarke received the telegram early in 1936 offering him the post in Bechuanaland, he had to find the place on a map. He did not realize that in many different ways fate had prepared him for a great opportunity. On two further occasions—in Sarawak and the Gold Coast—he was to be drafted in dramatically, to grasp a complex and difficult situation, and was to show that he had the personality, confidence and experience to rise successfully to the challenge. In 1936 he did not realize that his 16 years of rigorous training on Lugard's precepts, or his resolute but sympathetic and successful handling of the problems of Native Administration within the context of Lugard's Political Memoranda, were precisely the experience that was required in the ticklish situation in the Bechuanaland Protectorate.

In 1936 the fortunes of the territory had reached their nadir. For ten years Tshekedi Khama, the Chief Regent of the Bamangwato, a man of fire and vision, had been frustrated by the attitudes of many of the administrators of the Protectorate. He and his people had become increasingly alarmed by the continuing attempts of the South African Government to take over Bechuanaland and its sister protectorates Basutoland and Swaziland. Economic stagnation, drought, pestilence and growing political anxiety loomed over the almost melodramatic career of Tshekedi, but at a critical juncture Arden-Clarke made his appearance and the whole situation changed dramatically.

The background to the crisis of 1936 goes back almost to 1885 when Bechuanaland became a protectorate. In that year, feeling themselves threatened by German activity in South West Africa, by the advancing Boer trekkers and by the rapid movement of Rhodes' British South Africa Company along its road to the north, the Bamangwato people and their neighbouring tribes the Bangwaketse and Backwena accepted protectorate status. Under the terms of the treaties, the chiefs—including the great Khama, who became a christian—were left to rule over their own people, but almost from the beginning they were menaced by external pressures. In 1895 Cape Colony took over a strip of territory in the south of Bechuanaland including Mafeking, which, although it was thereafter outside the protectorate, remained its administrative capital. In the 1890s the chiefs protested successfully against being handed over to Rhodes' company. In 1905, the great Khama's fourth young wife bore him a son, Tshekedi, who was brought up at Serowe in an actively christian household. After schooling in South Africa and a college course at Fort Hare, at the age of 23, Tshekedi succeeded the great Khama as Regent for his nephew Seretse.

Tshekedi followed his father's example and ruled according to the best customs of the tribe, helping his people to stand on their own feet in the difficult modern world. Backed up by the London Missionary Society, Tshekedi firmly suppressed family and tribal feuds, and organized tax-collecting among the tribes.

The protectorates lay under the authority of the High Commissioner who, until 1928, combined the office with that of Governor General of South Africa, thus emphasizing the link with the Dominion. During the 1920s and early 1930s, the High Commissioner curtailed the powers of some chiefs, and deposed or banished others. Under the High Commissioner, the Resident Commissioner and his team of Resident Magistrates ran the country with an approach very different in emphasis to that used, for example, in Nigeria. The administration gave instructions to the native authorities, kept control of public money, and directly administered the extensive Crown Lands and all land belonging to Europeans. The whole administrative system appeared slow, inefficient and deliberately frustrating. It was made worse by generally indifferent staff, frequently recruited in South Africa, and with South African attitudes to native affairs, who saw little future in their careers because they expected South Africa to take over the territory at any time.

To a chief like Tshekedi, who witnessed and shared the sufferings of his people, and had the intelligence and initiative to see what should be done to improve things, the whole situation was doubly frustrating. The poverty-stricken protectorate suffered severely from the slump of 1930–1, and their sufferings were made worse by the cattle embargo imposed by South Africa. Because of the poverty, the slump and the drought, more and more able-bodied men were forced to go to the Union for work, a situation which exacerbated all the economic and social ills of the country.

Tshekedi first made his mark both nationally and internationally when, helped by his good friend and supporter Douglas Buchanan KC, he opposed the declared intention of the government to grant mining concessions in Bechuanaland to the British South Africa Company. Although the Resident Commissioner, Colonel Daniel, supported Tshekedi as an outstanding, efficient and forward-looking chief, the High Commission staff generally put pressure on him to agree to the concessions, and he was once told that if he did not agree 'he would be kicked out'. In 1930 he went to London to argue his case at the

Dominions Office. Lord Passfield reassured him, and in 1932 a completely new arrangement was drawn up which gave vastly improved conditions to the Bamangwato people—due entirely to Tshekedi's courage and determination.

In the following year, a native court which acted on Tshekedi's authority, caused a white youth to be flogged. He had an odious reputation in the area for seducing African girls, and his behaviour roused violent feelings among the people. To everyone's amazement, the acting High Commissioner Admiral Evans (Evans of the Broke), in order to teach Tshekedi a lesson, organized a special train to bring howitzers, guns and a strong detachment of marines up to Bechuanaland from Simonstown. The prospect of the Royal Navy operating in the Kalahari Desert gave considerable scope to a critical world press, and the Gilbertian element was enhanced when one of the howitzers was bogged down in the sand and Tshekedi's men had to come and retrieve it. The Resident Commissioner, Colonel Rey, suspended Tshekedi pending the investigation by Evans. This was an appalling misjudgement, for all the Europeans in the territory including the youth's parents, openly expressed support for Tshekedi. Tshekedi was actually on his way to Cape Town, under escort, when he received a telegram with a Royal Pardon from George V. Although he was re-instated by Evans—albeit with an ill grace—the incident did severe damage to Britain's reputation in Africa, and roused seriously hostile comment in the world press. The subsequent comment of Evans that he had taken decisive action because the natives were getting very much above themselves, drew further attention to the deep rift between the views of Tshekedi and those of South Africa and its supporters.

Such incidents focussed attention both on Tshekedi and on Bechuanaland, but, for the people of the territory they were overshadowed by the growing threat from South Africa to take over the area completely. At the 1932 Ottawa Conference N. C. Havenga raised the question openly and gave thinly veiled threats of stopping migrant labour into the Union. Here, again, Tshekedi's supporters Buchanan and Jennings helped. They travelled to London not only to clear Tshekedi's name over the flogging incident, but also to gain a clear assurance from the Government that the High Commission Territories would not be handed over to South Africa. In Whitehall they received a cordial welcome from Malcolm MacDonald, who initially admitted that he knew little of Bechuanaland or the Bamangwato, but before they left the emissaries received the assurances they required. In spite of this, South Africa, through Hertzog and Smuts, kept up the pressure and made more formal demands for the territories. Smuts quoted the Union Act of 1910, which clearly referred to the eventual admission of the territories, and he also quoted a speech by Lord Selborne in 1910, when he told the Bechuanaland chiefs that their admission 'would take place some day'.

Tshekedi played a useful role at this stage by publishing thoughtful and restrained booklets on Britain's responsibilities and Africans' trust. He stressed how much Bechuanaland valued the right of appeal to the Privy Council, which under the Statute of Westminster of 1931 South Africa had just cut off. Distinguished Commonwealth scholars engaged in the debate, and Margery Perham argued strongly against making the people of Bechuanaland pay the price of cordial relations between Britain and South Africa. At last an all party committee stated clearly that Britain had a moral obligation not only to consult, but to gain the consent of the peoples of the Protectorates, and that this was now more important than ever because of Hertzog's openly declared policy of white paramountcy.

In 1936 the new High Commissioner Sir William Clarke, backed by the Resident Commissioner Colonel Rey, pointed out that a more generous and more accommodating approach by South Africa might help to sway the peoples of Bechuanaland. Soon afterwards South Africa offered £36,000 to the three territories to help with their economic problems, but offset the value of their offer by stating that they expected to take over in two years. Malcolm MacDonald, now Secretary of State for the Dominions, stated clearly that because of the outrage caused by Hertzog's statement it would be best to leave the question in abeyance.

In the tense and highly charged atmosphere caused by these crises, another crisis now erupted. From the early 1930s Tshekedi had strongly opposed two new proclamations: on Native Administration and on Native Courts. These proclamations had angered and alarmed the people of Bechuanaland, and from 1933 Tshekedi had formally opposed them as a serious encroachment on native rights and native law. His argument, which was supported by distinguished constitutional lawyers, maintained that the peoples of Bechuanaland were not a conquered race, but had voluntarily entered into the protectorate agreements. Therefore the British government did not have the power to appoint or dismiss chiefs or to interfere in Native Law and Customs as the new Proclamations attempted to do. Hearing that he was in danger of arrest, Tshekedi fled with his fellow chief Bathoen to Cape Town and, on the advice of Buchanan, decided to sue the High Commissioner in order to prove the Proclamations illegal.

At this peak in his bad relations with the administration, he received the support both of Lord Lugard and of Margery Perham. They pointed out that elsewhere in Africa the British had gained the confidence of the chiefs and people, and, with tact and discretion, had encouraged the chiefs to work for the good of their people. In Bechuanaland, in contrast, the administration had signally failed to gain the confidence of the people, had not given them the guidance they needed, and appeared more and more ready to hand over the territory to South Africa. Margery Perham personally supported Tshekedi as an able and dedicated leader of his people, and she stressed the need for a complete change in the attitude of the administration. Significantly, Lord Lugard stressed the value of experience with the Native Administration system of Nigeria, and concluded that the peoples of the protectorate should be given as much responsibility as possible for running their own affairs.

While the debate raged in London and Whitehall the trial over the Proclamations took place before more than 1,000 of the assembled Bamangwato people. Tshekedi's adviser Buchanan had done his work thoroughly and was able to prove that Colonel Rey had drawn up the Proclamations without even consulting the chiefs on native law and custom. The judge realized the strength of Tshekedi's case, and quickly referred the matter to the Secretary of State. Although, considerably later, the Secretary of State was to give a ruling that His Majesty's Government was not limited by the treaty rights, Tshekedi had clearly won a moral victory.

In fact the Proclamations were altered in very different circumstances and in a very different atmosphere. Arden-Clarke arrived in Mafeking while this crisis was at its height. Colonel Rey was absent on leave, so immediately Arden-Clarke became acting Resident Commissioner. He set out at once for Serowe to see Tshekedi in his capital. They met and immediately established a trust and rapport which was never serously broken.

From his experience in Nigeria Arden-Clarke was able to see immediately what others perhaps saw later—that the key to much of the trouble in Bechuanaland was personal relationships. Tshekedi, a doughty fighter for his people and his principles, immediately responded to Arden-Clarke's firm, cheerful and relaxed approach. Having spent many years as a District Commissioner, Arden-Clarke immediately brought in the local District Commissioner, Captain Nettleton, for his initial talks with Tshekedi. A substantial contributing factor in the Tshekedi situation had always been the attitudes of the administrative staff. They were often men recruited as clerical officers who gradually worked their way up, and were not of the calibre of the Colonial Service officers who came to Bechuanaland after the success of Arden-Clarke. The old hands lacked imagination and drive, and in most situations fell back on the South African attitude of arrogant superiority towards natives.

Having made an excellent initial impact with Tshekedi, and having started work immediately on a temporary solution to the proclamations issue, Arden-Clarke set off as soon as possible to tour the protectorate; to meet the people, and to weigh up the nature of the problem which faced him. He followed this routine in three more territories: Basutoland, Sarawak and the Gold Coast, but the eagerness with which he always set off on trek suggests that he had not entirely lost the enthusiasm which he had had as a young District Officer for getting away from the office and out in the bush.

After a brief tour to get the feel of the territory, Arden-Clarke returned to tackle the issue of the proclamations. Having gained some time by a temporary measure, he set up a committee—not, as in the past, of government officials to lay down the law—but with himself, Tshekedi, Bathoen, with other chiefs and people. If his intial impact on Tshekedi had been good, the work on this committee convinced both chiefs and people that here they had a man of wisdom, foresight and experience. The chiefs had tried for years to set up treasuries for their people, but the government had always resisted their demands on the grounds that the people were not ready for such a change, and that such backward people could see and understand if their wealth was in cattle, but would not understand money which they could not see. Arden-Clarke, having struggled from his early days with the Madas and Mamas to establish financial responsibility among people far more backward than the Bamangwato, brought enthusiasm, experience and confidence to the relatively straightforward issue of the Native Treasuries. By 1938 a new Native Treasuries Proclamation was issued which brought deep satisfaction and substantial economic progress to the people. The proclamation set up a straightforward tax system, with a small Finance Committee staffed by professionals, with the normal departmental structure. At the same time the tribal courts were reorganized.

After this early work together, Arden-Clarke, who had been warned that Tshekedi was a very slippery customer, found him to be above all a man of his word. He said 'I could not have asked for a more staunch ally.' Their relationship proved even more important when, early in 1937, Colonel Rey retired, and Arden-Clarke became Resident Commissioner. In a letter home he said he would be glad when Rey had gone, because they had frequent differences of opinion, and although Rey had a quick brain and vitality, he lacked balance, judgement and patience in dealing with natives.

Having changed in mid-career from the Colonial Office to the Dominions Office, it was a remarkable promotion for Arden-Clarke to become Resident Commissioner at the age of 39. Clearly his success with Tshekedi and his handling of the Proclamations dispute had carried weight in his appointment. Having completed the groundwork on administrative reform, and having taken over from Rey, he left for a major tour in July 1937. His diary gives a vivid impression not only of the country and its people, but the sort of problems which faced a barren and drought-stricken area.

He left by train from Mafeking for Palapye where he transferred to a lorry and car. The local chiefs had been instructed to stop people begging from the train, but at Notwani he found an outrageous number of beggars. At Gaberones he met Arrowsmith[1] who reported the death of a chief, and then he went on to see the Bamangwato Cattle Improvement Scheme. Here he spoke to the animal husbandry officer and warned him—as he warned most of his staff—to be patient with Tshekedi and the chiefs, and to take time to win over the chiefs and people to new ideas. In a letter home he wrote:

> It is a truism of Native Administration, and the hardest one of all to follow, that you can only go as fast as the people will let you. It is a truth I am trying to instil into my Heads of Department . . . They try and press on too fast and ram their schemes down the peoples throats. As a natural result the people object . . . A few months spent in preparing the ground and in patient education will often make the people realize for themselves that the scheme is good, and in the end they will make it their own and see to it themselves that it works successfully.[2]

He also added that there was a bad tradition of long standing to be overcome.

When on trek, usually with a driver and two orderlies, they normally slept under the stars in spite of the intense cold—they often woke to find all their water frozen hard. He described how he went to bed with a cardigan, a great coat and a kaross of jackal skins on top of his blankets. After his years in Nigeria he found the cold difficult to bear.

His first stop was Serowe—Tshekedi's capital. Tshekedi was away on holiday, but he had useful discussions with the District Commissioner,[3] and emphasized the need to get in the Native Treasury Estimates as soon as Tshekedi returned. Serowe needed more quarters, and a Residency was also to be built. On the road again he met a family whose daughter's life had been saved by their newly installed wireless relay. He also met McIntosh the youth whose flogging had resulted in Tshekedi's temporary suspension. Arden-Clarke commented 'An incredible piece of administrative ineptitude.'[4]

His journey took him through the flat 'pan' country—formerly great

[1] Sir Edwin Arrowsmith KCMG.
[2] Letter to Family 4.7.37.
[3] The title had now been changed from Resident Magistrate.
[4] This and subsequent quotations are taken from a diary of the tour covering July and August 1937.

lakes but now flat dusty bowls. Game abounded here and he normally shot sprinkgbok to provide meat for the party. He was not a good shot and often ruefully referred to a vast expenditure of ammunition without any result. After a few days he met up with the DC, Ellenberger, and also Tshekedi's chief tax collector who was a member of the royal family and Arden-Clarke noted, when they were setting up camp in the bush, 'Like all ruling natives he is averse to doing any manual work and while Ellenberger and I were busy collecting wood for the camp fire he retired behind a thornbush and squatted down comfortably to rest.'[5] The next day he reached Gwata in an area of new territory handed over to Tshekedi as an increase in the Bamangwato reserve. New settlers were coming in, who had few complaints, except that lions were carrying off their sheep and goats at night. The country varied—some seemed promising, with plenty of water, elsewhere with water scarce it was near desert. After a grim drive through duststorms, he reached Rakops where he was able to get a bath in the house of the police corporal, but there followed several more days of desert driving, low gear work with the car radiator boiling until he reached Maun where a DC, MacKenzie, lived in a delightful house on the banks of a river, and with a tennis court.

At Maun he inspected the station, including a mission hospital run by Seventh Day Adventists. This needed expansion but its estimates had to be considered against other projects proposed by Sir Walter Johnson's report of 1937. He met the local people and traders and was able to assure them that funds were now available to rectify most of their complaints. He also attended a full dress Kgotla—the full formal meeting of the tribe—where the new chief Moremi expressed the tribe's wishes to move away from Maun. Maun lay on the southern edge of the great Okavango swamp, and Arden-Clarke met Jeffares, who was surveying the swamp, and needed the help of aerial reconnaissance.

On the journey from Maun, southwestwards some 200 miles to Ghanzi, he was stopped by a veldt fire—a serious problem, for the fires were destroying the vegetation and turning the land into desert. The first complaints from Ghanzi were that the radio operators from Mafeking and Maun left their messages to the end, and so they had to stand by for often half an hour wasting their precious batteries.

Ghanzi had a number of Dutch and poor white settlers—originally put there by Rhodes to stop German encroachment from South West Africa. The settlers claimed to have been promised all the land by the Resident Commissioner in 1898, and wanted the natives removed. Arden-Clarke refused to accept this, and added that everywhere in South Africa was this greed for land, and always at the expense of the native. Yet there was

[5] Diary 14 July 1937.

land to spare for all. None of the land was fenced, and sometimes when the pans in the interior dried out the Bushmen came over and occasionally stole cattle, though this was not a major problem. Colonial Development Funds had been used to develop a Karakul Sheep Farm under an enthusiastic Scot called Murray. Some extreme Calvinist Dutch farmers maintained that to breed and kill young lambs was sinful. Murray suggested they dropped some of their other sins and took up this one, and pointed out that out on the veldt they slaughtered all game with indiscriminate abandon.

At the time of this tour, Arden-Clarke was deeply involved in setting up and organizing the Native Treasuries throughout the Protectorate, but everywhere he went he found more work to be done, and the paper work had to be left until he returned to Mafeking.

One of the biggest projects, with the possibility of tremendous benefits for the country, concerned the Okavango swamps. A large river—the Okavango—flowed from the north into the swamps which had become a vast sponge, soaking up all its waters. Less than 100 years before, the waters had flowed right through the area, and the region to the south had been green and fertile. The current scheme was to get the Okavango flowing again, and to restore its waters to the arid desert area south of Maun. The Colonial Development Fund had given about £1,000 a year but, as Arden-Clarke commented, 'one might as well give a man a garden hose and tell him to wash away Mount Everest'.

The project, so far, had been operated by Colonel Naus, a temperamental Frenchman alleged to have fought with Sinn Fein. He had lived in the swamps for years on a pittance and, with just a few native labourers to help him, had achieved remarkable results. He took Arden-Clarke on an expedition into the swamps, along hippo tracks, in small dugout canoes. He had cleared a main channel and had made dams and sluices, but although more water was flowing, it was only scratching the surface of the main problem. Two days later Arden-Clarke, with the Government engineer, made an aerial reconnaissance over the whole of the swamps, and afterwards called a conference. He decided to stop the general scheme and concentrate the available money and effort on clearing papyrus from the River Taoghe, which would have immediate beneficial effects. He sent Naus to the coast for eight weeks leave, leaving for later the decision about the wider project of draining the swamps.

After the interlude in the swamps, Arden-Clarke returned to Maun to further discussions with Chief Moremi of the Batawana. He found them a truculent and difficult people but he made it plain that the government would not spend any money to move the tribe away from Maun. Travelling on, the next day he held a Kgotla at Kachikau. The tribe complained about the arbitrary conduct of the stock inspector, the difficulty of getting .303 ammunition for their rifles, and above all about the storekeepers, who would not pay them cash for their cattle, but merely gave them chits or 'good fors' to be used back at the store.

Beyond Kachikau he came to Kasane on the banks of the Chobe river and looking over the Caprivi Strip. This was a delightful spot with a few European bungalows and the Police lines. It had been a district centre, but there can have been little to do there except for shooting and fishing, and Arden-Clarke closed it down, adding that a lot of the old stagers were realizing that the old happy days of idleness had gone. Here also was a well run depot where boys from Barotseland were recruited for the Witwatersrand Mines.

After inspecting the station, and a forestry project, Arden-Clarke had lunch with two senior forestry officers. He wrote:

> It was ridiculous to hear these two men, both fifteen years my senior, addressing me with deference and calling me 'Sir', and referring to me as 'His Honour'. I suppose I shall get used to it in time but it does seem a bit fatuous . . . Everyone is a little taken aback when they first meet His Honour, the Resident Commissioner, and instead of a grey-haired elder of sixty, find me.

Soon after this he met the Duke of Northumberland and they were formally introduced—'His Grace', 'His Honour'. The Duke was about 30 and in filthy blood-spattered slacks having just carved a tusk from an elephant he had shot. He was accompanied by a real African character called Coombe, who had lost a leg after being mauled by a lion, but who continued hunting with his wooden leg. Some time later while out shooting, he was bowled over by an elephant and lay helpless, because of his wooden leg, while the elephant decided what to do with him.

Days in the bush and on trek were interspersed with serious policy discussions. One of the serious issues for the Bechuanaland Protectorate was the recruitment of their young men for the mines in South Africa. While still at Kasane, Arden-Clarke met one of the chief men from the Native Recruiting Corporation; he knew that there was an acute shortage of cattle in Johannesburg and that prices were soaring. He used this argument to convince Gemmill that the Union should allow cattle to be imported. He also suggested that Gemmill should apply for a recruiting monopoly, because his organization looked after their labourers well and repatriated them after their service.

Arden-Clarke's proposal arose from very serious concern about recruitment in the protectorate. There were too many recruiting agencies, which did not look after their workers, and which were taking away far too many able-bodied young men. He wanted to restrict recruitment to one or two companies, so that all their young men would be in one place, where he could keep in touch with them and see to their welfare. He hoped, if this was done, to arrange some sort of schooling while they were at the mines, In the protectorate 80 per cent of the pupils at school were girls, largely because the boys went off herding cattle at an early age and then went off to the mines as soon as they were old enough. He concluded:

Whether I shall ever be able to get my schemes through is another matter—there is much to be said for a dictatorship, provided, of course, one happens to be the dictator.

Early in August he left Kasane for Livingstone to see the Victoria Falls. On the way he passed a famous tree under which Livingstone is supposed to have slept. The trunk was plastered with government notices banning the import of arms and liquor. He immediately had them removed.

I hate to see a fine tree defaced like that, whether Livingstone slept under it or not—besides hardly a soul except an occasional native now travels this route and the native cannot read.

At the Victoria Falls he spent the afternoon prowling about by himself, and determined to bring Gina and the children up to see them. Here he got hold of a man who ran flights over the Falls, and interested him in running an air service from Livingstone to Maun to encourage tourists to go for shooting trips. His reasoning was far-sighted. If tourists started coming to Maun, where a hotel had recently been opened, he would be able to declare a game reserve and by doing this they would drive back the game—and also the tsetse fly which the game brought with them—away from the cattle grazing areas. After this discussion he was taken up on a flight over the Falls, and found they were even more magnificent from the air. He concluded 'See Naples and die. But first fly low over the Victoria Falls.'

After his detailed tour of the Protectorate, Arden-Clarke returned to Mafeking with a strong determination to galvanize the administrative service into action. While on trek he had seen much that dismayed him, and he felt that many of the problems stemmed from the attitude of the white administrators towards the native peoples. Here, as in other spheres, the key to progress lay in the lead which he could give with Tshekedi.

Together they organized schemes for the betterment of the people. To the Bamangwato and the other peoples of the Protectorate, prosperity depended on cattle and grain, and for both of these, new arrangements were made. To stop profiteering at the expense of the native peoples, tribal granaries were set up and in 1938 the Northern Rhodesia market was opened to cattle from Bechuanaland. Tshekedi, who had suffered years of frustration, now, with a Resident Commissioner whom he trusted and respected, became too impetuous and tried to drive his people too hard. Arden-Clarke realized that Tshekedi was antagonizing his people, and he frequently applied a restraining hand. Because of the climate and an abundance of land the people were easy-going and lackadaisical, and would not easily adapt to modern ways. Although the two had serious clashes, their deep respect and support for each other was never soured. The biographer of Tshekedi gives a shrewd appraisal of their relationship. [6]

'There were occasions that Arden-Clarke recalled to Tshekedi many years after. "You would suddenly get an almost devilish look in your eyes, Chief," he told Tshekedi, "and when I used to see that I would stop in mid-sentence and say—'Well, we'll leave this for the moment and go on in a week's time'. Tshekedi replied, "Well when I began to see the veins swelling in your neck, and you began fingering your collar, I would do the same'."[6]

The High Commissioner, Sir William Clark, on a visit to Serowe at this time, referred to the better understanding between the administration and the chief, and told Tshekedi in Kgotla: 'A new era has begun and I look for a period of peace and prosperity under your rule.'

'In this new era there was even a social innovation. To the dismay of his officials, and the horror of some wives, Arden-Clarke invited all of them to tea with the Tswana chiefs and their followers. However, everybody went, there were no noticeable ill-effects and the event became an annual one. But the times most appreciated by Tshekedi were those when he and Arden-Clarke went on trek together. Tshekedi would make his camp a little way off and, if invited to do so (he was meticulous and never went without an invitation) would join Arden-Clarke in front of the camp fire. Several officials have remarked that the trouble with Tshekedi was that he never relaxed, you could not sit down and have a drink with him and get on easy terms. Arden-Clarke did not find this: he would sit with his whisky, Tshekedi with his orange juice and they would discuss many things—tribal affairs, agriculture, education and wild game . . . Arden-Clarke asked him where the failure between him and the Administration had lain in the past: "In personal relationships" was the reply.'[7]

His maturing relationship with Tshekedi and some of the problems related to it, were described in a letter:

I have had the usual very full and busy week, the last three days being taken up with Chief Tshekedi. Our chief problem was that of the

[6] *Tshekedi Khama* by Mary Benson. Faber 1960.
[7] Ibid.

Masarwa, a servile tribe in the Bamangwato reserve, about whose status a lot of rubbish has been written, coupled with exaggerated stories of atrocities committed upon them by the Bamangwato. Hitherto the Chief had given the Government no support in dealing with the problem, but by the end of a long days battling I had won the Chief over and he has promised his active support of all the measures which I proposed. I am really feeling very pleased about it, and I think he will fulfil his promises. Now there is the compilation of the report for the League of Nations Anti Slavery Committee and the Aborigines Protection Society, a body of ill-informed and impractical idealists imbued with excellent intentions but of unbalanced judgement. The League of Nations Committee is mercifully much more sensible. [8]

By the end of 1937 Arden-Clarke clearly felt that he had achieved considerable success in the Protectorate, because so many new schemes were going forward and there was a positive and co-operative attitude between the administration and the chiefs. To some extent he felt the measure of his success was reflected in the complaint made in December 1937 by Hertzog the South African Prime Minister, about his appointment. Hertzog complained that someone more conversant with South African problems should have been appointed as Resident Commissioner.

Arden-Clarke revelled in the challenge of going on trek, with the excitement, the discomfort and the satisfaction of getting to grips with what were, in the end, his problems; but he was less happy on the more formal treks when he and his wife had to accompany the High Commissioner.

The most tiring part of all were the tea parties to meet all the European inhabitants at each place we visited. New people were brought up to one in a continuous stream, some of them completely speechless, others with their own axes to grind, yet others merely boring, but to each one had to give of ones best. And the same thing had to be repeated in our coaches at night when we entertained all we could fit in, to dinner. It's the social side of this job that I find most trying . . . Gina I'm afraid was a little overtired by the end of it. She stood up to the job like a little Trojan and did her share splendidly. [9]

Towards the end of 1937 Arden-Clarke went on trek with the Director of Education—Dumbrill. They visited schools and showed particular interest in the projects to build new primary schools. Often these projects were supported financially by the new Tribal Treasuries and they were often built by the 'tribal regiments'. This was self-help or forced labour—depending on which way you looked at it—but Arden-Clarke's

[8] Letter to Mother 3.10.37.
[9] Letter to Father 4.7.37.

comment was 'These people want schools and are determined to have them.'[10]

On this journey he had another meeting with Chief Tshekedi:

It really is a pleasure to meet Chief Tshekedi now. We disposed of all our business in a most amicable manner. There was one thing about which I expected trouble. I had to ask him to forget about his powers as Chief in accordance with native law and custom, and to proceed in a certain matter about which I knew he felt strongly, only through the court of the District Commissioner. It was really quite a lot to ask of a man so jealous of his rights and prerogatives as Tshekedi. Two years ago he would have refused point blank. Today he accepted my advice without demur. I think the whole secret is that we like, respect and trust each other.[10]

By this time Arden-Clarke had improved on his camping arrangements, and his expedition included a lorry and a Buick car. Even with this, progress was slow, the car frequently boiling because of endless low gear work through the sand. After several days of frustration they had the bright idea of taking off the bonnet. Although the driver strongly opposed this—thinking it was undignified for the Resident Commissioner to drive through the desert with a bonnet-less car—it completely solved the problem of overheating and they made much swifter progress thereafter.

On the third day—having, in the morning, seen an ostrich bury its head in the sand—they visited a new school at Loklakhane.

A tumbledown little grass hut in the veldt where about twenty four youngsters, mostly Masarwa, assemble to be taught by an untrained young man whose only qualification is that he scrambled through Standard VI. Dumbrill spent a happy hour or more putting the children through their paces and teaching the teacher how to teach. I wish Sir John Harris, the Secretary of the Aborigines Protection Society could have seen that school. He writes in the Spectator of the Masarwa as 'slaves under the British flag'. He should have seen his so-called slaves and their master going to school together.[10]

The school was in danger of closing because the people were migrating in search of the game, roots and berries on which they lived, but Arden-Clarke was busy getting them seed for their farms so that the 'cattle-post' schools could become more permanent and be staffed with trained teachers. At another school, where none of the pupils knew how to play games, Dumbrill taught them leap-frog and gave them a few old tennis balls. Again the problem was to teach the teacher to teach.

The whole district around Rakops suffered from severe drought, and

[10] Diary September 1937.

because grazing was giving out Arden-Clarke allowed intrusion, for grazing, on to Crown Lands. In some areas, too, lions were carrying off cattle and horses in large numbers. After days of hard travel and visiting small outstations, they came to the Botletle river about 14 miles from Maun. He wrote:

> There is a lovely moon, the reflection of trees in the water, the sound of water rippling over stones, the smell of water, the sound of frogs and plash of fish jumping—it's a poem and one comes on it so suddenly after the hundreds of miles of sand and dessicated wastes over which we have been struggling.[11]

After this pleasant interlude he reached Maun and met a South African general who had flown in to inspect the emergency air-strips and whose attitude—which Arden-Clarke tried to change—was that South Africa should try to strangle the Protectorates into submission.

Having established excellent relations with Tshekedi and the other chiefs, Arden-Clarke's chief role in the succeeding years was to galvanize his administration into action and to travel throughout the territory to ensure that his policies were being carried out. Many of the smaller chiefs were slow to understand the implications of the Native Treasuries and he often explained personally to a chief that, although he would get a regular salary, it had to be fixed at a reasonable level dependent on the tribal revenue. For years past the chiefs had been extremely suspicious of the government and the need to win their confidence was urgent.

For a country so dependent on its cattle, the advance of the tsetse fly into grazing areas presented a very serious problem, and Arden-Clarke travelled extensively with his Veterinary officers and supported their efforts to drive out the tsetse fly and to eradicate trypanosomiasis which it brought. Serious problems arose on the border with South West Africa and along the Caprivi strip because the authorities on the other side of the border were careless or negligent, and their inadequacy undermined the vigorous efforts being made in the Protectorate.

The presence of game features largely in the accounts of his travels. On one trip, a flock of vultures led the party to the carcass of a koodoo bull and a close view of three black maned lions. One of the party got in a shot, and severely wounded one lion but it got away and it was clearly too dangerous to pursue it through thick thorn bush. At the end of that day's travel they swam in the shallows of a river because there were crocodiles in the deeper parts.

With his personal interest and support, the scheme to re-route the Okovango River made substantial headway. The new engineer in charge, Drotsky, was a man of very different calibre to his predecessor, and was

[11] Diary September 1937.

prepared to devote his life to bringing back water to Lake Ngami. He hoped to find a diamond mine, and to present it to the government providing they devoted the whole proceeds to his scheme for Lake Ngami. He wanted nothing for himself. Arden-Clarke admired him and applied both to the High Commissioner and to the Colonial Development Fund for assistance with the project. At the apex of the triangular delta forming the swamp, a substantial improvement was achieved by re-opening the course where the Taoghe River joined the Okavango. Arden-Clarke described the Okavango as 'a grand river sixty yards wide, running swiftly between well defined banks and very deep'. Once he was about to swim in it when Drotsky pointed out three crocodiles. He travelled extensively in this area, often with Drotsky and other officials and was in camp with them when in September 1938 he heard on the radio the sombre news from Europe of the Munich crisis, and had to start thinking of his responsibilities should war come. To him, like so many of his generation who had been in the trenches, the idea of war was unthinkable.

The Ngami area presented violent contrasts—between endless miles of soft sand and blistering heat, and deep sluggish water courses blocked by towering walls of papyrus. Arden-Clarke, who had a sensitive eye for nature made some vivid descriptions of animal and bird life, together with humorous comments on the incidents which took place. Once having shot wildly and far too high at a buck, his driver said 'a good shot master, if the buck had jumped at that moment you would have hit it'.[12] On the same trip he wrote:

> There was some wonderful bird life to watch; giant kingfishers and the ordinary black and white pied kingfishers at their business of spearing fish, hovering with their long beaks pointed like lances and then dropping smack into the water and rising again swiftly, sometimes with a small fish in their beaks; two lovely jewels of birds which Mac. identified as malachite kingfishers, tiny things which kept visiting their nest almost at our feet, and a pair of gorgeous bee-eaters which perched on a branch above our heads paying no attention to us and occasionally flying off and performing incredible aerobatic feats in pursuit of some insect.[13]

While he thoroughly enjoyed travelling, and visiting the border posts all round the Protectorate, the new schools supported increasingly by the Native Authorities, the cattle development centres and the drainage schemes at Okavango, he was less than happy with the invariable request to say a few words. 'How I hate that phrase. "Will your Honour be good enough to say a few words."'

[12] Diary September 1938.
[13] Ibid.

Although Arden-Clarke's initial and most dynamic contribution to Bechuanaland affairs was in the field of personal relationships, of equal importance was his ability and determination to reorganize native administration so that it would operate for the benefit of the people. To achieve this he had many tough fights with Chiefs who saw their powers—and especially their financial powers—being whittled away, but having gained their confidence he also in the end gained their co-operation. In 1938 the Native Treasuries Proclamation was issued and was widely welcomed. It established tribal teasuries and gave each Chief a fixed stipend according to the overall revenue of the tribe. The tribal collection, or revenue, was divided up and 35 per cent went to the Native Treasury to be used in the tribal area. This immediately gave financial responsibility to the Chief and tribe, and with this money they accepted responsibility for education and agriculture. In the years after 1940 the funds of the Colonial Development and Welfare Act were channelled through these committees. Further reorganization, in parallel with these financial measures, and initiated at the same time by Arden-Clarke, finally emerged as the Proclamations of 1943 which adjusted the tribal machinery, recognized the Kgotla as the main consultative body of the tribe, and gave it legal authority to hold trials according to tribal law and custom. These changes facilitated co-operation between the Chief, the tribe and the District Commissioner.

In 1938 the High Commissioner set up a Joint Advisory Conference of the Resident Commissioners of Bechuanaland, Basutoland and Swaziland to study opportunities for co-operation between the territories and to consider their relationship with the Union of South Africa. The committee, including Arden-Clarke, visited the three territories in the course of 1938 and made their report in February 1939. They found that there was already substantial co-operation on a practical level between the territories and the Union, over such matters as police, customs and tax collection, locust control, prisons, as well as rail, air, telegraph and postal services, which were organized from the Union. The main recommendation, strongly supported by Arden-Clarke, was that the system of importing and pricing cattle, which led to large scale smuggling and violence, should be drastically changed. The Resident Commissioners established useful contacts with senior officials in the Union but Arden-Clarke was not sanguine about the outcome as the internal politics of South Africa were in such a rotten condition.

At the outbreak of war Arden-Clarke spent an apprehensive time while South Africa hesitated about coming into the war. If the articulate pro-German groups among the Nationalist Party had gained control, Bechuanaland would have been untenable, but thanks to the brave leadership of Smuts, South Africa joined the Commonwealth effort and played a significant part on the Allied side. Arden-Clarke's immediate problems centred on policing the border with South West Africa—formerly German—and preventing the incursion of disloyal Boers, though this danger lessened when Germany overran Holland in 1940. One Nazi agent had to be dealt with, but there was little real danger, and the tribes and Chiefs remained intensely loyal. Many officers naturally wanted to leave and play a more active role in the war, and it was difficult to persuade them that their most valuable contribution to the war effort was to stay put and help increase production in the territory.

In 1940 Arden-Clarke held a major conference of the Native Advisory Council, including the eight main Chiefs and 50 headmen. They discussed land tenure, nutrition, the cattle industry and the continuing problem of conditions in the South African mines. Following the conference he visited Johannesburg to see the gold mines. He visited the labour compounds and native locations, and went underground to see for himself the conditions in which the miners worked. He found that the gold mines treated their labour well, and fed them extremely well. He thought the miners were better treated than soldiers in England.

Bechuanaland responded loyally to the British war effort, twice raising £5,000 for the purchase of a Spitfire, and supporting whole heartedly Arden-Clarke's suggestion that the grant-in-aid from the British government which was running at £65,000 pa, should be repaid in full to help the war effort. He prevented South Africa recruiting men from Bechuanaland into their Native Military Corps, because of their attitude towards native people, but he helped to raise 4,000 troops to serve with the British forces as an Auxiliary Pioneer Corps. His own feelings—having served in the Great War—were divided. During a Christmas leave by the sea in Cape Province he felt the war was like a tragedy played on a distant stage.

He was to find throughout his career that because he was successful in one post he was rapidly promoted to tackle more serious difficulties in another. In Bechuanaland he had gained the willing and enthusiastic co-operation of Tshekedi and the other Chiefs, and had set the territory on the way to prosperous self government. For his outstanding work he received the CMG, but he was not destined to remain to enjoy the fruits of his labour. In 1942, because of his success he was transferred as Resident Commissioner of Basutoland.

Basutoland, with its desolate hills, tumbling streams and heavy rain—in many ways reminiscent of Scotland—had for generations been dominated by the ancient and formidable house of Moshesh. The current Paramount Chief, a vast and daunting female, followed by all the lesser Chiefs, fiercely resisted any intrusion into their domain, or interference in their highly profitable system. For decades the Chiefs had enjoyed the right to levy fines on their subjects and to pocket the proceeds. Arden-Clarke estimated that when he arrived in Basutoland the Paramount Chief had a salary of £2,000 pa from the British Government and a further £9,000 from the proceeds of so-called justice. The peculations of the Chiefs posed a doubly urgent problem—they took so much of the possible revenue of the country that there was little available for desperately needed development, and, secondly, the thousands of men who had enlisted in the forces and had travelled abroad, were not likely to accept such an archaic and unjust system when they returned after the war.

In Basutoland Arden-Clarke did not find the ready response which he had gained from Tshekedi in 1936—instead there was a withdrawn sullenness and a surly determination to oppose what he was trying to do. The Chiefs followed the lead of the Paramount Chief and did her bidding. He found so much wrong, when he arrived, that he had to undertake major reforms and reorganization straight away, although the administration was so badly understaffed that it was difficult to keep up the daily routine. He set out to reform the executive and judicial machinery of the Native Administration, and, above all, to establish a Basuto National Treasury.

He worked in close co-operation with the High Commissioner Lord Harlech, who clearly encouraged him to establish in Basutoland the system which he had set up and which was working so well in Bechuanaland. Harlech even proposed that a group of Paramount Chiefs should visit Tshekedi's capital at Serowe to see the system working. Harlech commented in 1943 that Arden-Clarke had scored a great personal success in carrying the scheme so far in such a short time and in the face of a good deal of opposition, but he added an admonitary note that the Basuto must not be hustled.[14]

The actual situation in the Basuto courts proved to be even worse than had been anticipated. There were over 1,300 courts and the fines were 'eaten' by the Paramount Chiefs, Chiefs, Sub-Chiefs and Headmen. The total fines 'eaten' in the course of the year amounted to nearly £50,000. Arden-Clarke proposed to reduce the number of courts to 136 and to maintain them with a salaried staff. Similar chaos reigned in the executive, where there were 250 Sub-Chiefs and over a thousand headmen—giving 1,300 officials superimposed on a population of 195,000. Arden-Clarke proposed to limit the amount paid for salaries to 5 per cent of the total revenue, and to terminate the salary of Headmen with less than 35 taxpayers under them. He expected and received tough opposition to these proposals. As an example the £11,000 income of the

[14] Memo, High Commission Office Pretoria, 28.1.43.

Paramount Chief was reduced to £3,500, and other Chiefs' salaries by a similar amount. He spent many months explaining, convincing and cajoling the different chiefs and councils, but gradually wore down the opposition. Addressing the Basutoland Council he said:

> The structure of any government may be compared to a three legged stool. The Basuto stool of self-government has got only two legs—the executive and the judicial—but it lacks the third, the financial, and a three legged stool with one leg missing cannot stand by itself. It is high time we fitted your stool with its own third leg, instead of using the Treasury of the Central Government as a prop to keep it upright. [15]

He had tackled the administrative reorganization with considerable urgency because he had been chosen to visit the soldiers of the three territories who were serving in the Middle East, and he had to depart in May 1943. He went first to Cairo and from there visited every unit with Bechuanaland, Basutoland or Swaziland soldiers, from the Turkish frontier to Tunis and Malta. They were mostly employed building roads, railways and airfields, guarding POW camps, and in fire fighting units. He found the troops eager to learn to read and write in English and showing a lot of interest in the Atlantic Charter and the Beveridge Report. He was concerned about plans for their demobilization and repatriation, plans for finding them jobs when they got home, and plans for using their abilities and skills in the rapidly developing local government, educational and health services. He brought them messages from their Chiefs, but found that lack of news from home was a critical factor in their morale. Many men thought their wives had gone off with other men or had gone to Johannesburg as prostitutes; others heard rumours of crops failing, cattle dying, and people starving. Having heard their complaints he organized a Protectorate Newsletter, he got the welfare services to provide what the troops really wanted—e.g. tins of snuff for the Swazis, but most of all suitable books—and he got the Churches at home to organize volunteer letter writers to help the illiterates. This arduous trip was followed by another in June 1945 when he visited North Africa and Italy to set up the arrangements for the troops to be repatriated.

On his return from the Middle East, he was plunged back into the reorganization of the administrative system and in linking it with the very substantial post-war plans. He outlined his plans to his DC's Conference in April 1944 and published them in detail in a circular dated 31 October 1944. [16] Giving a challenging address to his DC's he stressed that government in Basutoland was based on Indirect Rule, designed to help

---

[15] Minutes of Basutoland Council 10.11.42.
[16] Maseru Secretariat File 2258.

the native people to adapt to social and economic changes, and to strive for British ideals based on Christian morals, the political ideas of personal freedom and equity, and the rights and interests of the governed.

The Basutoland Council had agreed to the establishment of District Councils and it was planned to make the Basutoland Council more representative by having an elected representative from each District Council, with representatives of Agricultural Associations, traders, teachers and Ex-Servicemen. Government changes included two new district offices in the mountain areas, with a DC, police, dispensary and agricultural adviser—both of these to be linked with Maseru by motor roads. Reorganization in the Health Services included doubling the number of doctors, establishing 70 new health centres, together with new hospitals and ambulances. A special education commission was set up, and also a social welfare department to encourage youth movements, co-operative societies, community centres with radios, and other efforts to make rural life more attractive. It was emphasized that all of this depended on the earning capacity of the people and therefore changes in agriculture were crucial, as were the development of secondary industries based on water power. The Colonial Development and Welfare Fund had been approached for a grant of £100,000 all of which would be spent on development schemes, with the emphasis on agriculture. The country suffered severely from overcropping of land, from erosion of arable land, and from deforestation. Crop rotation, controlled breeding of livestock, the development of high yield cash crops and irrigation would all be introduced in an attempt to give all the families in the country about 50 acres of useful land.

This impressive list of plans, which sounds almost like a blueprint for setting up a new community, was merely a measure of the desperate situation Arden-Clarke had taken over in 1942. He had worked at a phenomenal rate to achieve this and had had the warmest co-operation from Lord Harlech. He was sorry when Lord Harlech left but was glad to hurry the plans so that someone who knew and cared about the territories could present them to the Colonial Office. During 1944 he also entertained a Parliamentary Delegation, who seemed sympathetic towards his hopes of getting £2½M to fund all his schemes. Later in the year he went to Pretoria to attend the swearing in of the new High Commissioner Sir Evelyn Baring. Baring came to Maseru, as one of his first formal engagements, to preside at the formal opening of the Basutoland Council.

Before this took place, Arden-Clarke had had a final showdown with the Paramount Chief. He wrote:

I have just told the Paramount Chief that I am no longer prepared to tolerate her conduct and that if she will not mend her ways and co-operate with the Government, I shall have to recommend her dismissal from office, a serious ultimatum that may cause a local crisis or, as I hope, effect some improvement. Anyhow, you will appreciate that though the war is remote life isn't all beer and skittles.[17]

Arden-Clarke had drafted Baring's speech, had told the Paramount Chief what to say, and then prepared his own speech. He was pleased that Baring followed his lead and took a tough and effective line with the recalcitrant female. He got on well with Baring, who had a genuine interest both in farming and in wild life, and the following year the Barings came to Maseru and made a remarkable trek through the mountains. Because of an old rupture, Arden-Clarke walked all the way—which amazed all the Africans he met—and he was rather proud of being one of the few Europeans, and the only Resident Commissioner who had walked across the breadth of Basutoland through the mountains which went up to 11,000 feet.

During the period when the war had ended and supplies started to come through, his schemes for the development of Basutoland began to mature. His routine work took him to Pretoria, to Durban and to Cape Town. He usually made light of his responsibilities but occasionally unburdened himself in his letters to his mother, and admitted a longing to throw aside for a little 'my responsibilities for this distressful country'. Another side of his character is shown in a short but moving letter to his mother:

You know Mother mine—when I came home after nine long and eventful years and saw you again I got a bit of a shock when I found you looking so much older and frailer than when I saw you last— stupid of me considering the length of time and all that happened in between—and then I found that mentally you were younger and had not grown old at all—you had kept your interest in new things, and new ideas and your sense of humour . . . It was good, very good to find you so unaged, alert and companionable, bless you, and still the wise understanding, beloved and loving Mother.

I have departed somewhat from the usual English stereotyped reticence but as I hadn't the guts to say it, I have written it.[18]

He had suspected for some time that at the end of the war there might be a 'general post' among the more senior and experienced men in the colonial field, and it came as no real surprise when he was appointed Governor of Sarawak and invited to Buckingham Palace to be knighted by King George VI.

[17] Letter to Mother 19.11.44.
[18] Letter to Mother 10.12.45.

CHAPTER FOUR

Sarawak

Arden-Clarke arrived in Kuching the capital of Sarawak on 29 October 1946. He and his wife had travelled out by ship as far as Singapore, and, after a brief stay with the Governor General Malcolm MacDonald, continued their journey in the Royal Navy sloop *The Black Swan*. Their immediate impression was of a sadly run down territory recovering very slowly indeed from the savagery of the Japanese occupation. Nearly all their staff—European, Chinese and Malays—had been interned for three years under the Japanese, but had generously offered to stay on to put the country back on its feet. The towns and villages, roads and bridges, had been devastated both by the Allied bombing and by the deliberate action of the Japanese before their withdrawal. The little cathedral at Kuching had been occupied as an arms store by the Japanese, who used the altar for flogging their victims. Conversations turned frequently to experiences of internment and especially of the notorious Changi jail in Singapore. The small hospital, which the Japanese had closed when they interned all the staff, had now re-opened.

When the Arden-Clarkes arived at Kuching, since both were martyrs to sea-sickness, they were glad the ship docked at night and that they had time to slip ashore and sleep the night at Astana—their future home. In the morning, they returned to the ship for an early breakfast, and then made their ceremonial arrival for the Governor's swearing-in at the Court House, in the presence of Malcolm MacDonald, the Chief Justice, the Chief Secretary and the assembled leaders of the local communities.

They soon settled down to life in Astana, which served as home, office and secretariat. They rose early and after a swim in their pool had breakfast—usually of bacon and egg or fried prawns. The lawns with tennis and badminton courts stretched down to the deep water of the estuary. In many ways it was an excellent home, for Arden-Clarke, however busy he was, managed to keep fit with swimming, tennis or badminton—and in the monsoons even fixed up a badminton court indoors.

The background to the complex political situation Arden-Clarke inherited, lay in the feuds of the Brooke family. In 1945, Sir Charles Vyner Brooke was Rajah of Sarawak. The Brooke family lived under complex legal and constitutional customs, and succession could only be to a male heir. Vyner Brooke had three daughters but no sons, and the succession could therefore go to his brother—about the same age—or to the brother's son Anthony, born in 1912. Anthony had joined the Sarawak service in 1936, and in March 1939 Vyner Brooke appointed him Rajah Muda—virtually heir apparent. Anthony aroused resentment by his use of public money and by his outspokenness, and he caused the resignation of a number of senior staff. In September 1939 the Rajah returned to Sarawak, and Anthony went to Rangoon where he married. The Rajah then divested him of his position of Rajah Muda, because of his irresponsibility, and sent him to England. This family feuding caused consternation and confusion in the country. When the war started Sarawak enjoyed considerable prosperity, and the Rajah, since the country was protected by Britain under the Treaty of 1888, gave several munificent gifts to help the war effort. In 1941 Anthony was back serving as a District Officer in time for the centenary celebrations of the Brooke Raj. The celebrations brought out deeply impressive demonstrations of loyalty and affection for the Rajah and Ranee, and were marked by a new constitution which established joint government by the Rajah and the Supreme Council. But this Council and the Council Negri were composed of senior Civil Servants or members appointed by the Rajah—not wildly democratic. At the same time Anthony was offered the succession but refused it because it belonged to his father. This refusal offended the Rajah who dismissed Anthony from the Sarawak service. In September 1941 the Rajah left Sarawak for Australia and was still there when on Christmas Day 1941, after a very brief campaign, the Japanese took over the country and arrived in Kuching. The suddenness of the overthrow left the people in a state of numb bewilderment, and they offered very little opposition to the Japanese. The occupation brought hideous atrocities—such as the massacre of 50 European women and children—but the Japanese put up little resistance when the Australian forces attacked in June 1945, and they finally surrendered in September. There followed a brief period of military rule until in April 1946 Earl Mountbatten handed over the government to the Rajah and Ranee. During the interregnum, The Rajah—Vyner Brooke—once again appointed Anthony as Rajah Muda and Head of the Provisional Government, but in October 1945 he again sacked him and stated publicly that the territory would be ceded to the Crown. Vyner Brooke formally made the offer of cession, and Britain accepted it. At this stage Britain had been accused of indecent haste, but it appears from the testimony of his wife that the Rajah hustled it through.[1] In February, without consulting the Supreme Council, he issued an edict handing over

[1] See *Queen of the Headhunters* by Sylvia Brooke. London 1970.

the territory. The interest on £1M—nearly half the accumulated resources of Sarawak—was set aside for the upkeep of the Brooke family. Anthony and his father violently opposed Vyner's decision and they gained substantial support in England both in Parliament and from such distinguished men as Winston Churchill and Arthur Bryant.[2] Vyner, incensed at an article by Arthur Bryant, effectively demolished the myth of the good old days in Sarawak. He maintained they were good days for the British residents and District Officers acting as little tin gods. The natives suffered from starvation because the British had replaced rice with rubber, there was no free press, there was a monopoly on mineral resources, and the only profit came from opium sales and gambling.[3] In spite of this broadside and the unseemly family wrangling, Anthony Brooke still obtained considerable support. Parliament debated Sarawak in March 1946, after two MPs, Rees-Williams and Gammans, had visited the area, and in May 1946 the Council Negri with its European, official and largely nominated members, voted in favour of cession by 19 votes to 16. This was the background to the sensitive and intractable situation which Arden-Clarke inherited.

No overt hostility was shown to the new British regime but Anthony Brooke and his wife were both active in different ways in encouraging the Malays to oppose cession to the Crown, and to demand their restoration as Rajah and Ranee. The people of the country were backward, bewildered and poverty stricken, and it angered Arden-Clarke that their chances of recovery should be hampered by what he saw as the selfish and mischievous activities of the Brooke family. Arden-Clarke immediately showed himself to be a positive, vigorous and effective governor, and he rapidly made his mark throughout the territory, but behind all his achievement lay the thought that Brooke in London was using parliament and the press to undermine his efforts, and was gaining some support even in the Colonial Office.

In December 1946 Brooke left Hong-Kong for Singapore and South East Asia. Singapore declared him persona non grata and then Arden-Clarke banned him from Sarawak. This caused a storm in London, where even Churchill backed Brooke's cause, but it caused very little stir in Kuching, where the people were responding to the active leadership of the new governor. He thought the colony was peaceful but sensed that there was real danger if someone was prepared to exploit the situation unscrupulously. Arden-Clarke was determined to ensure peace, order and good government, and to continue the ban on Brooke until the people had settled down. He wrote to his mother 'If this is tyranny (as

---

[2] Brother-in-law of Anthony Brooke.
[3] See *The White Rajahs* by Sir Steven Runciman, London, 1960.

one MP had said) then I am an unrepentant tyrant.'[4]

Although the rule of the Brooke family had been reasonably popular, they had done little to develop local government or to encourage people to stand on their own feet. Therefore Arden-Clarke had to start from scratch and to explain even the most basic essentials of his policy to the people. To get to know the people, and for them to know him, he had to traverse a territory of mountains and untamed jungle with appalling communications. Touring was largely restricted to the rivers, and of necessity had to become very informal. Gone were the spacious residencies of Southern Africa, and in their place the Governor and his retinue, when on tour, stayed in the Long-Houses and rapidly adapted to their way of life.

Going on tour provided considerable excitement. The fast flowing rivers had to be negotiated in a prahu or canoe, usually about 90 feet long and three feet wide, crewed by 30 paddlers and carrying up to 18 passengers. In the prahu Arden-Clarke sat amidships on a plank, looking a little incongruous, with a mackintosh and a waxed paper umbrella. Journeys in the prahu could last several hours, passing waterfalls, foaming rapids and towering jungle trees. On one of his earliest visits to an Iban long-house on the Rejang river, after a long trip in a prahu, he was taken up a side stream and from its banks had to climb up a steep slope to where the long-house was perched. The Headman of the House met him at the river bank and presented him with a spear, which served as a walking stick going up the steep and slippery path in the pouring rain. An archway of welcome greeted him half way up the hill, and an old woman threw rice—in the traditional greeting. She was supported by five bare breasted maidens in beadwork collars, high bodices decorated with silver coins, red sarongs and ornamental head-dresses. He commented 'They were very good to look upon.' At the top of the slope there were five steps up to the long-house and on each a pig had been spreadeagled. The biggest pig was on the top step, and it was his duty or privilege to kill it with his spear. Unfortunately, on this occasion his spear hit the jaw bone and bent. However, a quick twist, a savage thrust, and his honour was saved. Later he became so adept at killing his pig that he used to gain rounds of applause.

A long-house, which often housed hundreds of people, was usually perched high above the ground. It looked like a thatched barn on stilts, with an open platform, about 15 feet wide, at the front, running the full length of the house—often several hundred yards. The platform gave on to a covered verandah some 30 feet wide, also running the length of the house, and off the verandah stood the long row of family rooms, each

[4] Letter to Mother 14.12.46.

about 15 feet square. The verandah constituted the main road for the house—the place where people met and gossiped and passed the time of day. Above the rooms were large lofts where the young bachelors lived, while on a lower level behind each room lay the kitchens. Borneo had been notorious for headhunters, and most long-houses had blackened human skulls hanging in the eaves. Originally the long-houses had been built off ground and in very large units, for security against headhunters, but they were always built close to the river which provided water, transport and other amenities.

Having killed his pig, Arden-Clarke went into the long-house and was greeted by the village priest, who gave a blessing and sprinkled rice. Then the Governor moved down the verandah, greeting every family and shaking hands; at each door the house holder sprinkled grain over him and the wife offered him a glass of arak. Normally the drink would have been tuak—a pleasant rice beer—but the harvest was late, rice was in short supply, so Chinese arak was provided instead. The drink, fortunately, only had to be tasted and then handed back. After every family had been greeted, the Governor's party sat down with the priest at a table decorated with cane mats and finely woven cotton rugs. Then a cock was slaughtered and each visitor was touched with a blood-smeared feather. That finished the religious part of the ceremony and afterwards the attendant maidens brought more drinks and refreshments. More and more Headmen (Tuai Ruman) arrived in the long-house until there were over 500 people present.

The Iban people in this long-house were fairly prosperous, as they owned rubber gardens and padi fields. Although there were blackened heads hanging from the roof, the rooms had beds, clocks, pressure lamps and other modern conveniences. The family rooms, even when allotted to a visiting Governor, had little privacy, and three ladies watched him as he took down his trousers, wrapped a towel round him, and went down to the river for a bathe. After a bathe he changed and prepared for the evening's festivities. At first he sat and talked to the priest and people. Then the pigs, which had been killed, were cooked, and Arden-Clarke with his two colleagues Snelus and Barcroft ate their meal of pork, beef and chicken in the welcome privacy of their own room. After dinner there was a meeting on the verandah with all the Headmen from the area.

Arden-Clarke spoke about the government's policy to encourage the people to run their own affairs through local councils, while the government would provide specialist help, irrigation, development plans and dispensaries. Under the old regime there were few schools, and the people were eager to obtain teachers in the long-houses. The government encouraged this, and were starting to train suitable teachers. Finally he warned his people that they would have to be patient because the neglect of 100 years could not be overcome in a few months.

In the morning, after another orgy of handshaking, he slithered down the slope to his canoe, bade farewell to the Headmen, and paddled off down the river.[5] During this period he was spending nearly half his time touring the outlying districts of the colony. He wrote:

At each district HQ or government station I meet the leaders of the local communities, the Chinese and the principal traders, the Malay Datus and the Dyak Chiefs and Village Headmen. We have a meeting in the local court house when I hear 'requests' from any member of the public who has something to ask of me or the Government, and I talk to them all about local problems and the Government's plans for the future; The Resident of the Division and the District Officer sitting beside me as consultants and advisers. I inspect the Government offices, the various schools and anything else of interest and importance, hear what my officials, European and Asiatic, have to say, and give advice or decisions to the best of my ability. The evenings are devoted to the social side of things and one is very ready for bed at the end of it all. The people want to learn who and what a Governor is and I have to learn about the people and the problems of the country I am here to govern.[6]

In a subsequent letter to the family he gave some interesting views both about his job and about Anthony Brooke. Having described the drinking ceremonies associated with a visit to a long-house he added:

I have come to the conclusion that the chief qualifications a Governor needs in this part of the world are a strong head, an asbestos stomach, and a cast-iron sit-upon. Of course it isn't all killing cocks and tippling tuak. At every place I sit in open court and hear requests, some of which are a bit difficult to answer, and talk to the people about the Government's policy and plans, and deal with any false reports or mischievous rumours put about by Anthony Brooke's supporters . . . The only people who want Anthony Brooke are a small section of the Malays and the Malays altogether are less than one quarter of the population. As far as I can see ninety percent of the people of Sarawak are quite content with cession, so when you read in the papers about poster demonstrations, protests and a people seething with discontent, do not pay any attention to it. The small minority opposed to cession make a great deal of noise and receive most of the publicity but they do not represent the people. If they were not egged on by Anthony Brooke and his supporters in press and Parliament the whole thing would fizzle out.[7]

[5] Malcolm MacDonald, another intrepid traveller, in his fascinating book *Borneo People* in a chapter headed 'Life in a long-house', describes a tour he made with Arden-Clarke to the Iban people.
[6] Letter to Mother 10.2.47.
[7] Letter to Mother 11.4.47.

One of Arden-Clarke's most urgent priorities was to get over to the people of Sarawak, the benefits of British rule, and to show them how much the resources of the Commonwealth could help them. He used an RAF Sunderland flying boat, which he found convenient but noisy, to visit Sibu, Brunei, Labuan and North Borneo. He also made a most successful public relations exercise out of the visit by the Admiral of the Pacific Fleet, Sir Denis Boyd, on HMS *Alert*. After the ship anchored opposite Astana, the Admiral came ashore to make his formal greeting. The Governor then, to return the compliment, went aboard but found his plumes rather difficult to manage in the restricted space of a small ship. He then cast off in the Governor's sampan and stood at the salute while the ship fired a 17 gun salute—it went smoothly except that the blast from the guns nearly toppled him out of the sampan. The Naval visit had been designed to contact as many sections of the community and to make as much impact as possible. The first evening the Governor held a dance to which the local residents were invited. A small cabaret included a Malay girl dancer, five Chinese girls doing a traditional dance, and the spectacular Dyak dance by three Dyaks from the local police. All of these made an excellent impression because such entertainment had never happened before. The Governor led his cricket team to victory against the Admiral, and the ship's footballers beat the stars of the Kuching Chinese. The finale came with a cocktail party on board and a tattoo with flares, fireworks and the band of the Royal Marines.

It is perhaps easy today to criticize such junketing as irrelevant and anachronistic, but there is no doubt that the peoples of Sarawak, looking back over years of suffering during the Japanese wartime occupation, and facing the uncertainty caused by the Brooke family, took heart from such an occasion, just as the up-river Ibans did from the Governor's frequent visits. The Governor's personal finale to the Naval visit came when he was standing in his sampan prior to pushing off from the ship, and the Admiral's daughter came rushing down the accommodation ladder and gave him a big kiss—to the delight of the assembled crew watching from above.

1 July 1947 was the first anniversary of cession, and a time of some apprehension. The Colonial Office produced a booklet but it was almost a year too late and practically valueless. They had also delayed in sending out medals and awards for bravery during the Japanese occupation, so that at the King's Birthday parade many awards could not be made. During this period Lady Arden-Clarke had gone to South Africa to be with their children during their school holidays. On the way she stopped at Mauritius and visited the house where Sir Charles' mother had once lived. While Lady Arden-Clarke was away in South Africa, rumours circulated in Kuching that the Arden-Clarkes were leaving and that

Anthony Brooke would be coming in their place.

The ramifications of Brooke's activities were widespread. During a conference at Singapore Arden-Clarke and Malcolm MacDonald had to deal with a crisis caused by a totally inaccurate and unfounded statement by Brooke that Britain proposed to amalgamate Sarawak and Brunei. Arden-Clarke encouraged MacDonald not to see Brooke again, since it merely flattered his vanity and encouraged him to make more mischief. In contrast to the high level problems in Singapore, Arden-Clarke found evidence of Brooke's mischief when he visited a group of Land Dyaks— a very backward and indolent people who had been oppressed by the local Malays. They were subjected to considerable anti-cession pressure from the Malays, forced to contribute money, and forced to buy photographs of Anthony Brooke at exorbitant prices. In Kuching a large number of loyal Datus (headmen) were having a difficult time at the hands of the anti-cessionist forces. In order to support the loyal ones, he found the names of all those who were disloyal and sacked them. This caused some outcry from the local Malays, but brought general satisfaction.

A vivid impression, both of the country and of the problems he faced, is given by his tour to Bintulu District in July 1947. He set out by flying boat; this trip convinced him that the flying-boat was a godsend to Sarawak, and that he should argue against a land-plane service from Singapore to Borneo. He took the flying boat to Bintulu and travelled for the rest of his tour on his launch *Karina*.

Bintulu was a typical Sarawak trading centre with a long line of Chinese shops forming the bazaar, with a Malay or Melanau Kampong attached to one end, and at the other end the Government quarters and offices. In 1945 most of Bintulu was completely destroyed by Allied bombing, and quite unnecessarily, because the Japanese had already left. The day of Arden-Clarke's arrival he visited schools, the bazaar and the temporary court house, and in the evening had a Chinese dinner which consisted of over thirty different dishes—which fortunately were passed to him to taste first. Next morning he heard 'requests', first from the Asiatic staff and then from the local people. Requests included demands for schools and dispensaries; complaints by Malays that Dyaks had grabbed their land; complaints by Dyaks about the extortion of Chinese towkays (shop keepers); demands by the Chinese for vengeance on Dyaks who took Chinese heads during the guerrilla fighting against the Japanese; and requests about the price of rubber and supplies of padi because their own supplies had failed. He gave a ruling that all land grabbed during the Japanese occupation was to be returned to its rightful owners. Leaving Bintulu on the launch, he travelled for several hours up river to Sebauh a centre of the attractive Iban people, who accepted some hard decisions quite cheerfully. Here, too, he had to sit through a huge Chinese lunch and a huge Malay and Iban dinner in the evening. All the villages he passed through were gaily decorated and gave him a warm and spontaneous welcome. To the people, he was the new Rajah and he was usually addressed as 'Tuan Rajah'. The old Rajah never visited the country districts and so Arden-Clarke's tours made an excellent impression. He took the launch up the river as far as Tubau the centre of the shy Kayan people, who were so elusive and so scattered in the jungle that little could be done for them. Arden-Clarke heard their requests and offered to get them a teacher—they wanted an Iban teacher and had no time for the Malays. On returning to Bintulu he worked out a scheme for the Iban people to have two Native Authorities each with its own Treasury. When the Japanese came, the Ibans had grabbed the lands and the long-house of the Punan—a very shy and primitive people. Now Arden-Clarke insisted on the land and property being returned, and to emphasize his decision he stayed in the Punan long-house, a rickety and tumble down affair, with holes in the floor through which he could see the ground 20 feet below. Throughout the tour there was no trace of anti-cession activity and everywhere he received a sincere welcome as the new Rajah. Arden-Clarke described one incident:

> An old Iban said 'We have heard about the King, but he lives far away. What we want to know is who gives us our orders, who is our Rajah here.' Abandoning the niceties of constitutional theory, I tapped my chest and said 'I am. You obey me.' 'Good,' he said, 'that suits us and that's all we want to know.' It's a pretty fair summary of the attitude of the majority of the people of this country. [8]

It frequently became apparent that the previous regime had made no attempt to teach the people to run their own affairs, and from the start Arden-Clarke urged his staff to encourage their people's self reliance. Teams of his officers set up native councils and native treasuries, [9] and did all they could to modernize their thinking. He used the facilities of the Royal Navy, and one survey ship kept open house for the local people, put on nightly cinema shows, and ran a free dispensary in the ship's surgery.

[8] Letter to Lady Arden-Clarke 30.7.47.
[9] Having set up Native Treasuries (NTs) in Nigeria, Bechuanaland and Basutoland he continued his good work in Sarawak, but was disappointed that only the Dyaks and not the Chinese or Malays responded. With hideous rhymes and excruciating puns he adapted the old rhyme 'There was a young fellow called Sharkey . . .
There was an old fellow called Cla'ak
Who had an affair with Sara'ak
First result of his squeeze
Were six little NTs
But no Chinese, no Malay—all Dyak:

While his wife was away in South Africa with their children, he missed her very badly. He was also nostalgic for the 10 happy years they had spent there, and he seriously considered retiring to the Cape Town area. He reckoned that the country would not blow up in their life time though he thought it would eventually unless the Europeans changed their racial policies. The problems of long separations, the problems of caring for their children and for 'the Grannies' weighed heavily upon him. He concluded one letter:

> I must to bed my darling. I hate these long separations. The higher one gets the more one needs companionship, and the lonelier and more isolated one is. I want you so much my dearest dear.[8]

During August and September 1947 the Brooke affair caused further serious crises. Brooke had taken out a libel suit against a local paper and used the court case as an excuse to try to get into Sarawak. Telegrams flew between Kuching and the Colonial Office, and in the Governor's words 'The Secretary of State wobbled violently', and demanded to be consulted before any decision was made. Arden-Clarke replied that the decision had already been made, and made it clear that if his decision was reversed, and Brooke allowed in, he would resign. The anti-cessionists and Mrs Anthony Brooke, who was visiting Sarawak, had stated confidently that Brooke would be in Kuching on 24 September and that the Governor would never dare to keep him out. In fact he was kept out, the Court refused to adjourn, and Brooke's cause received another blow. Arden-Clarke's own comment was that a lot of rats were now leaving the sinking ship.

In July Mrs Brooke arrived in Kuching, and the anti-cessionists went out to her ship to greet her, in gaily decorated canoes. Arden-Clarke invited her to Astana but she replied that she would be delighted to accept when she was accompanied by her husband and that would be soon. After a fairly quiet start to her visit, Arden-Clarke received reports that she was touring the Dyak areas of the Upper Rejang river with a band of irresponsible scallywags, and was causing a lot of trouble. He was not unduly bothered if a few Malays were beaten up as a result, but he was concerned at the political repercussions should anything happen to her. He began to think that she too would have to be banned from the territory, though he was uncertain of the reaction of the Secretary of State, Creech-Jones. Malcolm MacDonald came to Kuching to discuss the issue and backed up the Governor completely. Creech-Jones had put forward several points, which Arden-Clarke totally rejected, and in a lengthy telegram, he set out the whole issue and demanded complete discretion to handle the situation.

A few weeks later Arden-Clarke unofficially had two very long discussions with Mrs Brooke. They got on well and were able to discuss things quite openly. Her main reason for being in Sarawak was to help her husband's cause. There appeared to be problems in their marriage because of another woman in Singapore, and she hoped to win back her husband by forwarding his cause in Sarawak. She had come out on her own initiative and, in fact, he had tried to dissuade her. She had been convinced that her husband would arrive in Kuching on 24 September, and felt badly let down when he did not. Left to her own devices she would probably have left, but now felt too much part of the movement. Arden-Clarke then told her 'If her intention was to stay here until her husband arrived she was in for the hell of a long stay. She had much better get out quietly and peacefully and I gave her the reasons . . .'

> She just has not begun to think things out: She is guided by sentiment and entirely irrelevant personal considerations, and has not faintest conception of the larger issues involved, or of her responsibilities as a person, who in Sarawak has a special status and position in the eyes of the people. At the end of it all she was certainly shaken and asked time to consider whether she would quietly pack up and go, as I advised, or would stay on indefinitely, knowing that I might take action to throw her out with all the resulting publicity and nastiness that would ensue . . . She will shut her eyes to facts and sense, and blindly follow her sentiments. I'm inclined to think that she imagines that by doing this stint in Sarawak she will win the esteem and gratitude of her husband and so win him back. I treated it all as a comedy last night but it is much nearer tragedy. I am afraid a lot of people are going to get hurt before this show is through and it is all so unnecessary.[10]

He next informed Creech-Jones that it would be wiser to allow her to remain, rather than have the adverse publicity of putting her out, but when she asked if she would be allowed to go to England and return with her children he raised strong and serious objections, because her position as a Brooke would be exploited and would aggravate the danger of violence. He was afraid that her health might crack up and if that happened he intended to have her taken to hospital in Singapore. His private view was that once she was out he would do his damnedest to see she stayed out, and she certainly could not be permitted to come and live in Sarawak with her family.

In spite of the upheavals caused by the anti-cessionist support for the Brooke family, Arden-Clarke continued his vigorous programme of visits to the outlying parts of the colony, on two occasions accompanied by Malcolm MacDonald, who would often call in and stay the night even if there was no urgent business—showing his awareness of the lonely and

[10] Letter to Lady Arden-Clarke 4.10.47.

isolated role a governor played. They found many areas where the District Officers left over from the Rajah's service were having difficulty coping with their new responsibilities, and in others, such a dearth of experienced staff, that Arden-Clarke had to carry out the routine organizing himself. During one of these visits MacDonald suggested that Arden-Clarke should take on additional responsibilities as High Commissioner of Brunei, and that Brunei should draw its staff from Sarawak instead of Malaya. He had also recommended that Arden-Clarke should be promoted KCMG in the New Year's Honours List. When this news was formally announced he wrote a personal letter saying:

> We owe a tremendous lot to you for your firm and constructive handling of Sarawak affairs during the last year. You have given the new colony the best possible start in all sorts of ways, undeterred by various difficulties. The peace and friendliness, and the people's stout support for the new Government, which mark the country today are due very largely to your energetic and commanding efforts.[11]

In 1947 South East Asia had been rocked by the upheavals of independence in India, Pakistan, Ceylon and Burma, and the world was emerging into its strongest anti-imperial and anti-colonial phase. Arden-Clarke, almost a classic imperial figure—and certainly an unrepentant one—never doubted the wisdom or the justification of the policy he administered, and which—as he saw it—had never varied from his earliest days with the Madas and Mamas in Nigeria. Sarawak, although on a small stage, highlighted many of the real Colonial issues since it only became a British colony in July 1947, three months before he became Governor. It therefore presents a good and clear opportunity to sum up the pro's and con's of colonialism and exploitation. Although he did not see it as such, Arden-Clarke's speech in December 1947 to the Council Negri was also in its way a classic—a clear statement of what had been achieved after a year of colonialism and what was planned for the future welfare and development of the people. Tough, clear, hard-hitting and factual it was his credo. He was saying, as Luther had before him, 'Here I stand.'

He reminded the Council of the urgent need of Trade Union legislation so that the colony could benefit fully under the terms of the Colonial Development and Welfare Act, which had already funded most of the beneficial schemes already started. The colony was financially buoyant because of the unexpectedly rapid recovery of trade, but the problems of reconstruction had been exacerbated by shortages of technical staff and of supplies. Of the revenue of 11M dollars, 64 per cent came from the

[11] Letter from Malcolm MacDonald December 1947.

export of rubber, and the country was far too dependent on this single commodity. Expenditure estimates of 13M dollars for 1948, using 2M dollars from the reserves, tried to balance the need to press on with reconstruction, against problems of staff and material shortages. Although the situation was encouraging there was no room for complacency, for there was an urgent need to build up the health and education services, and to diversify the economy. Further demands on the revenue would come from the war damage commission and from salaries for public servants, though another commission was investigating ways of increasing the general revenue.

The Colonial Development and Welfare Fund, started in 1940, had allocated substantial sums to Sarawak. It had already funded a soil survey and a census as necessary prerequisites of future development schemes. A grant of nearly 1M dollars had been made to set up 18 static and mobile dispensaries, and to get local people trained as doctors. Another 1M dollars had been granted to set up a teacher training college and secondary school, and a long-house school for the Iban people. Nearly all the future developments in the country would depend on the qualified pupils going through the secondary schools, and because of the urgency of this need, the training college and school would not wait for new buildings, but would be established in the Batu Lintang camp used by the Japanese as an internment camp. It was hoped to admit the first pupils in seven months. He paid generous tribute to the Rajah, Sir Charles Vyner Brooke, whose gift of £50,000 would be used to provide permanent accommodation for the education complex, to be known as The Rajah Brooke Training Centre. The imaginative scheme for a long-house school was being established at Kanowit. In addition to being a school, it would provide a two year course of general education, hygiene and modern agriculture for 30 married couples drawn from all over the Iban areas. The expectation was that they would carry back the new ideas and disseminate them in their own long-houses. The government had also provided funds to open seven new government schools, 15 new mission schools, and 22 Chinese and Dyak schools, and it had provided scholarships for people to go abroad for technical training.

All these projects had come from the Colonial Development and Welfare Fund, which had also provided for an aerial survey to help the lands and forestry departments, and to prospect for mineral resources. The Naval Survey had already brought practical benefit by enabling a 9,000 ton cargo ship to anchor in the Rejang river and take on an export cargo of timber, and a fisheries survey was helping to develop the fishing industry and a fish meal industry as well. A socio-economic survey had been carried out to ensure that the various measures proposed would fit in with the stage of development of the different peoples and be in their best interest. He paid tribute to the prompt, practical and generous help from the specialist agencies of the Colonial Office and the Colonial Development and Welfare Fund, which had financed all these schemes as well as others to provide clean water in the villages, to re-establish the Constabulary, and to eradicate malaria.

The encouraging development in education had not been shared by the Malay community. In December 1946 all government servants including teachers had been given the option of resigning if they wished. Thirteen per cent, all Malay and nearly all in Kuching, had done so, and as a result 22 Malay schools had had to close. It appeared that most had resigned because of fear of reprisals and boycott in the Kuching Kampongs (markets). These threats came in false rumours which had been deliberately circulated about the return of Anthony Brooke, and had enabled unscrupulous people to extort money, and damage the community. His own visits to every part of the colony had shown that there was widespread satisfaction with cession, and that the opposition was confined to a small minority of Malays and Muslim Melanaus. He regretted this division and gave his word that his government would do its best to heal the breach.

His main hope was to develop soundly based local government, by which the people would run their own affairs and learn to handle their own finances. He strongly encouraged local citizens to go into the higher reaches of the Government service and to participate in local government. Five local authorities with their own Treasuries were being established at Bau, Batang Lupar, Sarisbas, Sibu and Sebauh. He warned people to tread cautiously because different people were at different stages of development. He concluded:

> Measures have been initiated to develop the country's natural resources, diversify its economy and improve the standard of living of its people. The first steps on the long road that leads to self government are being taken. My final words to you are that you, by your labours in this Council room and by your deeds, your words, and your influence in whatever part of the country you reside, have your part— and it is an important part—to play in the progress and development of Sarawak.[12]

This meeting of the Council Negri set the seal on 15 months of determined work and effort, and placed the colony on a clear path towards fuller development. The great problems that were to bedevil South East Asia—the establishment of communist China, the communist subversion in Malaya, the emergence of Sukarno, Indonesia's confrontation with Malaya, and the upheavals of Vietnam—had not so far

[12] Governor's Speech 8.12.47.

emerged, and the main menace to the peace of Sarawak remained the activities of Anthony Brooke.

The Governor was alone at Astana over Christmas and entertained the temporary and permanent bachelors of Kuching. He enjoyed some relaxation into the New Year, and came in for some congratulatory ribbing when his KCMG was published.[13]

In the meantime Malcolm MacDonald, on his way to Canada on leave, challenged the Colonial Office on the Brooke question. He wrote a thoughtful and reassuring letter back to Arden-Clarke agreeing that, after the stand he had taken, it would be right to resign if his ban on Brooke was over-ruled, but that he should not consider resignation over Mrs Brooke, which was a less important issue. He enclosed for Arden-Clarke extracts of letters he had written and gave a summary of his discussions with the Colonial Office. He wrote:

> People remotely and comfortably situated in Whitehall should not place the Governor in such a position, (i.e. over-rule the ban), *and he felt that the Colonial Office were walking into a trap if they allowed Mrs Brooke and the children into Sarawak. He concluded,* Your threat of resignation is an extra inducement to our bosses in the Colonial Office to remain sane.[14]

In London some help came from T. Stirling Boyd MP, a former Chief Justice of Sarawak, who tried to discuss the matter with Brooke's chief protagonist David Maxwell Fyfe. He got no response and felt that the Tories who supported Brooke were being purely political, and they didn't really care at all about either Sarawak or Brooke. In January 1948 Mrs Brooke stayed at Astana prior to sailing for England. Arden-Clarke found her a reasonable and decent person. Really she was sick of the whole business, but continued to be manipulated by her husband and his advisers. In March Lord Listowel, from the Colonial Office, visited Kuching, met the anti-cessionist leaders, met Anthony Brooke in Malaya, and sturdily upheld the Governor's view and fully committed the Labour government to that view.

Arden-Clarke summed up the background to the problem as follows:

> 1. There is little doubt that in the early stages the Malays refrained from active demonstration against cession because they were well aware that their conduct during the occupation was, to put it mildly, suspect, and it was only when it became apparent that there was not to be an orgy of witch hunting that their confidence returned and they started to organize opposition; hence the obvious lack of interest in

---

[13] He was promoted from Knight Bachelor to Knight Commander. One facetious governor, misquoting Mae West, wrote 'Twice a Knight—and at your age!'
[14] Letter from Malcolm MacDonald 16.2.48.

the Cession Bill at the Council Negri. (i.e., the meeting of 17 May 1946 when the Cession Bill was passed.)

2. Dossiers of a large number of Anthony's most vociferous supporters would make sorry reading.

3. I do not think anyone can deny that the series of events leading up to Cession were unfortunate, but family feuds cannot be allowed to affect the interests of the country, and to air them merely discredits, and I think unjustifiably, a romantic and on the whole successful chapter in the history of the Empire.

4. As regards your final question, I am convinced that Anthony Brooke's presence in Sarawak would be undesirable and would endanger the peace. I agree that a ban of this sort on any normal citizen would be an infringement of the liberty of British subjects to travel wherever they like within the King's dominions and take active interest in local affairs, but Anthony Brooke in Sarawak is not an ordinary citizen. Less than two years ago he was heir-presumptive to the throne here. He has not renounced his claim to the line of succession to the throne. On the contrary, he is openly maintaining agitation to undo cession and restore Brooke rule, encouraging his supporters in Sarawak to regard him as the active leader in that cause, and signing himself in letters and photographs as Rajah Muda and permitting his supporters to declare him publicly to be the next Rajah. If he enters Sarawak his purpose will be to pursue this political aim by all means possible. This is at present his sole object in life which he freely admits. Once he entered Sarawak it would be impossible to get rid of him again unless he committed some criminal offence. The political principle and practice described above as generally applicable to all British citizens therefore does not apply in this particular case. In Sarawak he is a pretender to the throne and the banning of a pretender from the country of his claim is supported by countless precedents. [15]

In the spring of 1948, to his great delight after a long period as a grass-widower, he had his wife and all the family with him. The girls entered vivaciously into the social life of Kuching, and his son Paul, waiting to go to Exeter University, accompanied him on a strenuous tour to Bintulu, Sibu and Brunei. The happy family interlude lasted through most of the year, and included a visit from his brother Hubert who stayed at Astana on his way to Hong-Kong, and his old friend Hugh Bousted with whom he had served on the South Russian front in 1919. On 1 May at a truly regal ceremony in Brunei, he formally assumed office as High Commissioner. The Sultan of Brunei welcomed him, and the Royal Commission was read. A message also came from Malcolm MacDonald, who on the same day, became Commissioner General for South East Asia. Arden-Clarke spoke at length to reassure the people of Brunei that

[15] Letter to Malcolm MacDonald 6.4.48.

they remained as a protected state and they were not in any way being taken over. As High Commissioner he hoped to be able to give them help and advice. He had already arranged for places to be made available for students from Brunei at the new Sarawak Training College and at a training College in Malaya. During the celebrations he visited the Silversmiths Guild where he was presented with a casket, and was also entertained by the Malay, Chinese, Arab and Indian communities. [16]

In June 1948 Malcolm MacDonald stayed in Kuching for the Sarawak and Brunei Residents' Conference. After it he wrote:

> It revealed the tremendous creative work you yourself are doing in Sarawak. You are the fount from which has flowed all the constructive and coherent policy on political and economic affairs which has marked Sarawak during the last eighteen months. I congratulate you on a very notable achievement in the history of British Borneo. [17]

While Sarawak remained peaceful, increasing reference was made during this year to the troubles in Malaya and to attacks by communist terrorists. In August Arden-Clarke went to Kuala Lumpur to visit a group of Dyaks who were attached to British Army Units to act as guides and trackers to help in catching the bandits in the jungle. In September in a mood of pessimism he summed up the situation and reverted to Anthony Brooke. He said that there were enough problems in the aftermath of the Japanese withdrawal, from communist subversion emerging in so many places, from parrot cries of independence, and racial jealousies and animosities. Yet Anthony Brooke chose to fish in these troubled waters, and was claiming that in 1841 the lands were entailed on the Brooke family in perpetuity and could not be ceded. He was seeking the land for himself, while proclaiming his loyalty to Britain. Arden-Clarke considered this to be arch-hypocrisy.

Arden-Clarke's passionate determination to bring self government and financial responsibility to all areas of his domain involved him in frequent energetic tours. In November 1948 rough seas prevented him from travelling by boat and he therefore made a long and tedious overland journey. If he had not, he felt he would never have got the backward Melanaus to set up their own Council and treasury. Later on this tour, he developed a high temperature and his staff virtually forced him to give up a visit to the Dyaks which would have involved him in a march of 18 miles through steaming jungle and in pouring rain. He had spent seven months on tour since October 1946 and hated falling down

---

[16] Arden-Clarke got on well with a very wide variety of people but he found the Sultan of Brunei very difficult. He always appeared to be whining for more money, and Arden-Clarke found their brief meetings quite odious.

[17] Letter from Malcolm MacDonald 2.6.48.

on this trip, because he realized what trouble the Dyaks would have taken to welcome him.

Having suffered so much from the Brooke family, and its opposition to the cession of Sarawak to the Crown, Arden-Clarke shrewdly made the most of developments in the Royal Family and, to mark the birth of Prince Charles, he put on a magnificent celebration at Astana. The grounds were decorated with Union Jacks and the Sarawak Flag, and the whole population of Kuching was invited. Most of them seemed to come. The local press considered that the occasion outdid the centenary celebrations of 1941, and there was no doubt that politically it did a great deal of good.[18]

Later in the month, he wrote to his wife just before he had to address the main annual meeting of the Council Negri:

> I have got the needle badly and feel sick in the pit of my tummy. It really is ridiculous that after all these years and all the practice I have had, I should feel sick before making a major speech.

Halfway through the speech he paused to take a sip of water and found his hand was still shaking. He took no more sips because he was afraid it might 'detract from the air of firm and confident leadership a Governor is supposed to inspire'.[19] For the first time, defence matters were mentioned in the speech, and as Mao Tse Tung and the Communist forces tightened their grip on China, there was considerable apprehension about increased communist pressure all over SE Asia.

Being on his own at Christmas he gave his usual bachelor party on Christmas Day. His staff proposed his health, hoped he would have a good leave in England, that he would return soon, and that on no account would he get transferred elsewhere. There had been rumours, which he considered quite unfounded, that he might be transferred, but it pleased him that his staff appeared genuinely to want him back. He spent the slight break over Christmas doing a lot of 'sorting'—one of his favourite phrases—prior to going on six months leave in January 1949. He felt Sarawak had got over its teething troubles and he did not anticipate any major problems during his leave that his number two Dawson could not handle, though he was a little concerned to find how reluctant Dawson was to have to make decisions by himself. In the last weeks before he left, Brooke again wrote, and it appeared that another press and parliamentary campaign was imminent. Arden-Clarke did not feel at all certain about the Colonial Office, and wrote to his wife:

> I place little reliance on the staunchness of those at home or their will

[18] Sarawak *Tribune* 18.11.48.
[19] Letter to Lady Arden-Clarke 29.11.48.

to govern in the interests of the people if, by giving way, they can dodge a row in Parliament. Perhaps we shall be going on a pension earlier than we thought.[20]

After a series of farewell events and a final sundowner for 200 people at Astana, he left on 20 January 1949 to attend a major Governor's Conference at Singapore, under the chairmanship of Malcolm MacDonald, and attended by Gimson (Singapore), Gurney (Malaya) and Twining (N. Borneo). In describing the conference, Arden-Clarke wrote:

There was quite a schoolboy atmosphere of ragging and leg-pulling after living in the splendid isolation and exalted loneliness of our governorships.

The realistic Gurney and I shot down with speed and precision all the more fantastic schemes launched by Malcolm and Twining, and we came to a number of useful and practical decisions.

An Under-Secretary from the Colonial Office was flabbergasted at the speed with which they dealt with items that would have taken the Colonial Office a month. Arden-Clarke concluded:

I don't think he appreciated that we all knew what we were talking about, and the Colonial Office rarely does.[21]

Perhaps his staff had used the grapevine before their final toast to him, for he had not been on leave for long when Creech-Jones offered him the daunting challenge of becoming Governor of the Gold Coast. After wrestling with his conscience, as he always had to because of his total involvement with the people he governed, he accepted, though he threatened to resign unless he could go back to Kuching for a month to tour the Colony and to explain the situation to all the people. He was wise to insist on this, for when he reached Kuching in July rumours were rife. Two of the most powerful rumours were that he was going in order to make way for Anthony Brooke, or alternatively that he was being replaced by a Governor who would not obstinately maintain the ban on Anthony Brooke. Almost immediately he left for a tour of the whole territory including Brunei. He spoke to the people and told them that a change of governor did not mean a change of policy, and his successor would care for them just as he had done. He emphasized the need for goodwill and mutual trust between the government and the governed, and he warned the Chinese community that there was no place in

[20] Letter to Lady Arden-Clarke 21.1.49.
[21] Letter to Lady Arden-Clarke 25.1.49. Malcolm MacDonald realized Arden-Clarke's heart really lay in Africa. He told the author an amusing and perhaps significant anecdote about this conference. Someone referred to the three territories—meaning Sarawak, Brunei and N. Borneo. Arden-Clarke, who had been day-dreaming, suddenly came to and said 'you mean Bechuanaland, Basutoland and Swaziland'.

Sarawak for the divisions of mainland China. After a hectic tour, farewell dinners, and a cricket match especially arranged in his honour, he left on 26 July for talks with his friend and mentor Malcolm MacDonald in Singapore, and flew on to England the next day.

There was a savage and tragic post-script to all his struggles over Anthony Brooke. The new Governor Duncan Stewart arrived in Kuching in November 1949 and, following Arden-Clarke's example, lost little time in going on tour. On 3 December he arrived at Sibu by launch and as he stepped ashore a young Malay stabbed him. This tragedy hurt Arden-Clarke deeply because he realized the attack had been planned for him. The assassination horrified the colony and outraged the sense of decency of the Malay community. Its effect was to curb and finally destroy the anti-cessionist movement, but it was not until 1951 that Anthony Brooke told his supporters not to demonstrate any more, and to accept the British government.

CHAPTER FIVE
The Gold Coast—Crisis Measures

In February 1948 the Gold Coast erupted in terrifying violence. Riots, which first flared up in Accra, quickly spread to all the other major towns. Mobs made vicious attacks on European stores and offices, as well as on the shops and homes of Indian and Syrian traders. This outburst of arson, violence and looting, with sombre racial overtones, took the British administration almost completely by surprise.

As the rioters overturned the cars and looted the big stores, they little realized that they were putting an end to the great age of Imperialism in Africa. Even less did they realize that they were starting a revolution which in a few years was to free two hundred million fellow Africans from the domination and control of Europeans. Their acts changed the map of Africa from a kaleidoscope of European colours—British, French, Belgian and Portuguese—to one of proud but often poverty stricken independent African countries. A map of Africa in 1939 shows Liberia, a small speck on the coast of West Africa, as the only part of the continent ruled by its indigenous people, for even Ethiopia had been overrun by the Italian fascists. By 1965 the only territories not ruled by their own people were the beleaguered states of southern Africa under white minority governments, and a few outposts of Spanish and Portuguese control.

The Gold Coast in the years immediately after the war appeared prosperous, contented and cheerful—the ideal colony. For decades it had been more prosperous than its neighbours. Blessed with substantial deposits of gold, diamonds and bauxite, the country had been wisely developed by the benevolent policy of successive British governments and by the activities of many substantial trading concerns. While minerals played an important part in the economy of the colony, the main source of its prosperity came from cocoa, the sturdy and intelligent peasant farmers of the forest region accounting for more than half the world's supply. The export trade on which all else depended relied on the efficient functioning of the port of Takoradi, with its artificial harbour. The rest of the coast, pounded by Atlantic breakers, had had no good harbours and the only rival to Takoradi lay in the surf boats of Cape Coast or Accra.

The war had brought prosperity to the Gold Coast, not only from the demand for its main primary products, but also from the British and American military installations and the incomes of nearly 50,000 men recruited into the forces. These men—the clerks and mechanics from the southern towns or Kumasi, the fighting soldiers mostly from the Northern territories—were destined to play a key role in the history of their country. Brought at the beginning of the war from remote and primitive villages, trained and educated in the army, taken to the Far East where their two divisions, the 81st and 82nd West African Divisions, acquitted themselves bravely against the Japanese, these men were unlikely to accept everthing as it had been. Before the war the superiority of the white man had hardly been challenged. Soon it was to be challenged in an unexpected way.

The colonial administration and the army had made some attempt to use the reservoir of talent and experience provided by the returning soldiers. In the Northern Territories an imaginative attempt to raise the level of agriculture by training former NCOs in the use of bullocks and ploughs failed because no candidates came forward. Throughout the colony as a whole, less than half the ex-servicemen were provided with jobs. Their meagre gratuities soon disappeared. Their glamorous war-time skills seemed to bring them few prospects in the difficult post-war world. They had lost, too, the regular meals, the regular pay, as well as the relationship of trust which they had enjoyed with their officers. Their frustrations did not accord with the high hopes of the future of the colony which had been encouraged by the 1944 Plan for the Development of the Gold Coast.

In 1946 the able, experienced and popular Governor, Sir Alan Burns, after detailed and prolonged discussions with both European and African leaders, introduced a new constitution which gave an absolute majority to the elected African members in the Legislative Council. The new council consisted of the Governor, 12 official or nominated members, and 18 elected members. At first sight this appeared to be a dramatic hand-over of power, and caused great excitement, but in practice the Governor retained the veto and retained considerable further control. Burns and most of his staff publicly expressed confidence in the good sense, loyalty and dignity of the people of the Gold Coast. They realized that the new constitution would give power and influence to the chiefs and to the men of property and education, but failed to foresee that the elected members were inevitably condemned to the role of sterile opposition.

In spite of the high hopes of the new 'legco', Burns had already expressed his serious concern about the general state of the Colony. Because of the demands of the war, his staff had been severely depleted. Those who stayed on, usually the older ones who were not fit for active service, had been seriously overworked, and had taken very little home leave. The acute shortage of all types of supplies and materials in the years immediately after the war meant that many development schemes were indefinitely shelved. For these reasons the morale of the expatriate staff in 1946 and 1947 reached a dangerously low pitch.

In the stable pre-war days, the Colony had operated effectively under a system which virtually divided the administrative service into two; the Secretariat under the Colonial Secretary; and the Chief Commissioners with their field staff under District Commissioners. With rapid post-war change, when speedy collation and dissemination of information was essential, this division proved a serious hazard. When new younger men joined the service after the war, a new and unfortunate division emerged. The older and more senior staff—for example T. R. O. Mangin,[1] who had been in the colony since 1918—appeared to be old fashioned and autocratic in their approach. In 1946 the younger group protested, not only at the high-handed way they were treated, but at the autocratic approach of senior officers to the highly complex political situations then emerging. Burns rebuked the protesters and stood by his more senior colleagues, but their protests proved to be well founded.

Deep and serious frustrations in many parts of the community seriously belied the superficial assumption of the administration that the colony was cheerful, prosperous and content. World wide inflationary pressures in the years after 1945 became more acute in the Gold Coast. High prices for cocoa meant more money in circulation at a time when few goods were available, and the resulting inflation brought severe hardship to many sections of the community. A large black-market flourished. The Sachs Report, 1948, on the import and distribution of goods, levelled serious criticism at the Government for giving so much power to the big European firms. In a period of inflation and of short-ages, this discrimination appeared even more severe, and the Government seemed to favour the Association of West African Merchants (all Europe based firms) over the allocation of Import licences.

The Gold Coast, because of its greater wealth and because of the policy propounded initially in the 1920s by Sir Gordon Guggisberg, who founded Korle Bu as a teaching hospital and founded Achimota School, had a better education system than most of its neighbours. The African educationist Aggrey, who under the leadership of Rev. A. G. Fraser, the first Headmaster, helped to build up Achimota on the philosophy of full co-operation between black and white, also encouraged schools in other areas. At the top of the educational scale the educated African enjoyed an easy and relaxed relationship with Europeans, but this dangerously

[1] Later Sir Thorlief Mangin KCMG.

masked the frustration of the elementary school leaver, who now found few openings to satisfy his new aspirations, and who had to compete with the ex-serviceman, educated by his travel and experiences in the army overseas.

Several groups of intelligent, literate and articulate people, who had often been critical of the shortcomings of the Chiefs' rule, had been seriously frustrated by the Native Authority Ordnance, passed by Burns in 1944. This law bolstered up the power of the Chief against the criticism of his people, and showed that there was little future for the common man in this field of local politics.

In 1947 the administration faced a further blow through the repercussions of the notorious Kibi ritual murders. Four years before, at the funeral ceremony of a paramount Chief, Sir Ofori Atta, a Minor Chief had been murdered. Eight culprits were arrested, tried by jury and condemned to death. J. B. Danquah, the doyen of the wealthy and articulate African middle class, and a relation of Ofori Atta, led the defence and used every legal tactic to delay and prevent the executions, by appealing to the Supreme Court, the Privy Council and the King. In March 1947, the House of Commons, in an atmosphere of emotional misunderstanding, intervened and exacerbated an already difficult situation. The British government signally failed to support Burns, who offered his resignation, but was later persuaded to withdraw it. Although his policy and his integrity were vindicated in every respect, the whole administration in the Gold Coast was seriously damaged by the spectacle of a governor as powerful and experienced as Burns, being publicly pilloried and not adequately supported from Whitehall. Finally three culprits were hanged but the rest reprieved.

Deep antagonisms had been stirred up by the Kibi murders and their long drawn out aftermath, but these were soon to be overshadowed by the Swollen Shoot crisis. In 1943 the virus disease of Swollen Shoot had been identified in the cocoa trees of Ashanti. The disease spread rapidly, and in 1945 the Government embarked on the policy of 'cutting out'—that is to cut down and burn all infected trees and neighbouring trees. The policy brought immediate and fierce opposition from the cocoa farmer, who, just when cocoa prices began to go up, found his whole livelihood threatened. Throughout the forest region the drums and the mammy lorries spread the message of opposition, and the colonial administration—not well served by its Public Relations Department—mishandled the Swollen Shoot issue. As gangs of government labourers marched into the cocoa areas, both grievances and acts of sabotage multiplied. In March 1947 an African member of the Legislative Council proposed compensation for the cocoa farmers but this was refused by the British. A season of drought which followed, not only reduced the harvest of other crops to which the farmers had turned, but favoured the rapid increase of the mealy bug which spread the Swollen Shoot disease. Through misunderstanding, and lack of adequate explanation, in many areas the policy of cutting out was increasingly associated with an unsympathetic white government in Accra. A Committee of Inquiry set up in September 1947 suggested some initial improvements, but the crisis continued, to be used by Nkrumah the following year, and to be a major factor in the handing over of political power in the 1950s.

The discontent over Swollen Shoot largely effected the rural areas, but discontent over inflation and the exorbitant price of imported goods affected the country as a whole. A wealthy Accra contractor Kwabena Bonne,[2] who had become a minor chief of the Ga people, now came forward to lead the demand for substantial price reductions, or failing that a boycott of imported goods. In October 1947, his public stand against high prices gained immediate and enthusiastic support, and the majority of chiefs and councils throughout the Colony and Ashanti gave him their support.[3] The Government, faced with a mass movement on such a scale, remained amazingly inactive. If their inadequacy in the field of Public Relations was surprising, their incompetence in economic affairs was disastrous. The administration employed no economist and its own statistics were virtually useless. It even appeared to ignore the most obvious danger signs. Bonne's anti-inflation campaign, receiving massive support but achieving no reduction of prices, proceeded in December to the threatened boycott of imported goods. Bonne broadcast a New Year Message, strongly anti-European in tone, and opposing the exploitation of the people by the white man. The supporting resolutions, from different parts of the country—'We declare civil war', and 'We shall conquer our common foe'—illustrate the intensity of feeling. The boycott started on 26 January 1948, but even then it was February before Scott,[4] the Colonial Secretary, met with Bonne's committee. After careful discussions the main firms in the Association of West African Merchants agreed to cut their gross profit margin from 75 per cent to 50 per cent. Here again the Government failed at a crucial moment, because it failed to explain to the people what sort of price cuts this would mean. The idea rapidly spread that prices in the shops would be halved as soon as the boycott was lifted on 28 February—even the European community expected cuts of 30 per cent.

Meanwhile the Ex-Servicemen's Union, concerned at the effects of inflation and the high level of unemployment, organized a petition requesting the Governor to take action on behalf of its members, who

[2] He became known as the Boycott Hene.
[3] D. Austin *Politics in Ghana* p. 70.
[4] Later Sir Robert Scott KCMG.

had given loyal service to Britain during the war. The police granted permission for the procession to go to the Secretariat in Accra, but not to the Governor's Residence at Christiansborg Castle. The lifting of the boycott and the Ex-Servicemen's procession took place on Saturday 28 February. The police anticipated some difficulties and were apprehensive because many of their men had been called away to deal with violence in the Swollen Shoot areas. Troops in Accra garrison were on the alert at dawn.

On the day, the procession started peacefully enough but was joined by rowdy elements, and rapidly became an aggressive and menacing mob. Instead of going to the Secretariat it took the road to Christiansborg. A small detachment of police under Superintendent Imray quickly drew themselves up to bar the road to the castle. Imray shouted an order to halt but the crowd moved on. He grabbed a rifle, and after a warning shot in the air, gave the order to fire. Two men were killed and five wounded. Those few shots were to release pent-up forces which started the African Revolution. The crowd quickly dispersed and returned to Accra. There the shoppers, outraged at the paltry price reductions, readily joined in a spontaneous explosion of anger. Rioting crowds attacked the big European and Syrian owned stores, looting and burning shops and destroying cars.

The Watson Commission which investigated the February riots and reported in August 1948 summed up both the long term and the more immediate causes of the revolt. Burns had retired in July 1947 leaving a dangerous hiatus until Sir Gerald Creasey arrived in January 1948, only a few weeks before the riots. Mangin, the Chief Commissioner of the Colony,[5] and Scott, Colonial Secretary, dominated this period and were severely criticized in the Watson Report. The problems of staffing, supplies and general frustration, previously highlighted by Burns, had increased. Mangin's autocratic and reactionary attitudes had hardened when he was in control, and he noticeably lacked Burn's ability to integrate the two parts of the service and to co-ordinate information on which critically important decisions could be based. Thus Watson emphasizes that Creasey was very badly informed and given wildly alarmist reports which resulted in unwise and precipitate action. Creasey quickly publicized the assumption that the riots had a sinister Communist pattern, and links with overseas organizations. In a year which saw the intensification of the Cold War, the Communist emergency in Malaya and the coup in Prague, this might have been understandable, but these views, which proved to be unfounded, were passed on

[5] The Gold Coast, at this time, was divided into three sections The Southern Section called The Colony, the Middle Section Ashanti, and the Northern Section called The Northern Territories.

uncritically to London. In a Commons debate a government Minister hinted to the Communist MP Gallagher that he would not like the facts when they were established.[6] A significant factor in the 1948 situation was that Creasey had no field experience before, and Scott, upon whom he relied substantially, had recently arrived from Palestine. Neither they nor their senior colleagues appeared to grasp the significance of the forces of nationalism with which they were faced.

In the longer term the Watson Report put forward strong criticism of the system of indirect rule and of the political power of the Chiefs. As a result of the Report the Government made drastic changes in policy. It dissolved the Association of West African Merchants, it granted to cocoa farmers compensation for replanting, it abandoned the policy of compulsory cutting out and appointed an all African commission under the distinguished Judge Coussey to report on the Constitution.

In view of the dramatic political changes which followed, it is remarkable that during the crisis the Government did not call a meeting of the Legislative Council. Later its members were extremely critical of Mangin and Scott, but in a more light hearted vein wished to pardon Creasey as a first offender. Creasey left the Gold Coast in March 1949, and in spite of the strong and public criticisms of the Watson Report, Mangin and Scott once more took charge until the arrival of the new Governor in August 1949.

Having been briefed by Creech-Jones with the sombre warning 'I want you to go to the Gold Coast. The country is on the edge of revolution. We are in danger of losing it', Arden-Clarke flew out to Accra in August 1949. He faced a daunting task. The Colonial Office still thought in terms of a Communist inspired uprising, and his own experience had involved him in both civil and military action against the Communist insurgents in Malaya. He realized that after the disasters of 1948 in the Gold Coast, and the long interregnum after the sudden departure of Creasy, his initial impact would be important. He was therefore less than happy, after a 22 hour flight via Tripoli, Kano and Lagos, to arrive in Accra feeling 'crumpled, scruffy and heavy-eyed'.[7] A huge police guard of honour and the whole Executive Council together with Chiefs in state finery met him at the airport. After greeting them, he drove in the Governor's Humber Limousine—stopping at the town boundary to meet the Accra Town Council—to Christiansborg Castle which was to be his home for the next eight momentous years. A former slaving castle, it perched on a rocky promontory, with surf breaking at the base of the castle walls. Although he had been Governor of Sarawak, he was deeply

---

[6] Parliamentary Debates, House of Commons. 1 March 1948.
[7] Letter to Lady Arden-Clarke 14.8.49.

impressed by the magnificence of state occasions in the Gold Coast, and by the pomp which surrounded him at the castle.

He had less than two weeks between his return from Sarawak and his arrival in Accra, and he had asked the Colonial Office to provide the detail for his inaugural speech. He was not pleased therefore to have to compose and dictate it on the afternoon of his arrival, and before the ceremony the following morning. In his inaugural speech he promised that he would not rely on reports but would get out to meet and consult the people. He was aware of the economic problems and realized that the problem of Swollen Shoot which threatened the whole cocoa industry needed strong leadership from the government, and also from the chiefs. The Coussey Committee report would shortly be published and he emphasized that all future constitutional progress depended on the healthy development of local government, adding that the changes proposed by the Coussey Report would be acted on as expeditiously as possible, but that any attempt to influence events by violence would be dealt with very severely. In conclusion he quoted the speech of King George VI at the opening of the Colonial Exhibition, 'Progress depends upon a true sense of partnership between all sections of society . . . each giving of its best to the common weal;' and he made a final promise that it would be his prime endeavour to achieve mutual co-operation and goodwill.

Later he commented:

It was all very magnificent and I hope I did my part satisfactorily, despite that horrible sinking feeling in one's tummy and a shaking in one's hands and knees. At the end of the speeches some 300 people were presented and my right hand felt a bit sore—too great a proportion seemed to think that a forceful grip was required.[8]

The next day, Saturday, he inspected the Secretariat, bought a tennis racket and golf clubs, and in the afternoon attended the Accra races, driving down the course with an escort of Police Lancers. He wrote, in a letter to his wife:

It seems that out here they love panoply and plumes. Wherever I go I am expected to hold a Durbar in full uniform, and give huge sundowners and garden parties etc. They want a Governor, someone they can see and shout at and talk to, someone who will give them the pageantry and the occasion for fine clothes and ceremonial that they love, and someone too who will give them a lead. I get the impression that the Press build up, intended to be derogatory, that I am 'strong' and 'tough' is not unwelcome to the people . . . Apparently the announcement I made in my speech that I proposed to get out among the

---

[8] Letter to Lady Arden-Clarke 14.8.49.

people to see things for myself, followed by the news next day that I am to set out on a short tour on Thursday has gone down with a bang. What an enormous amount of play-acting there is in all this, the Governor's state, the doctor's bed-side manner, the all-in-wrestler's ferocity—and the people see through it but love it. We have a new role to play here, darling, and I'll need your help a lot.[9]

Official visits, protocol, ceremony, garden parties—though a critical part of his role, masked to some extent the appalling weight of responsibility he had undertaken. His whole administrative service, still at a desperately low ebb, felt vulnerable and insecure; Accra still contained all the ingredients of political revolution. It was here that Arden-Clarke really began his distinctive and unique contribution to the future and to the destiny of Ghana. He might have appeared, from his activities with the Madas and Mamas in the early 1920s, as a harsh and brutal imperialist, but his experience in Southern Africa, and more particularly in South East Asia, had changed his whole approach. His conversion into a governor, still as positive, but with a highly flexible mind, would appear to come from the influence of Malcolm MacDonald, and his years in Sarawak when he had seen the growing influence of nationalist movements, and where he had learned to be sensitive to new and complex political currents. This experience gave him the confidence to provide the leadership that was so urgently required in Accra where, because of the highly volatile political situation a single false move could have brought disaster.

He soon experienced the political situation at first hand. Leaving Accra exactly a week after his arrival he travelled to Cape Coast, Sekondi and Takoradi. Here posters emblazoned the walls demanding 'Self Government Now' or 'S. G. Now'.

At a Durbar I held yesterday at Sekondi an organized band of young toughs boo-ed all the way through my speech and there was organized booing as I walked round the railway workshops, and again at Takoradi harbour. As demonstrations of political feeling they were not convincing—as public exhibitions of boorishness and disrespect to the King's representative they are alienating all respectable and moderate Africans from the cause of 'S.G. Now' and so serve a useful purpose.[10]

Such a reception added to the pressures on a new Governor, and a few days later he suffered equally offensive behaviour from the Paramount Chiefs at Bogoso in the mining area near Tarkwa. At an informal meeting with the chiefs, because he was not in full uniform, three chiefs

[9] Op. cit.
[10] Letter to Lady Arden-Clarke 21.8.49

remained seated, giving as their excuse that they normally recognized the Governor by the feathers in his hat. He gave them a stiff rebuke, adding that such behaviour was as strange to him as it was foreign to the natural courtesy of the people of the Gold Coast. He refused to continue the meeting and left at once.

His immediate attempts to get the feel of the country were overlaid by the urgent need to brief himself as fully and as rapidly as possible about the political situation, before taking the critical decisions on the Coussey Report dealing with the political and constitutional future of the Colony. He had the draft report to study before the end of August and there followed a period of intensive discussion before its official publication in October 1949. Political briefing led inevitably to Nkrumah, but although Arden-Clarke and Nkrumah, between 1951 and 1957, were to play a dramatic dual role at one of the most important moments in African history, their initial contact could not have been more unfortunate and inauspicious. The senior advisers of the new Governor took a highly prejudiced and almost contemptuous view of Nkrumah, and at first this inevitably coloured Arden-Clarke's opinion. In a letter of 16 September 1949, referring to some alarms and excursions and a midnight council of war, he wrote:

> Nothing much has happened, a few minor disturbances by unruly mobs of hooligans and some stoning of cars, all quickly suppressed by the police. It was caused by a case brought against a man called Nkrumah—the extremist leader who is aping Hitler—for contempt of court. Judgement was given yesterday and he was fined £300 or four months and was given a fortnight to pay—a sensible judgement. I did not want him jugged for a month or two. The excitement has died down for the moment but the general idea is that there will be a real flare-up when the Coussey Report is published. That is the situation we are planning to meet. I think we'll be able to cope effectively with it.[11]

Such a view illustrates vividly enough the inadequate information upon which Arden-Clarke initially had to rely, for by September 1949 Nkrumah was already a serious and significant political figure. Born in 1909, Nkrumah, after attending a Roman Catholic Mission School, went to Achimota College. In 1931, when he finished at Achimota, he went to Elmina Catholic School which lay almost in the shadow of one of the great slaving castles. His passion for local history, politics and current affairs had been noted at school and it received a tremendous fillip when he heard Dr Azikiwe lecture in Accra in 1934. Azikiwe, then the leading African Nationalist, undoubtedly inspired him to continue his education

[11] Letter to Family 16.9.49

and in 1935, helped by a relative who prospected in diamonds, Nkrumah left for Lincoln University, Pennsylvania. He already held positive views. He wrote home saying that no African who visited America could return without being determined to liberate Africa from ignorance, poverty and the chains of imperialist exploitation. At Lincoln he proved himself an able, intelligent and extremely conscientious student who gained his Bachelor's degree and was encouraged to stay on for further semesters to do theology. At Pennsylvania University he took Masters degrees in Philosophy and Education, and he made a name for himself as a forceful preacher in the local Presbyterian Churches. Appointed a lecturer on the staff of Lincoln University he gained fame as a passionate protagonist in the struggle for the Negro cause and the struggle against colonialism. A flattering biographer wrote that he had embraced the philosophy of service before self, and this became the guiding principle of his life. This convinced him that he should give up his career in America and dedicate his life to Africa.

In June, 1945 he returned to London and enrolled at the London School of Economics as a PhD student. He neglected his studies and embraced wholeheartedly the cause of Africa and the Pan-African movement. Playing a leading part in the West African Students Union, which contained many future African leaders, he attended the Pan-African Congress in October 1945. This gathering of 200 delegates set up a Secretariat to co-ordinate the nationalist movements of Africa and to help federate the territories of West Africa. Nkrumah wrote fierce and provocative articles attacking colonialism and imperialism. He quickly formulated his method of attack. His Four Points were:

to organize the masses; to abolish political illiteracy; to prepare agents of progress; and to establish a nationalist press.

What already marked out Nkrumah from his fellows was his brilliant power of organization. This had been shown in America and in London but for the first time was to be really tested when he accepted the post of secretary to the United Gold Coast Convention, which had just been founded by Dr Danquah.

Nkrumah, after visiting Freetown and Liberia on the way, arrived at Takoradi in December 1947. He had two weeks rest with his mother and some old friends, and in January 1948 at Saltpond, went to his first meeting of the UGCC. He had been offered £100 a month but cheerfully accepted £25 and gained a reputation for being indifferent about money. Even at this first meeting, he showed that his views were very different from those of the leaders of the movement. He immediately proposed the appointment of members of a Shadow Cabinet, the co-ordination of every native organization, the establishment of party branches in every town and village, and the organization of training week-ends for party leaders. This basic organization was to be followed by demonstrations, boycotts and strikes in support of the demand for self government. When Nkrumah had taken over, there were no active branches of the UGCC, but he quickly travelled the country addressing meetings and setting up branches wherever he went. His fame spread rapidly and every class rallied to him, seeing through his dynamic approach the solution to their varying frustrations. Accepting conditions that would have appalled his well-to-do backers, he stumped the country often begging lifts on mammy lorries and sleeping in the ditch beside the road.

Nkrumah had been so heavily occupied in setting up his office at Saltpond and in organizing new branches throughout the country, that he had hardly heard of the boycott organized by Chief Bonne. He had certainly had no part in it and the leaders of the boycott had certainly not become members of the UGCC. While the boycott was still operating Nkrumah travelled to Accra on 20 February 1948 to address his first public meeting in the capital at the open air Palladium Cinema. His career could easily have been jeopardized at this point because his car broke down and he was hours late but thousands of people waited and listened enthralled as he spoke on 'The ideological battles of our time'. Danquah, who was to become his most hated rival and eventually to die in one of Nkrumah's prisons, supported him and told the people that Nkrumah would never fail them. Nkrumah urged them to stand together and fight for their freedom and independence, and they responded wildly to this confident, challenging and authoritative leader.

Immediately after the riots of 28 February 1948, although he was not in Accra at the time, Nkrumah cabled the Secretary of State demanding the recall of the Governor and immediate self-government. He copied his demands to the UN Secretary General and to the world's press. A few days later the police arrested Nkrumah and found an unsigned communist party card—this had little significance but contributed to the massive official misunderstanding of the nature of the February riots.

After the capture of Nkrumah all six political leaders were taken to Accra Airport, flown to Kumasi, and quickly herded into the gaol. During this period of imprisonment it soon became clear that Nkrumah disagreed with the others on every major issue. They even blamed him for the riots and for their detention. The youth organizations which Nkrumah had set up in Kumasi, hearing of the imprisonment there of all the leaders resolved to attack the prison and release them This plan, under the leadership of Krobo Edusei, was thwarted by the government which quickly removed the six by bus to Tamale the capital of the Northern Territories. From there they were spirited away to six different places and kept in solitary confinement for a period of about six weeks.

The period of imprisonment brought to a head the deep differences between Nkrumah and the other UGCC leaders, and soon after their release Nkrumah moved towards a decisive break. In September 1948, with one assistant and a few boys he started a modest single sheet newspaper *The Accra Evening News*, which rapidly became a most powerful political instrument. Every issue immediately sold out and was passed from hand to hand among the people. At a meeting in Accra, Nkrumah addressed a vast concourse of people on 'The Liberty of the Colonial Subject'. His prestige grew dramatically and in July 1949—a month before Arden-Clarke's arrival in Accra—he formally and publicly broke away from Danquah and the UGCC, and formed a new and completely separate party, the Convention People's Party or CPP. The party started with a six point programme: to achieve 'Self Government Now'; to remove undemocratic oppression; to maintain the unity of the country; to obtain better working conditions; to create a country where people will live and govern themselves as free people; and to obtain a united self-governing West Africa.

The CPP became the first and, virtually, the only effective political party in the Gold Coast. Supported from the first by the mass of the people and by youth organizations, the party covered the whole country with a network of party branches, with its party colours of red, white and green. Relying on the support of the largely illiterate masses, the party organized loudspeaker vans which toured even the most remote villages. Party members spoke to all the people in their own tribal tongue about the new and exciting challenge which faced them. In the towns of Accra, Sekondi and Cape Coast, newspapers based on the successful model of *The Accra Evening News* kept up a constant stream of encouragement, of information and of party propaganda. Against the wild excitement which swept the country in support of the CPP no other organization stood a chance. Against the radical, forward-looking and aggressive nationalism of the CPP, the policy of Danquah and his associates appeared middle-class, backward looking, and fatally compromised on the vital issue of colonialism. Their taunts about Nkrumah and his communists, verandah boys and hooligans—referring to the large number of ignorant and uneducated men who had jumped on the CPP bandwaggon—made little impact at the time, when the whole country was caught up in a wave of excitement, joy and self-confidence.

In these heady days it seemed that nothing was impossible. A brilliant leader had come—experienced, educated, determined and, above all, dedicated to his people's good. A man who could and did galvanize the whole energies of his people; an African patriot with the chance to prove to an interested and sympathetic world that Africans could run their own country. The CPP took to heart its leader's word—organize—and soon in bye elections and municipal elections the CPP candidates began to sweep the board. Challenged by their opponents to define 'Positive Action' they quickly produced a pamphlet which outlined their plans. Positive Action would use every legitimate means—political agitation, the press, boycotts, strikes and non co-operation based on the example of Gandhi. This was the situation in September 1949 when Arden-Clarke, monumentally ill-informed by his staff, referred slightingly to some extremist leader aping Hitler.

The Watson Commission which investigated the 1948 riots had recommended that another Committee should look into the whole question of the constitutional future of the Colony. This new committee, composed entirely of Africans under the distinguished African judge Sir Henley Coussey, acted promptly and effectively. The main body of the Coussey Report was accepted and the constitution it proposed was 'a very constitutional advance'.[12] It provided, as Dennis Austin wrote 'semi-responsible government',[13] and made a dramatic change from the normal pattern of colonial legislature. The new Executive Committee, of which the Governor was chairman, had 11 members, of which eight were elected and were to become ministers in charge of departments. A substantial minority of the Coussey Committee favoured a bicameral legislature with the chiefs acting as a senate, but this view was rejected largely on the grounds that if the chiefs had a separate house they would become more and more isolated. Many of the Coussey Report findings were based on the assumption that political power would devolve upon the chiefs and the middle-class intelligentsia—an assumption that was rapidly to be proved false. The main feature of the proposed constitution as it finally emerged was an elected Assembly of 78 members with 72 elected members, plus the Colonial Secretary, Financial Secretary and Attorney General, together with three representatives of commercial and mining interests.

The Report reached Arden-Clarke at the end of August 1949, three weeks after his arrival. He wrote:

> Its publication, which cannot be delayed much longer than the end of September or the first week in October is expected to provide the signal for a general upheaval, with strikes, hooliganism and sporadic riots, but I am not so sure that these will actually take place. Anyhow I'm taking every precaution to see that if they do, we deal firmly and promptly with them. I am by no means despondent about the situation here, though we can expect a fair packet of trouble during the next few months.[14]

[12] Col No 250 Statement by His Majesty's Government.
[13] D. Austin *Politics in Ghana*, p. 85.
[14] Letter to Family 31.8.49.

By early September the Governor with his top advisers had worked on the Report:

> The last few days have been pretty grim—on Saturday and again on Sunday my 'working party', consisting of Scott (the Colonial Secretary) Branigan (the Attorney-General) and three others (Saloway, Loveridge and Hadow) met to work on the Coussey Report . . . and at 8 a.m. yesterday the results of our labours left by air for Whitehall. The trouble is that the Secretary of State goes on holiday the day after tomorrow until the 30th. I am pressing hard that when the Report is published we should at the same time publish a despatch from him showing just how far we are prepared to go towards the grant of full responsible government, which is not as far as the Coussey Report recommends. The despatch would provide an ordered programme of constitutional advance sufficient to satisfy and win the support of reasonable opinion in the Gold Coast and at the same time would firmly and categorically dismiss the fantastic claims of the demagogues and extremists. That is the general idea if I can get the Secretary of State to adopt it. He seems to hanker after a conference in London which would not work. We cannot delay publication of the Report too long and that means that the Secretary of State would have to sign the despatch within a week of his return from holiday. Naturally he is reluctant to commit himself to this procedure without full knowledge of what he is letting himself in for, so we have had to get the full picture to him, including a draft of the kind of despatch I want him to write.[15]

His urgent preoccupation with the Coussey Report was interrupted the following day by his trek to the Northern Territories. This country, of orchard bush thinning into semi-desert, reminded him vividly of Northern Nigeria. He saw again the dignified naked pagans, he heard Hausa spoken and delighted at the excellent work of the District Commissioners and Chiefs in improving the living conditions of the people. Here he heard no political clamour, no demands for 'self-government now', and he found it refreshingly like the good old days. After a busy few days meeting chiefs and attending conferences at Tamale and Navrongo, he returned to Accra on 11 September to receive the reply of the Secretary of State.

> The chief thing is that the Secretary of State has agreed to the procedures we suggested about the Coussey Report and we'll make ready a despatch for publication with the Report, but he has asked for publication to be deferred until 24th October, and to this perforce we must agree. Two of my advisers Saloway and Loveridge will fly to Whitehall on Wednesday . . . everyone is agreed that it would be

[15] Letter to Family 6.9.49.

inadvisable for me to leave the country at the present stage or to be associated too closely in the public mind with the decisions which the Secretary of State may make.[16]

Realizing that the success of the constitutional advance and the maintenance of law and order depended substantially on the administration having prompt and up to date information, in early September Arden-Clarke appointed George Sinclair,[17] as Security Liaison Officer in charge of a three man committee to liaise with the police and military, to tour all danger areas, to supervise Special Branch activities, and to recommend action to the Governor and to the chief Commissioners in the regions. Special Branch reports quickly built up information, especially about the CPP and its activities.

For a second time in a month the Governor had to break away from urgent constitutional discussions to attend a major Durbar. This formal meeting between the King's Representative and the assembled chiefs played a crucial role in public relations and Arden-Clarke took infinite pains to ensure its success. Ashanti had a proud history as an independent nation, and when he visited the Ashanti Confederacy Council on 27 September and spoke to the Ashanti Chiefs he chose his words with particular care. After formally greeting the 60 chiefs assembled with their followers, with heavy gold ornaments, bangles, crowns and lavish decorated umbrellas, he addressed them. He referred to the great interest in the Gold Coast's advance to full responsible government within the British Commonwealth, and in the Coussey Report, but stressed that such changes demanded a heavy load of preparatory work and responsibility not only by the government but by regional councils, in a spirit of trust and goodwill. Any resort to violence would only postpone and delay the process. On the question of law and order and the responsibilities of the chiefs he said 'I rely on you to do your duty as you may rely on me to do mine.' He continued with references to the new Kumasi hospital, the establishment of a Regional technical college, housing development, food production and, finally, the inevitable issue of the campaign to save the cocoa industry from the ravages of swollen shoot. Ashanti produced half the colony's cocoa but so far it had not suffered severely from swollen shoot.

In the future the policy of Arden-Clarke and Nkrumah was to receive its stiffest opposition from Ashanti, and particularly the Ashanti newspapers, but on this occasion the intrepid *Ashanti Pioneer* played down the whole political issue and merely headlined the question of housing for African civil servants.

[16] Letter to Family 12.9.49.
[17] Sir George Sinclair, CMG, OBE.

In a letter home, after his successful visit to Ashanti, Arden-Clarke listed his commitments—visits by the C in C of the Belgian Congo, by a member of the French government, by the Governor of French Togoland and then preparations for the formal opening of the Legislative Council.

> And so it goes on, with all the real work of governing the colony in the midst of a constitutional crisis and threats against its internal security, to be done behind the scenes.[18]

Arden-Clarke had quickly given his own style and imprint to the administration and particularly to its public relations. Early in October he gave an informal party for the Press, and this created considerable goodwill. The *Spectator Daily*, not renowned for its sophisticated approach, commented:

> His Excellency proved to be a good conversationalist and his humorous remarks kept the gathering very much alive.[19]

It was noted that, almost alone, the Accra *Evening News* was not represented.

So often in the period of decolonization the Imperial power lost all initiative and appeared to be fighting a rearguard action, moving grudgingly and reluctantly towards the grant of political independence, but Arden-Clarke, even while the country was seething with excitement over the Coussey Report, took a very positive constitutional step by handing over the Presidency of the Legislative Council to the respected African barrister Mr E. C. Quist. Arden-Clarke had planned this move soon after he arrived and it was carried out with full pomp and ceremony. He drove to the King George V Hall in full ceremonials and with a bodyguard of Lancers. After inspecting the guard of honour he entered the hall accompanied by the full Executive Council and watched by a vast concourse of spectators. The new President, preceded by the famous gold mace, approached the Governor, and his commission was handed over in a brief dignified ceremony. Arden-Clarke wrote:

> There was a terrific ovation. To the majority of the spectators it had come as a complete surprise. There was no doubt about the genuineness of the applause. This was something that had gone home to them. The indications are that I have done the right thing at the right time, a comforting but rare event.'[20]

The press were almost unanimous in their approval, except for the *Morning Telegraph* which criticized the lack of consultation about the change and added:

[18] Letter to Lady Arden-Clarke 3.10.49.
[19] *Spectator Daily* 11.10.49.
[20] Letter to Family 12.10.49.

We would make it abundantly clear that no 17th century imperialistic chicanery is going to get us off our guard. We want Self Government with people of our choosing to steer the ship of state.

If we concede to this set up we shall still be broiling in the imperialistic frying pan and in the fire of Colonialism. [21]

The *Gold Coast Independent* gave a more representative view that it was a commendable step by the Governor and belied the initial supposition that he had been appointed to suppress the political aspirations of the people.

Arden-Clarke's moves in the Legislative Council, his easier relations with the press, and his vigorous programme of treks throughout the colony had impressed the people and ensured a sympathetic reception when he broadcast to the country on the day the Coussey Report was published, 25 October 1949.

He first thanked and congratulated the Coussey Committee for their excellent work which would lead the Gold Coast to responsible government within the British Commonwealth as early as possible. Such a development demanded the energy, good sense and co-operation of all the people in this great opportunity to shape their destiny. He asked the people to study the details soundly and constructively, and to realize that the democratic changes made in local government were equally as important as the more dramatic changes made in central government. In the proposed Legislative Assembly nearly all the members would be directly or indirectly elected. At the top the Executive Council, composed largely of African ministers, would formulate policy and would be collectively responsible to the Governor, but the individual African ministers would be responsible for their departments to the Assembly. The Governor retained a veto but could only use it with the agreement of the Executive Council or the Secretary of State.

He touched on the constitutional details in round terms, highlighting the more dramatic changes, and then in stern and challenging phrases demanded the sober and realistic endeavour of everybody to ensure the future of democratic government in the country. He reminded the people as a whole that the eyes of the world—both sceptics and well wishers—were upon them and this placed a heavy load of responsibility on them to ensure that the whole plan both centrally and locally was made to work successfully.

The press generally gave a most favourable reception both to his broadcast and to the Coussey Report, and in the ensuing months the Governor capitalized on this. At Speech Day at Achimota College, which produced large numbers of past and future leaders of Ghana, he referred

[21] *Morning Telegraph* 14.10.49.

to the distinguished work of Coussey, an old Achimotan, and in a challenging address to the pupils pointed out that, with discipline, enterprise and a spirit of service they could play a vital role in the exciting future of their country. To a European gathering at the St Andrew's Day Dinner replying to the toast 'The land we live in', he called for calm and understanding service in the new and challenging situation, in which there was no room for defeatists. He concluded with a prayer in rhyme:

> Lord, temper with tranquillity
> My manifold activity,
> And let me do my work for thee
> With very great simplicity.
>
> God send me sympathy and sense
> And help me hold my courage high
> And give me calm and confidence
> And please, a twinkle in my eye.

While the UGCC, whose senior members had been on the Coussey Committee, accepted the Report as a basis for constitutional advance, the CPP suffered no such inhibition and made the most of their opportunity. They boldly declared the Coussey constitution to be bogus and fraudulent and demanded Positive Action. Nkrumah who had been stumping the country speaking and distributing leaflets on Positive Action returned to Accra in November 1949 and called a 'Ghana Peoples Representative Assembly'. This meeting, which was massively supported, demanded immediate self-government with Dominion Status based on the Statute of Westminster. This situation posed a serious dilemma for Nkrumah who either had to take responsibility for a full scale revolt against the government or, alternatively, to accept the government's offer and fight the ensuing election which he would be likely to win. His more senior colleagues like Gbedemah and Casely-Hayford seemed to suggest compromise while the trade union element led by the Railway Workers Union counselled defiance.

The public rejection of the Coussey Report by the CPP and the drive for Positive Action alerted the administration to the need for vigilance. The Governor attended a large scale security exercise—Exercise Lion— held at Giffard Camp outside Accra. Officers from British and French West Africa attended, and the press publicized the high state of readiness of the security forces, and the valuable anti-guerrilla experience that had been gained in Malaya.

Arden-Clarke's concern at the rising political temperature and the growing influence of the CPP is illustrated by his second address to the Legislative Council, in December 1949. He referred to the enduring partnership between Britain and the Gold Coast, and to the good faith of the government in its determination to achieve responsible government as soon as practicable. He outlined his plans to ensure that, when the nine African ministers assumed office, they would be supported by a highly efficient secretariat system. He referred to Africanization which had various implications. He had already sent a thoughtful and reassuring memorandum to his senior staff to emphasize what a critical role they had to play in the hand over of power, and to allay their understandable apprehension about their future, and he pointed out to the Legislative Council that Africanization had to be considered in the context of the whole of an emerging country, and the government service should not take an undue share of the available talent. But his final and sternest message was to those who were sowing suspicion and mistrust, who were trying to engender bad blood, and who painted distorted pictures in lurid colours of an enslaved people struggling to be free from an oppressive tyrant. He called on all men of good-will to counteract the evil effect of political creeds based, in the words of the Litany, 'on envy, hatred, malice and all uncharitableness'.[22]

---

[22] Governor's address to the Legislative Council December 1949.

CHAPTER SIX

The CPP Emerges

During November the political situation had been exacerbated by industrial action. In September the meteorological workers, who had unsuccessfully negotiated for better pay since August 1948, sent the Government an ultimatum. The Government had reacted fiercely and dismissed all the strikers. The Gold Coast TUC, which was substantially represented on inner councils of the CPP demanded the re-instatement of the strikers, and, failing that, threatened a general strike. Again they received the intransigent reply that a general strike was illegal, and at this deadlock Nkrumah swung back to Positive Action.

By now it was clear to Arden-Clarke that the political situation had changed dramatically. From his own travels and more particularly from his highly efficient security committee he received accurate and up-to-date information. This showed that Accra, Kumasi and the other towns were coming increasingly under the sway of the CPP. Nkrumah gave a dynamic political lead, but as CPP influence spread, strong-arm elements came to the fore. They forced people to join the party, broke up rival meetings, beat up rival candidates and poured out slogans attacking the chiefs and attacking Europeans. At the same time the UGCC leaders like Danquah, who had confidently looked forward to taking over from the British, saw their support rapidly disappearing, and were unable to handle the political situation in which the CPP outbid them at every turn. While Arden-Clarke faced all these pressures in Accra, he also faced the formidable stand of the Chief Commissioners of Ashanti and the Northern Territories, who claimed correctly enough that the pace of political change set by the towns was in no way matched in the country districts, and that their areas as a whole were not in any way ready for headlong political advance.

On 15 December 1949 Nkrumah wrote to the Governor warning him that if the resolutions of the Peoples Representative Assembly continued to be ignored, a campaign of Positive Action would start, based on the policy of non-violence and non co-operation exemplified by Gandhi. On the same day he published a rousing article in the Accra *Evening News* and addressed a huge crowd in the Arena, where he again stressed that there must be no violence. Faced with this deteriorating situation, Arden-Clarke now took an important initiative. He instructed the Colonial

Secretary, Saloway,[1] a man of considerable ability and political insight, and with high level experience of the hand over of power in India, to discuss matters with Nkrumah.

Descriptions of these critical conversations vary dramatically. Saloway records that he convinced Nkrumah that the forthcoming election would be conducted fairly and that if the CPP had a strong following it could gain power by fully constitutional methods. He continued:

> Nkrumah publicly called off Positive Action and tried hard to get the Trades Union Congress to call off the General Strike, but the T.U.C. no longer had any control over the wild men.[2]

In contrast, Nkrumah recorded in his autobiography that Saloway warned him that he would be personally responsible if Positive Action led to violence, adding that the situation in India was very different and was not relevant to the Gold Coast. Nkrumah retorted that the people were roused, were determined to have their grievances redressed, and demanded that the Government must consider the resolutions of the Peoples Representative Assembly. Nkrumah then alleges that 'the same day an announcement was made over the local Radio that Positive Action had been abandoned'. To counteract what he maintains was a subterfuge by the Government, he called a meeting in the Arena and announced that 'Positive Action would start at once.' The political and social revolution of Ghana had started.[3]

Arden-Clarke gives yet another version:

> I have good reason to believe that some at least of the party leaders would have preferred not to resort to Positive Action but to await the results of the general election, of the outcome of which they were fairly confident. But they found themselves enmeshed in the coils of their own propaganda. The tail wagged the dog and 'Positive Action' was duly declared in January 1950.[4]

Although Nkrumah had stressed the non-violent aspect of Positive Action the movement rapidly assumed menacing proportions, and by 10 January 1950 two policemen had been killed in clashes with CPP supporters. The Government used radio and mobile police effectively, but as support for Positive Action swelled up, it became clear that firmer measures were needed. Therefore, after a number of meetings of the Executive Council at Christiansborg Castle, Arden-Clarke called an emergency meeting of the Legislative Council. His address to it was

---

[1] Sir Reginald Saloway, KBE, CMG.
[2] International Affairs October 1955.
[3] K. Nkrumah *Autobiography* p. 117. Nkrumah's precipitate action may also have been caused by Danquah's jibe that he had sold the country's future for an empty promise.
[4] African Affairs 1958 Sir Charles Arden-Clarke 'Eight years of transition in Ghana'.

significant. In contrast to the situation of 1948, when the Legislative Council did not meet, he took them fully into his confidence and addressed them with firm and authoritative leadership, appealing for their loyalty and co-operation. He pointed out that on his arrival in August there had been an atmosphere of distrust and suspicion, but as he had travelled about he had sensed a very substantial body of opinion opposed to the violence and intimidation of the CPP, and now sensed a growing confidence that the Government would uphold law and order. The majority of the people had realized what a very substantial measure of responsible government had been conferred by the Coussey Report, but when the CPP had rejected it and called for Positive Action the CPP leaders had been personally warned of the consequences of their action. He added, significantly:

> the T.U.C. had no mandate for a general strike, and did not call a general strike . . . the strikes that have occurred have been engineered by certain members of the C.P.P. . . . these are well known tactics advocated and practised by communists and others whose aim is to seize power for themselves by creating chaos and disrupting the life of the community.

He gave evidence of massive intimidation and referred to the two policemen who had been stabbed to death by CPP supporters. 'These men died in defence of the right of the free citizens of this country to go peacefully about their business without fear of molestation.' He paid tribute to the courage, bravery and devotion of the police. He reminded the Council that the eyes of the world were on the Gold Coast, to see if its people had the capacity and determination to shoulder their new responsibilities. It would be disastrous if the exponents of Positive Action were allowed to give the impression that they were going to take over, and everyone needed to show, not by their words but by their actions, their determination to maintain peace, order and good government in their land. He referred to the hooliganism, intimidation and violence, and to the attempts to subvert authority, to bring the chiefs into disrepute and to coerce the Government. He concluded 'I am determined that this state of affairs shall be brought to an end'.[5] In the debate which followed members gave unanimous support to the Governor's action in declaring a state of emergency, and not one voice was raised in protest. Soon afterwards Arden-Clarke received the warmest congratulations of the Secretary of State for his skill and resolution in handling the emergency, together with admiration and complete approval for his address to the Legislative Council.[6]

[5] Sir Charles Arden-Clarke. Address to Legislative Council 9 January 1950.
[6] Telegram 31 January 1950.

While the political crisis deepened, the rest of the country remained fairly calm. Arden-Clarke and his wife had had three days holiday over Christmas at a remote rest house in the hills of Togoland, and he had returned to a further round of official engagements. He gave a rousing address to the annual teachers' conference, referring pointedly to the danger of political indoctrination in schools. He seemed to gain confidence from being among the people, and he gave an inspiring address to the assembled chiefs and people at a durbar at Kibi just a few days after the state of emergency had been declared.

Some time later Arden-Clarke referred to these stirring events in a family letter:

> Sorry I have been so bad about writing but I have been rather preoccupied in dealing with our local Hitler and his putsch . . . Twenty four hours after I made the speech (to the Legislative Council) I gave orders to the police to put all those on our black list into the bag. This was done without any trouble or disturbance and now they are all standing their trials on various charges. [7]

Positive Action had rapidly developed into an ugly and threatening movement, but when the leaders, including Nkrumah, were put in gaol the country quickly returned to normal—clearly justifying the Governor's action. Although the threat to law and order had been removed, there remained the urgent task of completely reshaping the whole administrative system ready to hand over power to the elected ministers, and also to set up a completely new constitutional machine for the election promised by the Coussey Report. This again brought the Governor under pressure not from the wild men or purveyors of violence but from his own senior staff. He was, after all, asking them to create a system the main purpose of which was to eliminate their own positions. They quickly realized the top men would have to leave at independence, but they showed very loyal concern for the professional future of their more junior staff who would clearly have to change career in midstream. Arden-Clarke had the difficult task of keeping the balance between, on the one hand those whose prime concern was for the safeguarding of their expatriate colleagues and who were fundamentally unhappy about the pace of change, and, on the other, the vociferous elements of the press and people who were demanding an effective handover of power in the shortest possible time. This whole issue was highlighted in the decision on whether a European should retain control of a new Ministry of Local Government. This caused lengthy and heart searching discussions, and involved Arden-Clarke in correspondence both with his Chief Commissioners and with Creech-Jones and Cohen in

[7] Letter to Family 3.2.50.

Whitehall. He held firmly to the view that effective power had to be handed over, and that with the key Ministries of Defence and External Affairs, Finance, and Justice in European hands, and with his own reserve powers there was adequate protection for expatriate staff. He believed that any further constraints would undermine the Government's whole position and lessen its credibility.

The Governor also came under pressure from the large expatriate commercial organizations, particularly the United Africa Company, the cocoa firms, the Ashanti Goldfields Company and the exporters of bauxite and timber. In the past they had enjoyed very favourable conditions, had contributed very little to the revenue of the colony, and had retained a substantial say in any commercial regulations likely to effect their shareholders or their profits. Here, too, Arden-Clarke held to his lonely stand—that the success of this whole noble enterprise could not be jeopardized by the narrow interests of commercial firms.

He frequently reminded the people that the eyes of the world were on them—but, far more, they were on him. Much has been written of the experience of 1947 in India, but although Indian independence had been talked about from the early thirties, successive governments— particularly Churchill's—had dragged their feet, and only after Attlee's daring decision to send the brilliant Mountbatten to succeed the lugubrious and unsuccessful Viceroy Wavell did action start. Then after the Imperial Parliament and the Hindus and Muslims had agreed to partition, there was a headlong scramble for a few months to arrange the dual handover of power before independence in August 1947. There was little here to guide or influence the Gold Coast situation, and it is to the credit of Arden-Clarke that he withstood the pressures not only from the revolutionary political wing, but also from the reactionary elements among his own staff or in Whitehall, and maintained a reasonable, confident and dignified progress towards independence.

With the security situation firmly in hand, the emphasis on constitutional development is reflected in the Governor's address to the Legislative Council in February 1950. He emphasized the constructive nature of the task facing them and the necessity to ensure stable government and not mob law. Political independence needed to be based on serious and responsible local government. He then referred to the proposed Assembly and his remarks illustrate how dramatically the political situation was to change with the election of 1951. He said:

It is most unlikely that there will emerge from the first general election a single majority party capable of electing a Leader who could rely on an organized majority in the House, or capable of providing eight

Ministers to undertake the government of the whole country.[8]

He again reminded the Council of the importance of restoring world confidence in the Gold Coast, and stressed that politics was no substitute for hard work and economic development.

> Let us have (he said) no more waste of energy and breath on fruitless demands for a new heaven and a new earth in forty eight hours, let us have no more of the astonishing theory that political advance will come by letting millions of cocoa trees die of a disease which can be controlled and stamped out, let us have no more of the peculiar thought that prosperity will come through interrupting internal trade and cutting off trade with the rest of the world. Let the people rather get down to the job of making the best of the good earth they have and to the job of managing their affairs in an orderly and responsible way.[9]

The people as a whole responded well to this firm and positive approach, and the life of the country and the life of the Governor soon resumed its normal pattern. The press reported that HE[10] enjoyed a quiet Easter holiday in Ashanti—in fact this was a strenuous tour to Kumasi, Wenchi and Kintampo, involving three or four official engagements every day. He wrote:

> I liked the country most of which is very good farming land and I like the people, who for the most part seemed quite contented and prosperous.
> Easter Sunday found us at a little place called Wenchi where we attended evensong in the local school which is being used as a church by the Methodists until the building of their large new church is completed. The service started at 5.30 and we ensured a reasonably short sermon by inviting the Padre and his man who played the harmonium to come and have a drink with us at 6.30.[11]

Having shrugged off the political pressures, and having returned from Ashanti, he faced the formidable prospect of entertaining Lady Baden-Powell the World Chief Guide. In an unguarded letter he wrote:

> Fergie[12] reports that she was talking as she got off the plane, she talked all through the time she was meeting everyone, she talked in the car coming to the castle and she talked solidly from the moment I met her until after lunch . . . Then she had a press-conference in the dining room of the Castle with about thirty representatives of the Press,

[8] Address to Legislative Council 28.2.50.
[9] Ibid.
[10] His Excellency. The press frequently preferred this abbreviation. Other references included Sir Clarke and Sir Charles Noble Arden-Clarke.
[11] Letter to Family 16.4.50.
[12] His ADC Major Ferguson.

whom she completely defeated and sent out exhausted an hour later. At 6.30 she was all set and ready for the big reception when we had over 200 people in for a sundowner to meet her. The coloured lights, the lancers and the police band were all laid on and the people began filing in. Lady Baden-Powell insisted on speaking at length to every one of them as they arrived with the result that the queue was making no progress at all and stretched right down through the Castle courtyard on to the steps outside . . . Then she cruised round still talking hard and the only thing that stopped her was when the band played 'God Save the King'. She wanted to shake hands with everyone as they left, but this I firmly forbade, but then I am blessed if she didn't start shaking hands again . . . She is quite an incredible person and it is exhausting merely to watch the expenditure of so much energy.

The Chief Guide's visit included many most impressive parades, ceremonies and services, including an extremely high-church service about which Arden-Clarke wrote

All of us objected strongly to all the flummery that went on—the bowing and scraping, the changing of vestments and the incense. At one point when the incense bearer came parading down the aisle flapping clouds of incense into the faces of the congregation, Frankie Reed (the Chief Scout Commissioner) whispered 'Quite like a camp fire isn't it?' and Lady Baden-Powell whispered back 'Yes, and with only one match.' I discovered later that the incense bearer who had given me a special blast as he passed is the Chief Clerk in my own office. [13]

The press, upholding its tradition of frank criticism, referred from time to time to the imprisoned leaders, and became critical of the nominated element in the new constitution. It made an outcry about £10,000 being spent on each of the eight bungalows for the new Ministers and suggested that if the cost was halved the money saved could build more than 15 new village schools. The Ashanti *Times*, which later became a fierce critic of Arden-Clarke, commended his policy of meeting the people, but also referred to the growing number of CPP successes in town council elections.

In May HE made a lengthy tour of the Northern Territories and everywhere 'received a terrific reception from the Chiefs and people'. Durbars were held at many different centres, including Lawra the centre of the Lobi people. Arden-Clarke felt really at home here, remembering his days in Northern Nigeria, and he said:

It was a delight to be away from the tawdry politics of the coast and to be among chiefs and people who obviously welcomed the help of the European and were ready to work to help themselves. [14]

[13] Letter to Family 27.4.50.
[14] Letter to Family 21.5.50.

At the same time there was serious political significance in the vastly different standards and attitudes of the northern people. He described the tribal meeting at Wa, the centre of the Wala people.

At Wa, too, there was another tremendous show. After the usual meeting and speeches I went to the DC's bungalow and stayed on the flat roof of his porch under an umbrella while the Chief and the people did a ceremonial march past. First came three fetish (Ju Ju) dancers in horrific wooden masks completely covered from head to toe with headdresses, jackets and skirts made of masses of palm leaves dyed black, followed by the Chief on horseback and his mounted retinue. They wheeled round to face him while the sub-chiefs with their retinues, marched past between us in five companies. There must have been well over five thousand people including at least a thousand men armed with Dane guns. Every company had its own drummers and all were singing and dancing, while every now and then there would be a feu de joie from the gun men. The noise and the heat were terrific. The march past took half an hour and for the whole of that time the fetish dancers continued their dance in front of the Chief, an amazing feat of endurance.[15]

The village of Wa, with its District Commissioner and Chief illustrates well enough the British system of Indirect Rule, originally developed by Lugard in Nigeria, and by which many parts of Africa were ruled. The system which used the DC to bolster the authority of the Chief created a happy and dignified relationship in areas where tribal discipline was strong, but it came under fierce criticism from European administrators in Accra, and from the majority of articulate African critics and politicians. In Wa the Chief and his council of elders controlled most local government affairs including the court, the market and the school. The DC's team included a doctor, who ran a dispensary and a small hospital where he coped cheerfully with leprosy, yaws and a host of appalling tropical diseases. Of equal importance to the people were the veterinary officer—engaged in developing a cattle breeding area to overcome the tse-tse fly menace—and the Public Works Department officer who built the roads, the bridges, the deep ground toilets and the drinking water wells. The people lived a hard life in a hard land. With little vegetation, prolonged droughts, a diet of yams and cassava, they were none the less a cheerful and dignified people. Politically these people did not seek an end to colonial rule, or 'self government now'. In fact the reverse. In the years after the war when some Africans, who had been commissioned in the Army, became DCs the northern people generally opposed their appointment. They wished to keep their British

15 Ibid.

DC and did not with to be taken over 'by a southern savvy-boy'.[16]

Having returned from the Northern Territories, the Governor presided at the traditional Empire Day Rally of school children in Accra. He spoke to them of their membership of the great British family of nations, so old in its history but so young in its attitude to progress. After his speech more than 11,000 children marched past and he stood at the salute in full ceremonial dress.

Shortly after this he left for two months leave in England, during which he had an operation for gallstones. In his absence Saloway addressed the Legislative Council, announcing some very significant developments. Later, in the euphoric days leading to independence, the Volta River Scheme and the great Gonja Development Scheme, were hailed as the achievements of the new Ghana government, but it is important to note that they were both initiated long before the CPP came to power.

In the September meeting of the Legislative Council, Arden-Clarke gave further details of the constitutional advances that had been made. He carefully outlined the arrangements for the new ministries, emphasizing that each of the 11 Ministers would be responsible for his own department. Both the Legislative Council and the general public were slow to realize that the African Minister would be in charge of the department, and that the Permanent Secretary—a senior civil servant and at that stage usually British—would be there to help and advise but not to control. These senior civil servants, who were all vastly experienced in senior administrative posts had a key role to play, and Arden-Clarke appointed them early in order to set up the new ministries. This caused his first serious clash with the Legislative Council. Both it and the press, sensitive about any further posts going to Europeans, argued that the permanent Secretary posts should be open to public competition. Arden-Clarke made his own comments in a family letter:

By the end of the year our preparations for holding the first General Election in the history of the Gold Coast should be nearly complete and the elections themselves will probably be held towards the end of January. This thought seems to be affecting our local politicians, with the result that our legislators are beginning to make electioneering speeches instead of getting on with their job in a responsible manner. There were four critical decisions to be made at Leg. Co.; in three cases, after a lot of loose talk, they managed to behave themselves and do what was required. In the fourth case they passed a deplorable motion which publicly censured the Secretary of State, the Governor and the Public Service Commission because of certain Civil Service

[16] Conversation between the author and the Wa Na in 1946.

appointments and promotions made in connection with the new Ministries required by the new constitution. The aftermath of that is still with us and likely to be with us for a long time. I am not yet sure whether we can avoid a major crisis involving my over-ruling the Legislature and using my reserve powers. I am hoping that having vented their spleen the Finance Committee will vote the necessary money to establish the Ministries when they meet on 26th. If they fail to do so there will be all sorts of fun and games.[17]

Because of the political excitement, less attention was paid to the important economic issues announced at the same time. A ten year development plan costing £31M, with a further £15M for education and social services, was well advanced. Details were also available of the Volta River Scheme, which by damming the Volta River would produce enough hydro electric power to develop an aluminium industry based on local bauxite. The scheme would create a huge new lake, irrigation for the arid Accra plain, and a new port to the east of Accra. Such a vast scheme needed outside capital and outside technical assistance, and the Governor emphasized the need to curb political unrest and to restore world confidence in the Gold Coast.

One of the many impressive achievements in the Gold Coast prior to independence was the work of the Ewart Committee, which had the formidable task of setting up a complete electoral system in a country with no experience of democracy and where a large majority were illiterate.[18] The committee produced the closest co-operation between Europeans and Africans at a time when the government lay under considerable suspicion, and to produce the new system ready for registration to start in November 1950 was an amazing achievement. The judicial adviser A. C. Russell said 'How it was done, I still fail to understand.'[19]

A significant change now came over the political situation, which affected the future of the colony and particularly the future relationship between Arden-Clarke and Nkrumah. As the civil servants set out to register voters for the forthcoming elections, they were often met by truculence and suspicion. They were often saved from ignominy by the co-operation of the local CPP agent. With many misunderstandings—some serious, some hilarious—a new link was forged between the Government and the CPP. The CPP quickly showed that it was going to fight seriously in every constituency and it was going to make a genuine

[17] Letter to Family 20.9.50.
[18] Full details for this remarkable achievement are given in Dennis Austin's *Politics of Ghana*, the definitive work on this period.
[19] Rev A. C. Russell, CMG, quoted in Austin, p. 109. Russell later became Chief Commissioner Ashanti, and after he retired was ordained.

attempt to work the new constitution. Although Nkrumah and the other CPP leaders were in prison the party organization continued with remarkable efficiency. The foundation had been laid by Kojo Botsio and then after February 1950 the work was carried on by Komla Gbedemah, who completed a nation-wide structure of party branches. Support for the CPP grew rapidly.

The imprisonment of the CPP leaders had given a great opportunity to the UGCC but they totally failed to grasp it. They failed to adapt to the new political situation and, having expected power to drop into their lap, they seemed incapable of matching the vigour or the organizing ability of the CPP. Arden-Clarke summed it up as 'The distaste of some of the most able Gold Coast men for the rough and tumble of local political campaigning.'[20]

Although massive support welled up for the CPP, the party still faced formidable problems. It lacked decisive leadership and many local branches began to show an aggressively independent attitude. In October 1950 a demand was made to start the revolution in Kumasi, while at the same time other branches made fierce attacks on all expatriates and especially the police. These outbursts seriously embarrassed the leaders who were earnestly cultivating the image of a responsible national party fit and ready to govern.

The rapid political advance towards political independence formed the main theme of Arden-Clarke's address to the final meeting of the old Legislative Council in November 1950. He referred to the 1,800 extra staff working in all the areas, under the guidance of the DCs, to explain the new electoral system and to register the voters. The Government had printed nearly half a million pamphlets and leaflets in eight different languages, 14 cinema vans had been used, as well as frequent programmes on the local radio. The Governor and many speakers in the debate emphasized how much interested attention the world was giving to the forthcoming election. After the debate was over Arden-Clarke spoke a few valedictory words, thanking all members of the Legislative Council for their strenuous work and especially the work they had done on committees. During the past year members from Togoland and members from the Northern Territories had joined the Council which had been a major unifying force in a volatile political situation. He stressed the great economic changes and improvements which the Council had initiated, reminding them that the cocoa boards, the industrial development boards and the Agricultural Loans Board were just as important to the future of the country as the more glamorous political changes.

[20] Letter to Family 4.1.51.

Although the Government's security reports showed little evidence of communist activity in the Gold Coast, all the western nations had been preoccupied since June 1950 with the Korean War, and at the end of the year were facing the daunting danger of the colossal Chinese build up in North Korea. Arden-Clarke's concern with the wider issues of the communist danger is reflected in his speech to a predominantly Scottish and entirely expatriate audience at the St Andrew's Night Dinner. Making the point that as a Sassenach he qualified to be present because his wife was Scottish he said:

> We see today a group playing with the fires of war, caring nothing it would seem, for the ruin they could cause. They are blinded by their devotion to a perverted political creed—a creed which is a denial of the very foundations of freedom. Such is their lust for dominion for themselves and for their creed that they must, it seems, assault and pervert the whole world.

He continued by requesting Europeans to play their part in ensuring, in the Gold Coast, that the inexperienced could learn of democracy at the pace and in the manner best suited to them.[21]

Another side of the prevailing attitude and the communist bogey was illustrated by the official visit of two MPs—one Labour, one Conservative—in October 1950. They gave the impression that they knew everything and wished to learn nothing, they insulted or gave offence to all the senior staff they met, they caused a major crisis in the conclave of Ashanti Chiefs which necessitated the personal intervention of the Governor, and when they returned to London they wrote a damaging and wildly inaccurate article in the *Daily Telegraph*, entitled 'Red Shadow over the Gold Coast'. In this they suggested that the CPP were using the latest techniques of the politbureau and were also using tyranny, despotism and the Ju Ju of darkest Africa.[22] The Governor cabled the Secretary of State to dissociate himself from their statement and this he did.

As political independence in the Gold Coast drew closer, it highlighted the problem of the future of the mandated territory of Togoland. This former German colony had been divided between the British and the French, with scant respect for the wishes of the people or the tribal boundaries—particularly those of the Ewe people. During 1950 Arden-Clarke undertook preliminary discussions with the French High Commissioner and the Governor from Lome. He got on well with M. Cedile the Governor of French Togoland who came for a conference in April 1950. Arden-Clarke described their discussions.

[21] Speech, St Andrews Night Dinner, November 1950.
[22] *Daily Telegraph* 17.11.50. Mr A. E. Cooper, MP and Sir D. Gammans, MP.

This morning I had a good conference with Cedile about the future of Togoland. He is a very sound chap and is quite ready to tell Paris where it gets off, and this is unusual in any French Governor, who is more under the control of his central government than is a British Colonial Governor. We are united in a fixed determination to liquidate the interference of the United Nations in the colonial affairs of our territories. At first he was a little reluctant to follow the course which I regarded as essential but did not take a great deal of persuading. What our two Metropolitan Governments are going to think about our advice I don't know. I think the Colonial Office is ready to play but the French Government may prove a bit sticky.[23]

The discussions continued through the year and in November 1950 there was a further conference in which conflicting opinions caused deep divisions. Togoland continued to occupy much of his time even in the period running up to the vital first election. Before that he wrote an interesting family letter. He had had a strenuous tour to southern Togoland early in January. He enjoyed the attractive country and, as ever, had a quick eye for the amusing incident. At a meeting of chiefs there were present a number of scouts and one cub:

He was in uniform except for his hat and in its place he had substituted a small enamel chamber pot which he wore with pride, the handle sticking out over his nose and each time I passed him he sprang smartly to attention and gave me the Scout Salute. No one seemed to regard his headgear as in any way unorthodox or remarkable.[24]

He left this meeting for a conference with the governor of French Togoland, of which he made more serious comment:

The continuous interference of the Trusteeship Council of UNO in the affairs of Togoland which is a trust territory under the UN Charter, with its woolly-minded idealism and utter ignorance of colonial administrative methods and practice, and the difficulty of working in harmony with the French, make Togoland one of my major headaches.

He continued his letter saying that Max Aitkin MP, had encouraged him to think of standing as a Conservative when he retired, and he added some interesting personal comment:

The idea of becoming a politician in my old age does not attract me, and the more I have to do it the more I hate public speaking. Anyhow I am far too independent in my views and outlook, and far too accustomed as a Governor to getting my own way, to make a good party politician.[25]

[23] Letter to Family 2.5.50.
[24] Letter to Family 21.1.51
[25] *Ibid.*

On returning from Togoland he was host to the governors of the other three British West African colonies, Nigeria, Sierra Leone and the Gambia, who were almost equally preoccupied with the wider political effects of the forthcoming Gold Coast elecions.

In the weeks before the February election of 1951 the colony remained peaceful but the political excitement mounted daily. The administration had received growing respect not only for the meticulous and considerate work of the Ewart Committee in setting up the electoral machinery and deciding the constituency boundaries as far as possible in accordance with local sensibilities, but also from Arden-Clarke's clearly expressed determination to press ahead with the planned changes and to uphold firm and good administration in spite of criticism from many different quarters. Thus he rejected the more extreme and vocal demands for the immediate Africanization of the Civil Service up to the highest level, but also—backed by his own DCs—rebutted the claims of the UGCC that the CPP were using bribery, extortion and strong arm methods. He went out of his way to repeat the message that there would be a period of genuine partnership leading to independence, and during this time African Ministers would assume real responsibility, would be fully answerable to the Assembly for their departments, and that the Civil Service had the clear-cut responsibility to make this possible.

In the party struggle, the UGCC, in spite of tardy efforts to whip up national support along traditional lines, found its support dwindling away almost daily, and was outsmarted and out-manoeuvred at every turn by the CPP. Dennis Austin in his definitive work on the politics of Ghana, gives a remarkably detailed account of the 1951 election and describes the CPP as a nationalist movement in full cry, touched by the CPP's own magic. At all levels the CPP canalized the bubbling enthusiasm of the people, and rarely misjudged the occasion. Funds came pouring in from parties, rallies and dances held all over the country. The Accra *Evening News* and the party publicity department kept up a flow of apt and effective slogans: 'We prefer Self Government with danger to servitude in tranquillity', and, aiming at a different audience, 'Vote wisely and God will save Ghana from the Imperialists.' The strong anti-imperialist line helped the party against the UGCC, by making the Chief appear with the DC as the main agent of imperialism. The CPP also built up the cult of Nkrumah's martyrdom—languishing in an imperialist dungeon—and made effective use of their 'prison graduate' heroes. When CPP leaders came out of jail they brought messages from Nkrumah, who exhorted the people to support the party with grit, determination and loyalty, and even produced the party's election manifesto, smuggled out on toilet paper. The party cleverly cashed in on the cocoa farmers' discontent even though this eventuality had first been foreseen years before by the UGCC leader Danquah. As CPP candidates began to romp home in the Municipal elections the party studied its methods, learnt from its mistakes, and refined its techniques. All over the country, towns and villages were deafened by cars and lorries sounding the CPP slogan on their horns.

As the election approached, the Gold Coast administration looked ahead—calm, confident, well informed and well-prepared. Arden-Clarke had reminded the country that the eyes of the world were upon them, but world opinion had not yet adjusted fully to the idea of political independence for African colonies. In Britain, the after-effects of the Gammans-Cooper article still lingered on, and the press, inevitably effected by the renewed reverses of the Korean War, still looked with apprehension at the suspect left-wing techniques of the CPP. Capitalist enterprises heard with alarm some of the more unguarded remarks of the CPP spokesmen about expatriate businesses and neo-colonialism. In Africa itself, leaders and potential leaders of nationalist movements studied every detail of the election campaign with mounting excitement. By contrast, in South Africa, Dr Malan voiced the growing apprehension of the whites at this terrifying climax of doctrinaire British liberalism, while the hard core Afrikaner view was represented by *Die Transvaaler* which referred venomously to the absurd spectacle of half naked barbarians taking part in elections.[26]

After the months of intensive preparation the election was conducted with dignity and decorum, as if the people were indeed conscious of the role they were playing in history. The result, a resounding victory for the CPP, had been accurately forecast by the Government. The complex electoral arrangements worked out successfully. In Ashanti and the South, the CPP won 29 out of a possible 33 seats in the rural electoral colleges and all five minicipal seats. The Northern Territories had a separate electoral college which nominated 19 members. These could have caused serious problems for the CPP but, following the northern tradition of co-operation, went along with the new government. In addition, apart from the three ex-officio members and the six representatives of commerce and mining, there were 18 territorial seats to be chosen by the different area councils of chiefs. These nominations were made after the election results had been declared and enabled a number of respected UGCC candidates who had been defeated in the constituencies to become members of the Assembly after all—though to be treated with some derision by the elected CPP members.

Two results in particular show what a dramatic upheaval the CPP had achieved. In Sekondi, Pobee Biney, an active CPP member, a member of

---

[26] Quoted in R. Rathbone 'The Handover of Power in Ghana'. (unpublished thesis).

the Gold Coast TUC, and an engine driver, decisively defeated Sir Tsibu Darku, OBE, the Omanhene of Asin Atandasu, one of the most distinguished men in the country, who had been a member of the Legislative Council since the 1930s, was a member of the Executive Council, and also a member of the Coussey Committee. Secondly, in the constituency of Accra Central, although he was in prison, Kwame Nkrumah had been able to stand. He won the seat by 20,780 votes to the 1,451 of the UGCC candidate Ako Adjei, and in doing so presented Arden-Clarke with one of the most difficult, fateful and dramatic decisions that a governor can ever have faced.

Much speculation has been made about this momentous moment in African history—when Kwame Nkrumah was released. Many historians have assumed that such a decision must have been referred to the Secretary of State for the Colonies, James Griffiths. Richard Rathbone interviewed James Griffiths in August 1965 and he claimed 'he had a clear memory of such consultations'.[27] Arden-Clarke produced several pieces of evidence to the contrary. Soon after he retired, he addressed the Royal Empire Society, and was asked the critical question—had he consulted the Colonial Secretary about releasing Nkrumah. Lord Hemingford,[28] who clearly recalls the incident, said that Arden-Clarke paused, looked round, and then with a twinkle in his eye brought the house down by saying 'I can't altogether remember.' He did, however, in his own papers give a long and detailed description of these events, in which he makes it clear beyond all reasonable doubt that the decision to release Nkrumah was his alone. His description shows clearly, not only that the decision was his, but also illustrates the very clever tactical methods he used to obtain the maximum benefit from the situation. His words written as the drama unfolded give a more authentic ring than any of the other descriptions or recollections—even including Nkrumah's autobiography—which were made some five or 10 years after the events. They give such a meticulous description of these events that they must be allowed to stand in their entirety:.

'On Thursday, 8 February the first general election in the history of the country took place. There were 38 seats to be filled by popular ballot in the Colony and Ashanti, the Northern Territories having adopted a different system of election for their 19 seats. Most thorough and elaborate preparations had been made for preparing the people to cast their votes. The elections went off well and in a most orderly fashion, on the whole more orderly than an election in England. The results of the elections were startling. The Convention People's Party (the CPP), the

[27] R. Rathbone. Thesis p. 138.
[28] Principal of the Teacher Training College at Achimota.

extreme nationalist party, which went to the polls on the slogan "Self Government Now", made practically a clean sweep, winning 35 out of the 38 seats available with one of the remaining three a "fellow traveller". Most of the opposition candidates, even those contesting constituencies regarded as safe by the moderates, forfeited their deposits.

'A month before the election it had been expected that they would win anything up to 25 seats, but at that stage no-one, not even the CPP, expected such a wholesale victory. Indeed, when the CPP list of candidates containing the names of a number of ne'er-do-wells was published, the party stock suffered a momentary slump and many moderates, who had themselves done nothing towards establishing a disciplined political party, began to hope that the country would react strongly against the CPP list of candidates and send moderates to the Assembly. It was then that the CPP played a decisive stroke. They put up their leader, Kwame Nkrumah, who was still in gaol, as one of their candidates for Accra. They promised that if he was elected he would be released from prison. A great wave of enthusiasm spread through the rank and file of the party and they then threw all their energies into the final stages of the Election campaign. A few days before the Election began, my intelligence sources forecast 34 seats for the CPP and this coincided roughly with the last forecast made by the CPP Executive before the elections.

'Although there were 18 members still to be elected on the following Saturday by the Territorial Councils of the Colony and Ashanti and 19 members from the Northern Territories, a total of 37, it was clear that having regard to the ineffectiveness, lack of organization and local jealousies of the Territorial Councils, the CPP had in fact obtained a working majority in the House of Assembly and would be entitled to form the new Government, or, if they decided to go into opposition, would be able to wreck the new constitution before it had had a chance of starting.

'The CPP moved quickly. On Friday, 9th, they sent me a letter asking me to meet a deputation of their Executive Committee that afternoon to discuss the immediate release of Kwame Nkrumah, their leader, and other members of their party who were still serving prison sentences in connection with their campaign of "positive action" in January last year. I was not prepared to release anyone until after the Territorial Council elections were over on the Saturday. Also it was important that if Nkrumah and his colleagues were released it should be done as "an act of grace" rather than as the result of public pressure. Knowing that they would probably be attending the Territorial Council elections at Dodowah on Saturday morning, I replied that I would meet them on Saturday morning, in the hope that they would ask for a further postponement. This they obligingly did and asked me to see them on Monday. I agreed to see them on Monday afternoon and in the meantime made all arrangements for the release of Nkrumah and his colleagues at 1 pm on Monday. This took the wind out of their sails and enabled me to claim that the release of these men was in fact "an act of grace" and a gesture of goodwill. To my surprise it was accepted as such by the public and local press, "and e'en the ranks of CPP could scarce forbear a cheer". The decision, however unpalatable, was in fact inevitable. To have refused to release them would have undoubtedly led to a head-on collision and would have received little or no support from the UK press or Parliament. There were about a dozen journalists representing UK, S. African and American newspapers here at the time and I was kept informed of their views and the trend of their reports.

'Moreover, by acting quickly I put myself in a better position to resist the demand, which I knew would be made, for the release not only of the so-called "political prisoners" but also of the ex-servicemen and other party members who had been imprisoned for participating in riots and acts of violence. Sure enough on Monday afternoon when the CPP representatives came to see me, after thanking me for releasing their leader and others, they asked me to release the rioters. I said that I would examine each individual case to see if any grounds for remission existed, but that I could hold out little hope of anyone convicted of crimes of violence being released. Gbedemah, their leader, made the illuminating remark that, if they had only known in time what I was going to do, he would have advised Nkrumah and the others to stay in prison until I had agreed to release all, a remark that Nkrumah himself repeated to me in one of my later interviews with him.

'The whole of the fortnight from Sunday, 11 to Sunday, 25 was taken up with a series of interviews with the leaders and representatives of the various parties and groups which had been elected to the new House of Assembly. My objective was to arrive at an agreed list of eight persons whose names I could present to the House for its approval for appointment to ministerial office. The new Executive Council consists of 11 members, all of whom are called Minister. Three of them are officials (The Chief Secretary, the Financial Secretary and the Attorney General): the remaining eight must all be elected members of the House of Assembly. The Colony and Ashanti Territorial Councils had between them elected some half dozen or more CPP members and sympathizers and had thus ensured to the CPP an over-all working majority in the House, a fact admitted by all parties.

'The CPP line was that by virtue of their majority and in accordance with accepted parliamentary principles they were entitled to all eight ministerial posts, though they were prepared to give two or three of the 11 posts of Ministerial Secretary[29] to the Northern Territories and possibly Ashanti. The view of the Territorial Council members was that the constitution did not provide for government by a single political party and that a system of checks and balances allowing for the representation of all sections of the community had been intended. While admitting that the CPP had an over-all majority, they considered that only four ministerial posts should go to the CPP and the remaining four should be divided up between themselves. My own view was that, whatever may have been the intention of the framers of the constitution, party government had arrived, and that the responsibility for the Government should be placed fairly and squarely on the shoulders of the majority party, but that in the interests of national unity there should be a coalition and the party should accord representation in the Executive Council to the Northern Territories and to Ashanti, the Colony already being fully represented by party members. If my view prevailed, this meant that the CPP should have six of the eight ministerial posts available, Ashanti one and the Northern Territories one.

'The CPP finding that I was ready to give them the substance of their demand, i.e., an over-all majority in an Executive Council composed of three ex-officio and eight representative members, were quite co-operative, but wanted themselves to choose the Northern Territories and Ashanti representatives. I pointed out that the Northern Territories and Ashanti would say "Thank you for nothing" and refuse to co-operate on such terms. Eventually, chiefly because of Nkrumah's helpful attitude, they agreed to leave the choice of these representatives to me in consultation with the Territorial groups concerned.

'The Territorial groups were a very different proposition. At first they pressed hard for four ministerial posts, although they were prepared to admit that if I put their four suggested names forward the Assembly would reject them. When they found that I would not budge, they decided that they would not co-operate in the Government at all and would refuse any ministerial offices; instead, they would hold themselves in reserve to form an alternative Government if the CPP majority failed. They informed me that they were not a party, had not got any special policy, did not regard themselves as an opposition and were not prepared to form a coalition. I pointed out that this was hardly a clarion call to the country and was unlikely to win the support of the voters and that if they came out publicly with this kind of statement in the House they would be committing political suicide.

'For a long week talks and arguments went on until at last on Friday afternoon (23 February) the Northern Territories and Ashanti

---

[29] The local equivalent of the British Parliamentary Under-Secretary.

representatives agreed each to take one ministerial post and accepted the list which in consultation with them and the CPP I had prepared. On Saturday morning the Northern Territories representatives reappeared in my office and announced that they had changed their minds again and they would not take office. I allowed myself the indulgence of a brief but violent explosion which obviously shook them and then for an hour I wrought patiently with them. Finally they accepted my advice and agreed to take office. I told them that there could be no more changes of mind as I was now sending the list of names to the Speaker for presentation to the House of Assembly when it met on Monday, 26, and that if they did have any more second thoughts they could declare them publicly to the House and to the world in general.

'The House met on Monday morning. The motion for the adoption of the list of eight names was moved by Nkrumah and seconded by Sir Tsibu Darku, who had throughout been the chief opponent of that list and had in the background inspired most of the tergiversation of the Northern Territories representatives. The ballot on the names in the House was secret; all the names were accepted practically unanimously except one which was adopted by 48 votes to 29. Nkrumah, in selecting his list of five party members for ministerial office, he himself being the sixth, seems to have been guided in part by a desire to collect a team that would be able to understand and deal with the tasks facing them e.g., himself, Botsio and Gbedemah, but partly also by his wish to convince the outside world that the representatives of his party were men of standing and education, e.g. Hutton-Mills, Casely-Hayford and Dr Ansah-Koi. All those selected were university graduates. The two oldest members of the CPP team—Tommy Hutton-Mills and Archie Casely-Hayford—both come from families widely respected in the Gold Coast for their parts in early political movements. The two non-CPP ministers, E. Asafu Adjaye (Ashanti), one of our best barristers, and Braimah, a sub-chief from the Northern Territories, are both sound men and well respected.

'On Monday afternoon I held my first meeting of the new Executive Council and administered the official oaths to all the members. The first business was the election by the Council of the Leader of Government business in the House. Kwame Nkrumah was automatically and unanimously elected Leader.

'After the meeting I went into a huddle with Nkrumah and with the Chief Secretary to decide on the distribution of portfolios. Most of Nkrumah's suggestions were sound but he had got Ansah-Koi for the Ministry of Health and Labour, probably because of his medical qualifications, and this had to be changed. Again I found Nkrumah very reasonable and co-operative. So we gave Gbedemah Health and Labour and Ansah-Koi the thankless task of answering for the shortcomings of the PWD as Minister of Communications and Works.

'On Tuesday the portfolios were duly distributed, Ansah-Koi registering strong objections but getting no change. The first thing the Ministers asked for was time to settle up their private affairs. I pointed out that many of my functions were now devolved by law on their shoulders, but they replied that they hoped I would go on governing for a little longer until they were ready.

'I do not yet know what to make of Nkrumah. My first impressions, for what they are worth, are that he is an idealist, ready to live up to his ideals, but I have yet to learn what those ideals really are. Unlike most of his colleagues he seems quite genuinely to bear no ill-will for his imprisonment and is not venal. He has little sense of humour but has considerable personal charm. He is as slow to laugh as he is quick to grasp the political implications of anything discussed. His approach to questions is more that of a psychologist than a realist. He has proved he can give inspiration and I find him susceptible of receiving it but I fear there is a streak of weakness that may be his undoing. A skilful politician, he has, I think, the makings of a real statesman and this he may become if he has the strength to resist the bad counsels of the scallywags by whom he is surrounded.'[30]

Much has been written about the dramatic release of Nkrumah and his appointment as Leader of Government Business, but Arden-Clarke for all his prestige and success as a resolute governor was about to embark on a course more perilous than any he had tackled before. There was no precedent for the situation he faced. Colonial administration gave no preparation for the delicacy and political astuteness required in the new situation. No governor before had had to play the role of governor together with that of joint political leader and party manager. Nkrumah did pay tribute to Arden-Clarke by saying that the remarkable system of dyarchy could not have worked without the unique relationship and understanding that quickly developed between them. The relationship developed because they both were totally dedicated to making the system work and bringing the country forward to political independence. Though they disagreed and were—together and separately—under intense and varying pressures from different groups, they each trusted the other. Where failures occurred there was tact, patience and understanding to rebuild confidence and trust.

In March 1951 even before the formal opening of the New Assembly, Arden-Clarke toured the country and tried to meet as many District Commissioners as possible. He attended a Conference of DCs at Cape

---

[30] Letter to Family. Undated but probably 28.2.51.

Coast in order to reassure them about their new position and to guide them in their delicate and difficult new role. As the country progressed towards independence this became one of the most intractable and emotive issues that he had to face, and there were times when his staff in the field felt that he had identified himself too much with the CPP and the dramatic political limelight of the world stage, and that he had not backed them up as loyally as he should have done.

The formal opening of the new Legislative Assembly took place on 29 March 1951. Arden-Clarke with a shrewd stage-manager's eye ensured that this was a really magnificent occasion. He left Christiansborg Castle in plumes and full ceremonial uniform with two ADCs and a police escort. At the King George V Memorial Hall he inspected a Guard of Honour and went forward to meet the Speaker—Mr Quist, who had been Speaker of the former Legislative Council. From that point onwards the ceremony became a close replica of Westminster. The procession, preceded by the mace, stopped at the Bar of the House and then advanced to the dais:

'The Hall was absolutely packed and was a most colourful sight. The Members from the Colony and Ashanti were all dressed in their gaily coloured Kenti cloths thrown over one shoulder Toga fashion, with a coloured shirt underneath, the Members from the North in their robes and head-dresses of various kinds, the officials in white uniform with their decorations, with Branigan the Attorney General in full-bottomed wig, black robes, knee breeches, lace cravat and lace ruffles at the wrist. Among the spectators were military, police and civilian officers, all in uniform, judges in their robes and wigs and, of course, the ladies in all their finery. I had too much work to do and was too nervous to take in everything properly.

As soon as everyone was seated and I had removed my kid gloves and put on my glasses I rose and said "Mr Speaker, Honourable Members, I have it in command to deliver to this Honourable Assembly a gracious message from His Majesty the King". Then came a fanfare of trumpets, quite a long piece, excellently played by the police bandsmen and drummers, drawn up on a platform overlooking the entrance hall but unfortunately out of sight of all those in the hall, but in full view of the crowd outside. The crowd then added its own unrehearsed part to the proceedings by loudly applauding the fanfare and I had to wait a few seconds before reading the King's Message. As soon as I had done another fanfare was played. I sat down only to rise again immediately as the first gun of a 17-gun salute boomed out, and read a message from the Secretary of State. When this was over I sat down and the Speaker rose, formally welcomed the Parliamentary Delegation from the House of

Commons in a short and well-worded speech and asked them to deliver their message. Proctor,[31] Leader of the Delegation, rose and read a letter from the Speaker of the House of Commons, addressed to the Legislative Assembly. This, like the messages from the King and the Secretary of State, was very well phrased and excellent in tone and content. He followed this with a very good speech. When he had finished I rose again for the third time, to read our local equivalent of the speech from the Throne, the only paragraph of which I had provided myself was the first one, which made it clear that I was addressing the Assembly "in the terms advised by my Ministers and approved by my Executive Council". Unfortunately the blighters had prepared a very long speech for me, as every Minister wanted to have his own little bit inserted and despite our best efforts in Ex.Co. it was impossible to reduce it to a reasonable length. It took 36 minutes to read and as it contained little that was really interesting and many long-winded platitudinous statements of policy it must have been pretty boring to listen to, though I gather that the audience did not find it so.'[32]

In the following years Britain came under fierce criticism from anti-colonialist critics for trying to strangle the natural political development of a new nation by transferring all the checks and balances, the routine and machinery, the pomp and protocol of Westminster into an alien situation, but on this triumphal day no voice of criticism was raised.

In his own descriptions of events Arden-Clarke was quick to appreciate the juxtaposition of the momentous and the banal. The formal celebrations were hardly over before he faced the sudden crisis that, following a party decision, all CPP Ministers and members of the Assembly would have to boycott the Governor's formal dinner for the new ministers and the parliamentary delegation. He quickly gathered the ministers together, expressed his serious displeasure, and told them to go away and think about it. The next day they reconsidered the decision and duly attended.

The dinner—not only for the ministers and visiting MPs but for all the top dignitaries in the country—took place in the newly refurbished Castle dining room. The African ministers dressed in their Kente cloth looked most impressive. Arden-Clarke had decided that, ignoring precedence, European and African should alternate round the table, and he took some malicious pleasure in putting Nkrumah next to Sir Henry Blackall the President of the West African Appeal Court. Among the issues this distinguished gathering touched upon was the effect on the Gold Coast if the Conservative Party won the next election in Britain. The majority

[31] Sir D. Proctor KCB.
[32] Letter to Family 2 April 51.

considered that the Conservatives had no positive alternative policy, though African opinion definitely favoured the Labour government.

CHAPTER SEVEN
Arden-Clarke and Nkrumah

The real triumph of 1951 lay in the relationship of trust which Arden-Clarke and Nkrumah first achieved and which they quickly established in the workings of the Executive Council. In his autobiography Nkrumah later described his first meeting and his relationship with Arden-Clarke.

Although Sir Charles Arden-Clarke and I had been opposing each other for so many months past I had no idea what he looked like, for we had never met. I wondered how I should be received. Had I known this man before I should not have doubted the courtesy that would be shown me.

A tall broad-shouldered man, sun-tanned, with an expression of firmness and discipline but with a twinkle of kindness in his eyes came towards me with his hand outstretched, a hand that I noticed was large and capable looking. He welcomed me and asked how I was. As we both sat down I sensed that he must be feeling as alert and suspicious of me as I was of him. We lost little time, however in coming down to the business in hand. I did my best to make it clear to him that I would be prepared at all times to place my cards face upwards on the table because it was only by frankness that mutual trust and confidence could be established. He agreed with me wholeheartedly on this and I sensed immediately that he spoke with sincerety. He was, I thought, a man with a strong sense of justice and fair play, with whom I could easily be friends, even though I looked upon him as a symbol of British imperialism in the country.[1]

The atmosphere of trust was also confirmed by Mr Gbedemah, who had organized the successful election while Nkrumah was in gaol, and who recalled that, when he and his colleagues first went to the Castle, Arden-Clarke held out his hand and said 'Congratulations Mr Gbedemah. I don't mind telling you that you've given me hell!' From that moment onwards they trusted him and never regarded him as the enemy. They felt that he trusted them to play straight with him and the

---

[1] Nkrumah *Autobiography*, p. 137. Nkrumah's book has been criticised for being disjointed and self centred. In fact Mr Daniel Chapman, a distinguished Ghanaian who was Secretary to the Cabinet, suggested the idea of the book, and it was arranged that his secretary Erica Powell should go to Nkrumah when he had occasional free time so that he could dictate to her.

trust was never seriously broken on either side. When the CPP cabinet had to go to a meeting, they referred to him as 'The Guv.' or 'Noble Charles'.[2] From the time of the 1951 election, the CPP never seriously doubted that Arden-Clarke's aim was the same as theirs—to lead the country to independence and to achieve an orderly transfer of power.

The three Europeans who held ministerial posts in the new cabinet— R. H. Saloway, Minister of Defence and External Affairs, R. Armitage Minister of Finance, and P. Branigan Minister of Justice and Attorney General—accepted Arden-Clarke's lead and helped to make the Executive Council into an effective working committee. After it was safely established Arden-Clarke left for home leave after one of the most dramatic and gruelling tours of his career.

Returning from London in January 1952 Arden-Clarke had an interesting journey. At the airport he was delayed by Anthony Eden, and he met Sir Andrew Cohen, about to fly to Uganda, but distressed because his luggage had gone to Prestwick. At Castel Benito airfield he met Sir Godfrey Huggins, the Prime Minister of Southern Rhodesia and Sir Gilbert Rennie, Governor of Northern Rhodesia. In Accra he immediately had to play host to Pakistan's representatives, who had attended President Tubman's inauguration in Liberia, and to attend the first meeting of the Gold Coast Amateur Boxing Association. He had a long standing interest in boxing and did much to help Roy Ankrah the Empire Featherweight Champion.

In opening the new session of the Legislative Assembly in January 1952, Arden-Clarke outlined the policies and projects to which the Government were committed. It is particularly significant as the first major detailed policy statement since the CPP had fully assumed power, and it illustrates not only the sound and meticulous work carried out by the joint Cabinet team, but also the type of problems facing the colony as it set out on the road to independence. The Government gave the highest priority to the training and recruitment of Africans for the highest posts in the civil service, to the establishment of effective local government, to the expansion of teacher training in order to provide free primary education, and to the positive encouragement of technical education. Next, the Governor reminded the country, again, that the Swollen Shoot disease was still threatening the cocoa industry 'which was the life blood of the country', and he exhorted all sections of the community to support the necessary measures. Major building schemes included the extension of Takoradi Harbour, the initial foundation of Tema harbour east of Accra, the inauguration of the Volta River Scheme, and the planned extension of the railway into the Northern Territories as a major attempt

[2] Interview. Mr Gbedemah December 1978.

to raise the standard of living there. Improvements in communications included the establishment of an automatic telephone exchange in Accra,[3] new roads, bridges and water supplies, and irrigation schemes for the dry Accra plain.

After the formality of the speech from the throne, a more human and personal reaction was given in a letter to the family:

> There was a lot of cheering and shouting of the slogan 'Freedom' which is the battle cry of the C.P.P. After inspecting the guard of honour I was met at the entrance of the Hall by the Speaker in his magnificent new robes of office—black satin and gold—wearing a full bottomed wig. Old Quist has the presence and dignity to carry these trappings and they certainly added to the impressiveness of the occasion . . . It was as usual unbearably hot on the dais on which Quist and I sat and we were both mopping ourselves vigorously before my speech ended. They always seem to arrange the fans to play on one's feet and not on one's head, with the result that I am always wondering whether my glasses are going to get so misty that I shall have to stop reading the speech, take them off and clean them. As soon as I had finished the speech, I was escorted out by the Speaker's procession and got back to Castle just about an hour after I had left it, to enjoy a long drink of cold beer, followed by a bath.
>
> That evening I gave a big sundowner party to which all members of the Assembly were invited and which was attended by well over three hundred guests. We had it out on the big lawn which was surrounded and crossed by strings of electric lights, with the police band seated at one end of it. Part of the Castle and some of the trees were floodlit. We had a heavy rainstorm on Saturday evening and the lawn in consequence was looking its best. An added touch of colour was provided by the new garden party seats and tables . . . but the vast majority of the guests preferred to congregate in a tight bunch between the two bars.[4]

Early in February he wrote home to describe the ceremonies to mark the death of King George VI. Always conscious of his onerous responsibilities as the representative of the King—and then of the Queen—he was deeply touched by matters personally affecting the Royal Family. At the time he had two senior official guests and he commented 'I was relieved to see them both go. Both liked to talk interminably and neither of them were capable to talking audibly. I left them as much as possible to bore each other.' In contrast, he was looking forward to the

[3] In 1979, after more than 20 years of independence, the Accra telephone exchange hardly works at all—for example the telephone link to the university at Legon, six miles from Accra had been cut off for more than a year. The rail link to the north was never completed.

[4] Letter to Family 31.1.52.

visit of his fellow Governors from Sierra Leone and Nigeria. 'As this is about the only chance we ever get of meeting others as equals there is usually a considerable amount of joking and leg-pulling.'[5] In a subsequent letter he grumbled fiercely about the McCormicks who ran the violently anti-British *Chicago Tribune*, and who stretched his patience to the limit.

Once the new session of the Assembly had started, Arden-Clarke had to face the difficult and sensitive issue of the role of the British expatriate civil servants in the period of decolonization leading to independence. The experience of the hand-over of power in India proved to be of little value, and once again he had to pioneer the way in a situation fraught with danger. Here, too, Arden-Clarke and Nkrumah were thrown together and each helped the other in dealing with their more intransigent opponents. Nkrumah faced the dilemma that, having taken on the responsibilities of office, he appeared to his more extreme followers to have sold out to the imperialists; at the same time he had to restrain the party from attacks on British civil servants, especially the District Commissioners. Nkrumah also did his best to reassure the British administration, from the Governor downwards, that the continuing attacks at local CPP meetings were not encouraged or condoned by the party leadership. Three crucial departments—defence and internal security, finance, and justice—still remained under direct expatriate control and were staffed largely by Europeans. A revolution had taken place between 1948 and 1951 and not all colonial civil servants had fully adapted to the new situation. On the British side the police, in particular, remained suspicious of the intentions of the CPP and seriously feared that they might be handed over to a left wing dictatorship. Their apprehension is illustrated by such phrases as 'dictatorship of the proletariat' and 'commissar' in police reports at the time, and by the police action in keeping a very close surveillance on CPP party leaders, their political activities, and even their financial affairs.[6] Many senior British staff objected violently to the CPP Ministers divulging confidential information and confidential documents to party meetings.

On the African side, many of the CPP members and most of the Accra newspapers kept up a barrage of criticism of European staff. Leading articles constantly returned to the theme that a great political victory had been won—the main purpose of which was to get rid of the Imperialists—yet more expatriates were being employed. Nkrumah, while understanding these views, realized that, because of the desperate shortage of suitably qualified African staff at a senior level, and because of the development plans, European staff would be needed for many

[5] Letter to Family 16.2.52.
[6] Special Branch Summaries May 1951.

years to come.[7] A minority of Europeans who clung to outmoded attitudes and had it in their power to delay or frustrate the new policies, created severe problems both for Nkrumah and for Arden-Clarke.

During his leave in London the Governor had taken part in profitable discussions with the Secretary of State about the future of his expatriate civil servants. They had concentrated on the need to provide a continuing supply of expatriate officers to staff the substantial new economic and social developments, while at the same time making certain that the career prospects of those officers were safeguarded. On his return, Arden-Clarke—putting it forward as the policy of the Colonial Office—announced to the CPP Cabinet that Britain did not wish to impose British officers on the Gold Coast if they were not wanted, and, if that was the case, the officers would be transferred to other territories where their services were required. This partial bluff gave Nkrumah the opportunity to emphasize publicly how much the country needed the skills and experience of expatriate staff and how welcome they would be under an independent regime. CPP ministers followed his lead but although these firm statements helped, they did not prevent the morale of the expatriates, and especially the District Commissioners out in the field, from reaching a dangerously low level. Within a few weeks of these announcements Arden-Clarke had to warn the Executive Council that the Civil Service was on the verge of collapse.[8] Many senior officers were planning to resign or to seek transfers to other territories, but, more alarming still, because of the reports of the conditions in the Gold Coast, very few new officers were prepared to come and serve in the colony, and consequently many major projects were being starved of key personnel just when they were starting. In spite of the joint efforts of both Arden-Clarke and Nkrumah the situation steadily worsened. The Governor had to warn his ministers about their relations with the civil servants and appealed to both sides for courtesy and civility. He deplored the growing practice by rank and file CPP members of attacking civil servants in the Assembly because some favour had not been granted. This still did not solve the problem, and the civil servants organized deputations both to the Secretary of State and to the Governor. Arden-Clarke arranged for the deputation to meet Nkrumah so that he could reassure them. Although they were seriously worried about their professional security in the future, they had a reasonably strong base from which to bargain. They accepted the pledges of Nkrumah and his ministers but doubted how much weight this really carried, since personal attacks on civil

[7] Nkrumah *Autobiography* p. 148.
[8] Executive Council Minutes. 25.1.52. At about the same time transfers to other territories were frozen.

servants continued to be made both in the Press and at CPP meetings.[9] They also objected to the interference of politicians in the affairs of government and administration. Derogatory remarks and threats by CPP speakers about District Commissioners caused particularly fierce resentment. At a higher level, ministers often failed to understand the difference in their position as a minister and as a party spokesman, and they caused embarrassment and resentment in the different regions.

During the discussions at the Colonial Office, the Secretary of State—Lyttelton—had linked the position of expatriate staff with the issue of the next round of constitutional reform. He insisted that a fully detailed scheme for compensation for Colonial servants, as they were replaced by the policy of Africanization, must be worked out while he still held sufficient power to insist on this, and before the next round of constitutional reform took place. He based his demands on the scheme worked out for members of the Indian Civil Service in 1947. This strategy put Lyttelton in a strong position—and one with which the CPP Ministers did not quarrel—but he was aware that, following the lead of the Gold Coast, more and more African territories now sought independence, and the number of territories seeking an increase of expatriate staff was rapidly diminishing. The crises of 1952 during which Arden-Clarke, Nkrumah and Lyttelton strove together to find a reasonable and acceptable solution, led eventually to a complicated scheme. Formally announced by Nkrumah in July 1953, it attempted to be fair to the officers whose careers would be threatened or disrupted, and at the same time to prevent a sudden rush of resignations. The scheme worked reasonably well and fewer officers than anticipated left the service as independence approached. On returning from leave in May 1954 Arden-Clarke wrote:

> The Service generally seems to have accepted the scheme for retirement with compensation for loss of career as fair and even generous, and morale appears to be good.[10]

In the past, the District Commissioner had been a figure of immense power in his own area and some, who were slow to change their attitude, did cause serious resentment among the African population. For this reason Nkrumah changed the name from District Commissioner to Government Agent, thus emphasizing where their true loyalty had to lie. Looking back on this difficult issue, Nkrumah said that without the unique relationship and understanding he enjoyed with Arden-Clarke the problems could not have been solved.[11]

[9] Executive Council Minutes. 29.9.52.
[10] Letter to Family 25.1.54.
[11] *Autobiography* p. 147.

Arden-Clarke's close identification with the policies of the CPP seem to have followed a clear intellectual and philosophical decision that it was his responsibility as Governor to lead the country to an orderly handover of power. Mr Gbedemah and other CPP leaders including Mr Kojo Botsio and Mr Krobo Edusei emphasized this in interviews in December 1978. This commitment brought him under intense criticism from his own staff in the early 50s, and more violent opposition from Ashanti during the NLM period. His influence was powerful and, for example, in 1952 he was able to have Krobo Edusei transferred to another post. The Governor's involvement, and that of his senior expatriate ministers, made an important contribution to the smooth running of the government, and occasionally ensured its survival, but this was achieved at a considerable cost. More and more the opposition criticized him for not being impartial and, as the power of the opposition grew, the criticism became more outspoken.

In the spring of 1953 he visited London in order to hammer out new constitutional proposals, and his total dedication to the Gold Coast and its people is shown in a letter to his mother written from the Athenaeum just before his return to Accra:

> I have had a very busy time and, I think, successful. The opposition to my proposals was not serious and soon fizzled out and, unless the Cabinet here turn them down, the only battle that remains—it will be long, difficult and hard fought—is to get them accepted in the Gold Coast. There is no doubt that there is a powerful body of opinion in the highest quarters here who think that I am going too far and too fast but as no-one has been able to put forward an alternative policy that has the remotest prospect of working I am being allowed to have my way. Nevertheless there are those who will weep no tears if the Gold Coast comes a cropper and delude themselves with the idea that failure or a breakdown in the Gold Coast will provide them with an excuse to slow down the rate of political advance in Africa. They forget that you cannot slow down a flood—the best you can hope to do is to keep the torrent within its proper channel.
>
> I had an opportunity of putting forward my ideas, informally and off the record, to the editorial staff of the *Observer*, with whom I had lunch one day, and to a gathering of Unionist Peers in the House of Lords. I did not 'pull my punches' and I think some of the older fossil Lords were a bit shaken at times. [12]

During 1953 the country floated high on the world cocoa boom, and all the hopes and aspirations of the great CPP victory remained untarnished. For Arden-Clarke it proved to be a year of progress and consolidation. In April he opened the extension to Takoradi Harbour,

[12] Letter to Mother 19.4.53.

which provided valuable additional dock space until the opening of Tema harbour, not expected until the late 1950s. Although he had had some struggles with his staff over their terms of service, his relationship with them generally was sound and confident. Burden, the Chief Commissioner of the Northern Territories, stayed at the Castle on his way home to retirement. Arden-Clarke sincerely regretted his departure because he was a wise counsellor and was well liked and trusted by the people of the north. At about the same time he visited another senior colleague Loveridge, [13] who had broken a vertebrae in a fall and had to spend the three hottest and most humid months of the year in plaster from his waist to his neck.

> I asked Mrs. Loveridge whether he had not been intolerable to live with and she replied that he had been 'almost saintly'. As she is a fairly forthright sort of person this impressed me enormously. More particularly as I have never heard any of my unregenerate family apply that epithet to me. [14]

He was deeply distressed by an incident at Elmina which resulted in the death of a very promising young police officer, Edgar Brooks. The new local council at Elmina had attempted to enforce the collection of the local rates. Ignoring the instructions of the Government Agent (District Commissioner) the police had confiscated a drum. This unwise act had incensed the local people, and the next morning a mob of about 3,000, who had been drinking through the night, advanced on Elmina, in order to recapture the drum. Brooks who had been taking a normal police parade and was unarmed, went out to speak to them and was shot in cold blood. The whole country was horrified at the killing and universally condemned the senseless violence.

Anticipating that he would retire in 1954, Arden-Clarke had spent part of his leave looking for a suitable house, and in May 1953 he completed the purchase of Syleham House at Diss in Norfolk. This purchase, at a little under £5,000, taxed his resources and he wrote to the family with mock seriousness that ready cash would be in short supply for a few months. His impending retirement gave him a useful lever in another sphere. He heard, soon after the purchase of Syleham House, that he would be asked to extend his term of office but, coming at a time when he was deeply preoccupied with the new constitution, he made it plain that he was not prepared to serve a further term unless the British government adopted the constitutional policies which he advocated.

During May 1953 the colony was caught up in the final preparations for the Queen's Coronation. With his feelings of intense and personal

[13] Capt G. N. Burden, CMG, Mr J. A. Loveridge, CMG, OBE.
[14] Letter to Family 5.5.53.

loyalty to the Queen, as her personal representative in the Gold Coast, he gave an enthusiastic lead and undertook a gruelling programme of engagements described in a letter 7 June 1953:

I have a pretty strenuous programme to get through. On Sunday the 31st there is to be a Coronation Church service in the afternoon at the Sports Stadium here and on Monday evening I give a Coronation Ball for over 200 people at the Castle. That is scheduled to go on from 9.0 p.m. to 1.0 a.m. and at midnight during the first few minutes of Coronation Day I shall propose the health of the Queen. The present idea is that the buffet supper will be served downstairs and that all the guests bedrooms shall be cleared of their beds and have tables and chairs where the guests can go and eat. We cannot rely on the weather in June and have to be prepared to have everything indoors. On Tuesday, Coronation Day, there is to be a big Military Parade at the Stadium at 8.0 a.m. with trooping the colour and the saluting of the Royal Standard. After the Parade which is likely to be a lengthy affair we should be free to listen to the broadcast of what is going on in London until the afternoon when there is a race meeting and a regatta, I propose to attend the regatta, and then a terrific fireworks display on the old polo ground at 7.30 p.m. At 7.30 a.m. on Wednesday the 3rd June I fly up in a special Dove with the Prime Minister, the Whistlers and the Casely-Hayfords to Kumasi.[15] This will just give me time to change into uniform and appear at the big Coronation Durbar which the Asantehene is organising. Last Wednesday I flew up to Kumasi to discuss this Durbar, among other things, with the Asantehene. It is the first big Durbar he has held since I have been Governor and he is fairly spreading himself. All the principal Ashanti Chiefs, some thirty of them, will be present with their retinues. It should be a most colourful affair. The Golden Stool of Ashanti which is supposed to contain the soul of the Ashanti nation will be on parade and I shall be introduced to it. I gather the whole affair is likely to last $2\frac{1}{2}$ hours and most of that time will be taken up by my going round greeting the Chiefs and then the Chiefs each coming up in turn with their retinues to return my greetings. It looks as if I shall have to be on my feet most of the time and it promises to be a somewhat exhausting affair. In the afternoon I have to attend the final of the Coronation football tournament and then I give a reception to about 300 people in the Officers' Mess when we shall all drink the health of the Queen. Next morning early I fly up to Tamale where another big Durbar has been arranged for the morning and again I give a reception in the evening. On Friday the 5th June I leave Tamale airport at 7.0 a.m. and fly down direct to Takoradi, change into uniform at the airfield and then take a Military Parade afterwards going to the Officers' Mess for what they call light

[15] Lt General Sir Lashmer Whistler, GOC West Africa Command; A. Casely-Heyford Minister of Agriculture.

refreshments which in my case means a glass of cold beer. I motor through to Cape Coast in time for lunch and that afternoon at Cape Coast there is yet another Military Parade and a Durbar of Chiefs followed by yet another reception in the evening at Government Lodge and a nice restful day is brought to an end when I have to attend a Coronation Dance and present prizes to the winners of the Coronation high life competition. On Saturday morning I motor back from Cape Coast to Accra, attend a Coronation race meeting in the afternoon, give a big reception at the Castle for some 400 people at 6.30 in the evening and then go on to the Coronation Dance where I am to present the prizes to the winners of the Coronation Band competition. I have the weekend in which to recuperate before going on to Ho on Tuesday the 9th for the Coronation celebrations which will be held there on Wednesday 10th. I am glad that Coronations don't happen very often.

Among his many Coronation engagements, the great Durbar organized by the Asantehene at Kumasi is of particular significance. The Asantehene at the head of his Chiefs and people addressed the Governor most cordially:

Your Excellency,

On behalf of the Queen Mother, Chiefs and people of Ashanti, it is my privilege and pleasure to welcome Your Excellency to Kumasi on this eventful occasion.

I can assure Your Excellency that we are deeply appreciative of your visit, because we are aware of your many and varied engagements this week in connection with the Coronation of Her Majesty Queen Elizabeth II.

We are however very proud that for the first time in the history of the Gold Coast, the Governor of the Gold Coast is able to join us in Ashanti in a ceremony arranged to mark the Coronation of a British Monarch.

It is customary on an occasion like this to make known to the Governor the requests of my people. This time I have only one request to make. That is that Your Excellency should be pleased to convey to Her Majesty the Queen our unswerving loyalty to Her Person, our prayers that She may have good health, long life and happiness; and our sincere hope that freedom and progress in a spirit of peace, tolerance and mutual understanding will prevail in the world at large during Her auspicious reign.

Finally, from the depth of our hearts we welcome Your Excellency and wish you a very happy tour.

'GOD SAVE THE QUEEN'.

The Governor replied in another brief and heartfelt address:

Otumfuor Asantehene, Nana Asantehemaa, Chiefs and people of Ashanti.

This great gathering has met together today in honour of the Coronation of Her Majesty. I formally make known to you th; yesterday Her Majesty was crowned and has assumed the Style and Title of 'Elizabeth the Second, by the Grace of God of the United Kingdom of Great Britain and Northern Ireland and of Her other Realms and Territories Queen, Head of the Commonwealth, Defender of the Faith.' Representatives of the Gold Coast with those of Her Majesty's other Realms and Territories were present in Westminster Abbey to witness that crowning and among them was a representative from Ashanti.

Yesterday the Chiefs with their people were celebrating the Coronation in their towns and villages throughout the length and breadth of Ashanti. Nevertheless, many of you have made long and tiring journeys in order to be here to-day to do honour to the Queen and to greet me as Her Majesty's representative. I appreciate that and from my heart I thank you all for the cordial welcome you have given me to-day. I ask those Chiefs who live outside Kumasi, when they return to their homes, to convey to their people my greetings on Her Majesty's behalf.

In the Coronation Message that I issued to the Chiefs and people of the Gold Coast I reminded you that the Queen has dedicated herself to the service of her subjects and I asked that our response should be to give Her Majesty our unstinted loyalty. To-day, Otumfuor Asantehene, you have responded by asking me to convey to Her Majesty the unswerving loyalty of the Chiefs and people of Ashanti to Her Person and your prayer, which is echoed by all her loyal subjects, that She will live long to reign over us in peace, prosperity and happiness.

On behalf of the Queen, I thank you for your message and will ensure that it is laid before Her Majesty in person.

LONG LIVE THE QUEEN.

The warmth and spontaneity of his welcome by the vast crowds assembled in Kumasi contrast starkly and dramatically with his formal visit in 1955 when his car was stoned.

In addition to the Coronation tour, when he visited each regional capital, he spent much of 1953 on trek. The Northern Territories had a separate and different constitutional link with Britain, and as the colony progressed towards independence Arden-Clarke saw it very much as his duty to explain the situation to the Chiefs. He addressed a large gathering of Chiefs at Tamale in May, explained the legal details of protectorate status, and concluded:

The Gold Coast can only become a prosperous and successful self governing country as a single united whole . . . There is no future for the people of the Northern Territories if they are separated from their brothers in the South.[16]

Later in the year he visited a rather neglected area in Western Ashanti which the CPP Ministers had largely ignored. On his return he applied what pressure he could in order to get things done but added:

I wish I could be an old time governor again, able to give orders and ensure their immediate execution instead of having to work through inexperienced and often incompetent ministers.[17]

Again, in December 1953 he made a further two week visit to the North, travelling 1,500 miles in the new Rolls Royce. Its comfort substantially reduced the fatigue of such a trip and at the end of the tour he made his usual comment:

I thoroughly enjoyed my tour and view with dismay the prospect of returning to Accra with its cabinet meetings, files, interviews and other weariness of the flesh.[17]

He was particularly pleased that during this year some of the smaller projects to which he had given his personal encouragement came to fruition. In October he opened a Training Centre for the Blind, which tried to help some of the 50,000 blind people in the country, and in November he presided at the opening of a leper settlement. In the previous year 14,000 lepers had been treated and there was now reasonable hope that the majority could be cured by modern medical treatment. His wife shared his interest in these two good causes, but they both suffered considerable inconvenience in their formal engagements at this time because she had fallen and broken her arm in October, and he had suffered from a severe and prolonged attack of tennis elbow caused by shaking hands so often at the Coronation celebrations.

It had become traditional that he would propose the toast of 'The Land we Live In' at the Caledonian Society St Andrew's Night Dinner, and in 1953 he used the occasion to speak on a serious issue and to outline his own philosophy. Referring to the rapid changes taking place, about which some people had complained, he continued:

There are other and more important threads running continuously through the fabric of our actions in this land since Britain first assumed the full responsibility for its government. That event occurred comparatively recently—only some fifty years ago: that in human history, is only yesterday and is not so very long for a consistent pattern to be followed . . . When I came out to West Africa over thirty years ago as an administrative cadet, my masters were

[16] Speech 27.5.53.
[17] Letter to Family 20.12.53.

quick to teach me two things—first, that owing to my lamentable ignorance and complete inexperience of all things African I was quite useless and would probably remain so, and secondly, that however useless I might be it was my job to teach the African to stand on his own feet and manage his own affairs. And that is the job which with due humility I and many others like me have been trying to carry out ever since. This being so it always astonishes me when somebody suggests that there is anything new or revolutionary about the approach of a dependent territory to self-government and full independence. On the contrary, it is the fruition of a policy consistently held and practised by Her Majesty's Governments from the latter years of Queen Victoria to the present day of our young and lovely Queen Elizabeth, whose health we have just drunk.

There is, then, nothing new about the goal we are striving to reach and if we are approaching it with increased speed, that again is no cause for astonishment, let alone regret. I know that speed can be frightening and it is always an anxious time when the young, be they our own sons and daughters or a people under our tutelage, launch themselves into the worlds. That is the time when parent or guardian needs a cool head, but not cold feet.[18]

At the end of what had been a stable and successful year, he was able to have a break over Christmas, indulging what had become one of his main leisure interests. He went to Ada near the mouth of the Volta river, with Robert Jackson and Mr Lironi,[19] for a spell of game fishing. They fished for barracuda, yellow tails and tarpon and were delighted when one of the party, Lironi, caught a tarpon of 140 pounds. A few weeks later before he went on leave Arden-Clarke caught a tarpon of 160 pounds which stood as a record for some time.

[18] Speech 30.11.53.
[19] Sir Robert Jackson, Development Commissioner. Mr A. Lironi, Department of Information.

CHAPTER EIGHT
The Development Schemes

During the 1950s African leaders and left wing spokesmen became increasingly critical of imperialism and colonialism, and they backed up their criticism with fierce allegations about the savage exploitation of the colonies by Britain. Their criticism contained an element of truth but not the whole truth. Successive British governments with benevolent but complacent attitudes to economic affairs, had contributed substantial sums to the colonies, but their laissez-faire policies had certainly permitted industrial and trading companies of all sorts to make substantial profits out of the people. In contrast, many British companies—especially the large chocolate manufacturing companies—had a record of care for their employees that was admirable, and they could maintain truthfully that they had played a major part in developing the country. They had built factories, houses and villages in what had been native bush; they had created employment; they had provided schools and hospitals; they had trained local people and had given them secure well paid employment. They could reasonably ask if this was brutal exploitation.

A more serious and sustained criticism is that the Gold Coast, like other British colonies, was encouraged to export primary products—especially cocoa and timber—which were later manufactured in Britain. Thus Britain gained all the benefit of the manufacturing process, and the colony had permanently to pay high prices for manufactured imports. The Gold Coast's pattern of trade certainly played into the hands of the big multinational firms like Lever Brothers, which wielded substantial power over the small traders or the cocoa farmers of Ashanti.

The mining companies of the Gold Coast can reasonably be criticized under both headings. For decades they had been a law unto themselves and, while exporting millions of pounds worth of diamonds, gold and bauxite, and paying substantial dividends to their shareholders, had contributed little to the direct revenue of the colony. Even before the war, Chiefs had complained in the Legislative Council about the derisory fees paid to the tribes for the mining concessions, but they had been advised not to interfere in such matters. The reactionary leaders of the mining industry, with attitudes hostile to the political developments of the 1950s, were to become a major problem for Arden-Clarke. Like

Burns before him, he referred to the three mining representatives as 'the unholy Trinity'.

Nkrumah has often been given the credit for the development plan of 1951, and the subsequent Volta River Scheme, but both of these schemes were initiated by Arden-Clarke before Nkrumah came to power. The plan was launched in a promising economic situation. A favourable balance of payments (£90M exports–£60M imports), and a revenue of £29M which topped expenditure by £5M, gave sound cause for optimism. The 10 year development plan—to spend £73M over 10 years—concentrated on clear and straightforward aims. To facilitate the economic and social revolution demanded by the CPP, the highest priority was given to increasing the productivity of industry and to developing communications and transport. £2M was allotted to the enlargement of Takoradi harbour—then the only harbour in the country—and a further £16M to the building of a major new port and a new town at Tema on a site 14 miles east of Accra. Tema was designed not only to provide a large modern port for Accra and the whole of the Eastern Region, but was also linked to the biggest and most ambitious of all the development plans—the Volta River Scheme. Development of all sorts depended on good roads, and a new trunk road was planned to run along the coast from Accra to Takoradi, in order to encourage the development of the coastal area and to help in the supply of locally grown food to the ever rising population of the capital. Of the £8M spent on roads, a substantial portion went to the building of a trunk road from Kumasi, the capital of Ashanti, to Tamale in the Northern Territories, and to the building of bridges to replace the ferries which had caused traffic delays in so many parts of the country. A bridge, which was to have serious political significance, was built at Adomi on the lower Volta, and linked the Volta region with Accra.

No one disputed the importance of road transport, but some improvements were also made in the railway system. The old main line ran from Accra to Kumasi and Kumasi to Takoradi, but a new line was now built which reduced the journey from Accra to Takoradi by 160 miles. Another line, from Takoradi to the gold fields at Tarkwa, was substantially improved, and the antiquated pre-war locomotives were replaced by powerful new diesel engines. Simultaneously, came the vigorous development of the post and telegraph system as a necessary pre-requisite of industrial and commercial progress. Along the country's sea coast the picturesque and traditional fishing boats and 'bum boats' were gradually replaced by motor boats as a part of a deliberate policy to improve the fishing industry.

The dramatic political victory of the CPP produced loud demands for economic improvements and gave an impetus and momentum to the relatively modest aims of the development plan. Initially the development plan gained almost universal support as an attempt to bring real benefits to every part of the country, and the whole community seemed to be galvanized into action. In the field of public utilities the urgent need was not only for clean piped water, wells, reservoirs and sanitation, but for the large scale provision of houses. By 1952 a number of water and sewage schemes had been started, and the government had given backing to housing projects in all the main towns, together with low-interest loans for house purchase.

The development plans of the 1950s illustrate the contrasting characters of Arden-Clarke and Nkrumah. The 1951 Plan, initially under Arden-Clarke's firm control, was a model of sound and restrained development, which deliberately curtailed capital investment in order to prevent sudden inflation. At the same time he had sought skilled economic advice. In 1952 Seers and Ross presented their major report on 'The Financial and Physical Development in the Gold Coast'. They suggested that inflation should be countered by the positive diversification of crops—especially cash crops for export; that there should be a better balance between domestic supply and demand; and that there should be a greater investment in the infrastructure of the colony. Professor Arthur Lewis, the distinguished economist, concurred with this advice.

In contrast, Nkrumah was a man in a hurry. He demanded that the ten year plan should be completed in five years, and this was agreed. After this sucess, and as his political power increased, he tended to listen more and more to advisers with little or no experience of government. 'There is no evidence that Nkrumah had more than a hazy understanding of what was involved.'[1] Krassowski criticized Nkrumah for failing to see that it was not possible to turn Ghana into an advanced industrial country simply by increasing investment, and pouring money into the public services.

In the early 1950s, when the excitement and enthusiasm was kept under reasonable control, tremendous achievements were made, and many of Arden-Clarke's visits to different parts of the country were to inspect progress on schemes which brought real benefits to the people. The government made substantial investment in the development of coffee, rubber, copra and the palm kernel industries. Professional advisers criticized the system of subsistence farming for being wasteful and inefficient, and for failing to produce the surplus necessary to feed the growing population of the towns. Further subsidies were given to the study of irrigation, soil conservation, fishery development and tse-tse fly control.

[1] Krassowski, *Development and the Debt Trap*. London 1974, p. 22.

The Northern Territories, with its searing heat and near desert conditions, was the most backward and least productive part of the country, and much of it was scourged by the tse-tse fly, which made cattle raising impossible. The government therefore launched a number of large scale schemes to bring major benefits to this area. The Gonja Scheme, the best known, attempted to cultivate 30,000 acres, and drew on the experience of the Sudan-Gezira scheme and the Russian collective farms. It was hoped that this scheme would help to develop the growth of ground nuts, maize, guinea corn and rice at a substantial commercial level, and that, as the trunk road developed, these crops could supply the markets of Kumasi and the south, and, at the same time, bring much needed cash to the northern farmers. The determination of the government to achieve rapid agricultural development extended not only to large scale projects such as the Gonja Scheme but to the provision, in many parts of the country, of model estates to experiment with new crops and new skills, and to provide residential training schools for agricultural officers at all levels. A veterinary school was founded at Tamale, and others for pig keeping and poultry keeping at other centres. Many of these enterprises, while being a part of the development plan, also received help from the Food and Agricultural Organization of the United Nations, and from the United States Operations Mission. Arden-Clarke enjoyed his frequent visits to the north, partly because they got him away from the intense political pressures of Accra, but also because it was one of the most satisfying aspects of his work to see all these developments—which for the most part he had initiated—taking shape and bringing benefits to a people who really appreciated what was being done.

While these exciting developments in the north were taking place, there was a country wide drive to develop fisheries. On the coast the government surveyed fishing grounds, trained crews in modern techniques and in the handling of motor boats, and, where possible, built small fishing harbours. The development of Tema harbour included substantial provision for large scale fisheries. The coastal areas, although poor, had always enjoyed the advantage of eating fish—a valuable addition to a diet that was dangerously short of protein—but now fisheries were set up wherever the inland rivers could be dammed or reservoirs built. Frequently villages received piped water and supplies of fish, at the same time. Here again, Arden-Clarke, who developed a passion for big game fishing at the mouth of the Volta River, took a strong personal interest in the development of fisheries.

With these attempts to improve general living standards came a positive campaign to improve and widen the health service. The British colonial system had provided a service of able and dedicated doctors who, even in remote villages, had operated small hospitals and dispensaries. These doctors, together with colleagues in the larger companies, gave a valuable service to the people and took part in important research into tropical diseases. No sudden improvement was possible in the field of medicine because of the shortage of doctors and trained medical personnel, but the Government encouraged all communities to set up health centres, and to support schemes to educate the public towards modern concepts of hygiene and sanitation.

In a major policy speech, reflecting the agreed policy of the government, Nkrumah said:

My first objective is to abolish from Ghana, poverty, ignorance and disease. We shall measure our progress by the improvement in the health of our people; by the number of children in school and by the quality of their education; by the availability of water and electricity in our towns and villages; and by the happiness which our people take in being able to manage their own affairs. The welfare of our people is our chief pride, and it is by this that my government will be asked to be judged.

In the application of development funds to education Arden-Clarke and Nkrumah agreed wholeheartedly. Ghana had a number of excellent schools—notably Achimota where Nkrumah had been educated, Mfantsipim at Cape Coast, and others supported by missionary endeavour, and these schools through their former pupils had made Ghana both the leader and the symbol of African nationalism; but such schools catered for only a tiny minority of the children in the country. In 1951 90 per cent of the people were illiterate. The education system—copied largely from the British—seriously neglected all aspects of technical education, and there was, therefore, a glut of lawyers and clerks and a damaging shortage of nearly every type of skilled tradesman and artisan. If the country was going to achieve a revolution in its standard of living, it needed far more mechanics and technicians. Higher education repeated the same pattern—with a crippling shortage of medical staff, engineers, architects and economists. One of the curses of Africa had been that any bright pupils from the villages, who were fortunate enough to be educated, rarely wished to study agriculture or to return and serve the village community by helping the peasant farmers shake off what was virtually a stone age bondage.

With almost universal support, the Government embarked on a major educational programme. A substantial school building scheme was started, primary school fees were abolished, and the facilities for teacher training rapidly expanded. In the five years after 1951, the number of primary schools increased from 1,000 to over 3,000, and the number of pupils in both primary and secondary schools increased from 200,000 to over 500,000. Increases in the primary schools obviously had to come first, but far sighted plans linked this with the enlargement of secondary and technical education. The new technical schools provided five year courses in industry, commerce, technology and agriculture. Where the country lacked specialist facilities, students received generous scholarships and grants to take them to Europe or America to obtain technical qualifications.

Arden-Clarke became personally involved in the most important single project in technical education, the establishment of the Kumasi College of Technology in 1951. It offered London University degree courses in agriculture, applied science, engineering, architecture, pharmacy and other subjects. Here, clearly, was the answer to the old problem of too much emphasis on purely academic subjects, but Achimota still had a role to play. Adjacent to its splendid site outside Accra, a new university was founded, with close links both to the school and to the Teacher Training College. Soon these institutions were employing their own graduates, as well as Ghanaians who returned from Britain and America to play a part in the inspiring new developments.

Both Arden-Clarke and Nkrumah, who spoke on the radio themselves, realized the importance of radio for educating the older generation and the country at large, and they therefore set up a countrywide broadcasting system, closely linked with the government information service. Initially based on relays from the BBC the new Ghanaian service deliberately developed locally produced programmes, and gave news and information bulletins not only in English but in Twi, Fanti, Ewe, Ga and Hausa. From the start emphasis was placed on developments in Ghana and Africa rather than London, Washington or Moscow, and the programmes were aimed at audiences throughout West Africa. To back up the radio service, the Government also provided a fleet of more than 40 mobile cinema vans to bring news and information to every corner of the country. Before independence all these services did much to educate and unite the country in the great endeavour, but as, later, Nkrumah veered more strongly towards dictatorship they became both dangerous and sinister.

Just as the Kariba Dam, dramatically spanning the Zambesi, stood as the symbol of Central African Federation, so the whole movement towards an independent Ghana—depending on the co-operation and leadership of Arden-Clarke and Nkrumah, of Britain and Ghana—was symbolized by the Volta River Scheme—the apex and pinnacle of all the development schemes. Before its completion it was to run into squalls of international politics and international finance, and to face unforeseen economic difficulties because of a world surplus of aluminium. In a later moment of crisis President Eisenhower was personally to intervene, but few of these dramas were anticipated when the scheme was launched in the early 1950s, with the enthusiastic backing of all sections of the government and the country, as the one great development scheme that would revolutionize the standard of living of the Ghana people and create in Ghana a modern industrialized society.

The ambitious and imaginative Volta River Project aimed to dam the River Volta not far from its mouth and, from this, to develop the whole eastern region of Ghana and far beyond, with hydro-electric power, bauxite mining, aluminium production, new port facilities at Tema, the irrigation of the dry Accra Plain, together with road, rail and water transport. The project included the Akasombo dam, over 300 feet high, which would produce a lake and reservoir 300 miles long and would engulf one ninth of the whole area of the country. A hydro-electric power station, producing 750,000 kilowatts, would provide sufficient power for an aluminium smelting plant producing over 200,000 tons a year, and based on vast local bauxite deposits. There would be enough surplus power to supply cheap electricity throughout the country, to speed up the whole process of industrialization and to get away from the dangerous over-dependence on cocoa. The project was capped by the proposed new deep-water port of Tema which was to act as a major port for Accra and the Eastern Region, and to handle the export of both cocoa and aluminium.

The Volta River Scheme as a whole came to fruition after independence when, to boost the morale of the doubters, Nkrumah said 'Its my baby', but, even before 1957, substantial work had been completed on the port and new town of Tema, and the Volta bridge at Adomi had been built. After independence, when the restraining hand of Arden-Clarke was removed, Nkrumah embarked on a series of wasteful, grandiose schemes which rapidly ate up the country's accumulated assets and left it deep in debt, but the real monument to Arden-Clarke is not only the Volta River Project, but the thousands of more modest schemes which were launched and brought to fruition prior to independence, and which brought immense improvements to the lives of the people.

One unfortunate legacy of the Legislative Council system bequeathed by the British is that politics appeared to consist solely of talking. Many of the new CPP ministers suffered from this illusion, and it took many weary lessons from Arden-Clarke and his civil servants before the new men realized that the more important aspect of their newly found responsibilities in Government was the unending hard work of efficient and uncorrupt administration. While Ghana's independence is Arden-Clarke's greatest achievement, a balanced assessment of his Government must not overlook the benefit the country gained from his example of realistic and down to earth planning backed up by dedicated administration—an example followed with unselfish devotion by his staff of public servants.

CHAPTER NINE
The New Constitution

The Coussey constitution which had brought the CPP to power in 1951—even though Nkrumah had called it 'bogus and fraudulent'—had also laid down guide lines for substantial changes in local government, and had certainly envisaged another constitution, within four years, to establish a fully democratic system for the country. Discussions in the cabinet and with Whitehall had taken place as early as 1952, when Lyttelton, the Secretary of State, had made it clear that a scheme of compensation for expatriate civil servants had to be agreed before further constitutional advance took place. Discussion continued during 1953, when Arden-Clarke visited London prior to the publication of the White Paper in July.

The debate on the constitution highlighted the problems which Arden-Clarke faced, and gave an initial indication of the opposition he was to encounter before independence was finally achieved.

The Development Plan with its massive capital investment had attracted considerable attention in the world money markets. It had been launched in the tense atmosphere of the Cold War, the Korean War, and at the time of Moussadek's take-over of the great oil complex at Abadan. It was natural that doubts and fears should be expressed. The Tory press in Britain—led by the *Daily Telegraph*, which through General Spears had ready access to information from the Ashanti Gold Fields—questioned the integrity of Nkrumah and the CPP, and expressed fears of a CPP take-over of the mines as political independence approached. The *Daily Telegraph* gave examples of corruption, of threats to Europeans in the mines, and quoted some of the wilder speeches of CPP supporters. Such an approach forced Arden-Clarke on to the defensive, and he became the chief spokesman for the CPP government on the international stage. Parts of the pique expressed by British business interests may well have come from the growing interest of American, West German and other European firms and investors in what had long been a British preserve.

In the atmosphere of the Cold War, the danger of communist infiltration had to be taken seriously, and Nkrumah's left-wing background seemed to justify the fears that were expressed. In fact he was strongly anti-communist, took extremely strong measures against the import of communist propaganda material, banned the *Daily Worker* and purged the CPP of all left-wing elements. Few people realized what intense pressure Russia was putting on Nkrumah at this time by trying to inundate the country with leaflets and propaganda. Nkrumah acted vigorously and stated publicly 'We have no intention of coming under the influence of another outside power, which we believe to be ruthless, just when we are putting off an imperialist yoke that is sitting very lightly on our shoulders.'

In view of the extreme left wing dictatorship he established after Ghana became a republic in 1960, this may seem surprising, and it raises the significant question whether Nkrumah was aiming all along to establish a communist state, and whether, during the struggle for independence, he hoodwinked Arden-Clarke and his colleagues in the government. Some historians have suggested this,[1] but the idea has been strongly refuted by those colleagues who worked very closely with him. In discussions in 1978, Komla Gbedemah, who was Nkrumah's Finance Minister for the eight years up to 1962, in referring to this precise question, maintained that although Nkrumah was always generally orientated towards socialism he did not have a positive or coherent philosophy. In the period before 1957 he did not at any time discuss the matter, and it would not be true to say that in any sense he hoodwinked Arden-Clarke or anyone else. The CPP ministers were thinking of independence, more or less as it was achieved, and to the exclusion of any other major philosophical notions. There was completely free and open discussion in the CPP Cabinet throughout the whole period up to independence, and the issue of communism was never mentioned. This view was confirmed by Robert Gardiner who held high positions in the Ghana goverment, who worked with both Arden-Clarke and Nkrumah, and who subsequently served in the United Nations. He said that although Nkrumah had some vague left-wing ideas, in the 1950s independence was the sole and total issue, to the exclusion of everything else. There was no way in which Nkrumah had any overall plan for a lurch to the left—he was essentially a politician and an opportunist. Among the CPP leadership there was no general acceptance of a socialist ideology and there was no serious discussion of it. There was no thought beyond independence. Gardiner emphasized, too, that Nkrumah lacked any overall philosophy and always picked up ideas from other people. Thus in the period up to 1957 Arden-Clarke—a figure of massive trust and integrity—had the paramount influence, but later on, after independence, Nkrumah came under the influence of Bing and other left-wing figures, but, even then, there was very strong criticism of

[1] See C. L. R. James *Nkrumah and the Ghana Revolution*, London, 1977.

the communist elements. Nkrumah had no real grasp of economic affairs nor did he appear to be interested in economic problems. He naively believed his own slogan that, if you grasped the political kingdom, all else would be added to it. With this situation, Gardiner believes that Arden-Clarke was a real mentor and friend to Nkrumah, and went far beyond what he needed to have done, to guide and influence Nkrumah, to help him avoid the pitfalls and to see what was required and, above all, to ensure the success of the drive towards independence. Nkrumah had an exaggerated idea of his own importance, a feature kept sternly in check up to 1957. This, together with his naivety, was later illustrated during the Congo crisis in 1960, when he sent top secret telegrams to Patrice Lumumba via Brussels and was surprised both that Lumumba never received them or that the Belgians knew about the contents.

While the communist scare affected Ghana's image abroad, the local government reforms raised deep and fundamental issues at home. The CPP stood as the party of modern democracy and had always opposed the power of the chiefs. Although the Coussey Report is best remembered for its proposals for the new constitution, it had at the same time proposed fundamental changes in local government. In place of the old Native Authorities it suggested new local councils, more democratic in composition, in order to face the new problems of a modern state. These proposals had been made after detailed discussions with chiefs, DCs and people throughout the country, but at the time few observers appeared to realize what significant changes were being proposed. The scheme started quietly, but in the five years after 1951, 26 district councils, 14 urban councils, and 238 local councils were set up. The Coussey Committee had realized that the reforms would curb the power of the chief locally, but intended that the chiefs would have a central or national role to play in some form of second chamber. The chiefs had long been suspicious of the CPP and its assault on their powers, and when local government reforms were accompanied by the continuing party propaganda of the CPP they felt more and more threatened. The first formal protest came from the Asanteman Council as early as 1952.

The apparently innocent local government changes, thus, affected both the role of the chief in an independent Ghana, and the relationship between central government and the regional administrative system. The Chief Regional Officers (formerly Chief Commissioners) had a monthly, and often stormy, meeting with Nkrumah, when they had the opportunity to present the case of their chiefs, of their staff in the field, and the aspirations of their own regions. At a lower level the DC—renamed Government Agent—came under fierce attack and criticism from CPP spokesmen, who saw him above all as an agent of Imperialism. In this uncomfortable situation the DC and the Chief drew together, protecting, as they saw it, their own people's interest and welfare, and all the important standards in public life, against the despicable attacks of ignorant rabblerousers. The DCs increasingly looked to their Chief Regional Officers for support because the hierarchy in Accra appeared to have become so completely identified with the CPP government. This attitude—understandable though it was—caused Arden-Clarke considerable distress, for he was above all a man of loyalty and integrity, and it added substantially to the pressures under which he worked.

The rumblings of discontent from his field staff and from the regions lingered on until they were overtaken by the National Liberation Movement, but they were temporarily eclipsed by the excitement of the constitutional White Paper and the general election of 1954. The new constitution established a single chamber legislature of 104 members, directly elected on a secret ballot, from separate constituencies. The Cabinet was to be drawn from the elected members and appointed by the Governor on the advice of the Prime Minister.

Although straightforward in itself, the constitution covered a number of fundamental constitutional changes which had been discussed from 1952 onwards. The new Cabinet excluded the three ex-officio British Ministers. From the start, Arden-Clarke had positively supported this as a necessary step towards a fully independent government. but, even so, he still retained his veto and had adequate safeguards on Defence, Security and External Affairs.

The establishment of a directly elected single chamber brought two significant changes—the six members representing the mines and commercial interests, and the indirectly elected members were all eliminated. General Spears, the mining lobby and the *Daily Telegraph*, had all actively criticized this proposal; the chiefs had opposed the elimination of the indirectly elected members, since that was the way most of them obtained their seats in the 1951 parliament. These objections had given rise to lengthy discussions about a second chamber for the chiefs, for the mining and commercial interests, and for distinguished local citizens, but after consideration by the Cabinet it was turned down, and Arden-Clarke concurred with this decision.

There was already some apprehension in the country about the attitudes of the CPP towards the independence of the Judiciary, and this was assuaged by the new ruling that the Governor should appoint a Public Service Commission, and then on their advice, after consultation with the Prime Minister, should appoint the Judiciary. Concern about the Judiciary was to be expressed more than once before independence was finally achieved, but Arden-Clarke reassured the critics. All remained well while he was Governor, but their worst fears were realized in the years after independence.

Discussions about the new constitution had brought out the growing fears of the Northern Territories, that, as independence approached, they would be dominated by a party which was southern based and which could easily neglect their interests. The Northern Territories enjoyed Protectorate Status and they were most reluctant to give up this special relationship. Arden-Clarke twice visited the Northern Territories—once with Nkrumah—to explain the need for a strong and united Ghana to go forward to independence, and to assure the northern chiefs and people that they would not be let down or neglected. Describing his role he wrote:

My chief task is to prepare these people for the general election which will be held in six months time, warn them to resist the blandishments of the politicians, and impress on them the vital importance of electing their best man to represent them in the Assembly, and of ensuring that their members stand united and speak with one voice for the North. I am afraid Nkrumah and my other ministers will not like what I am doing but these people are entitled to honest and impartial advice from their Governor and that is what they are getting.[2]

One responsibility which the new constitution specifically reserved for the Governor—and which he would gladly have handed over—was the Trust Territory of Togoland. Its difficulties had dogged his footsteps since 1949, and as Ghana moved another step towards independence the issue of Togoland had to be faced.

Togoland's problems had been created—as were those of the Middle East—by the shortsightedness and ineptitude of the Versailles Settlement. After 1918 the German colony of Togoland had been placed under the mandate of Britain and France, and had been neatly divided down the middle from north to south. This decision—neat and convenient for the League of Nations administrators—divided the Ewe people between three territories: the Gold Coast, British Togoland and French Togoland. After 1945 the UN Trusteeship Council took over the former mandates and quickly became highly critical of the colonial powers. It listened readily to complaints and seemed to encourage local protesters. In 1949 and 1950 Arden-Clarke had discussions with the Governor of French Togoland, and they were both highly critical of UN interference.[3] During 1950 a small minority party started to demand a separate state for the Ewe people and this gained some support at the UN. Arden-Clarke believed that the UN had foolishly encouraged an unwise and artificial demand, since there was no way of creating a viable

[2] Letter to Family 12.12.53.
[3] See page 114.

Ewe state. When the UN sent a visiting mission, Arden-Clarke, in the cabinet, spoke bluntly:

> I must say that I do not welcome their intrusion into our affairs and I do not think it serves any useful purpose. In fact by giving scope to local agitators and politicians to play off the United Nations against the administering authorities, these missions can cause quite a lot of harm.[4]

Through his personal contact with the French, he set up an Anglo-French Council to monitor the Togo situation and to facilitate discussion. Two issues clearly stood out. The Accra Government was now fully committed to the Volta River Scheme and its success would depend very substantially on the riverine people. If a separate Ewe state was created the Volta Scheme would be impossible. Arden-Clarke, with the close co-operation of the CPP, therefore created a new region of Trans Volta Togoland under a Chief Regional Officer based at Ho. This enabled a considerable sum of money to be channelled into the region in order to convince the people of the benefits of the British connection. Although the region came under the energetic direction of George Sinclair,[5] and the CPP mounted a positive propaganda campaign, these efforts encountered considerable difficulties. The people of South Togoland did not take kindly to paying taxes, and the Togoland Congress, which supported the demands for an Ewe state, encouraged them in their refusal. There followed a period of violence, with frequent fights between the CPP agents and supporters of the Togoland Congress, and each incident was assiduously reported to the UN. A delegation of the Ewe people, accompanied by George Sinclair, then went to the UN in New York. Nkrumah had explained that the plan was for British Togoland to be incorporated into an independent Ghana, and it was, therefore, hardly an Imperialist trick. This helped to improve the atmosphere and to obtain a reasonable decision. On a lighter note, Krishnon Menon—the Indian delegate on the Trusteeship Council—was highly amused at George Sinclair's role with the delegation and told him 'You must be the white catspaw of Black Imperialism.'

In the midst of the serious UN discussions, Arden-Clarke wrote an interesting letter home which throws some light on his own humour and also on the level of debate in the Trusteeship Council:

Dear Family,
    A certain Dr. Armattoe recently addressed the Trusteeship Council of U.N.O. about Togoland affairs. He does not like what the Gold

[4] Cabinet Minutes 19.4.51.
[5] Sir George Sinclair. His nickname in Accra during this period became 'The abominable Ho man'.

Coast Government is doing in British Togoland and he does not seem to like me. I think you may be interested in what he had to say about me:

> So low has British honour sunk that Sir Charles Clarke could sit like a Moghul Emperor on his wooden throne and not a flicker of discomfort cross his smooth face nor the stench of the vast pile of corruption and scandal shake one follicle in Sir Charles's hyper-aesthetic nostrils. British knighthood has indeed come down in the scale of chivalry in the course of one single generation. . . . We have ceremonially been buried alive and sentenced to death by the Prime Minister and his Cabinet of the Gold Coast without Sir Charles raising his delicate and well manicured fingers in protest.

I take it hardly that no single member of my loving family has ever told me that my nostrils were aesthetic, much less hyper-aesthetic, or referred to the delicacy and the beautiful manicure of my fingers, and that I am left to learn about these good points of mine from a complete stranger—but possibly this is because the stranger and I have never met.[6]

The United Nations seemed finally to be convinced that British Imperialists were not trying to dismember the Ewe people, and although the Togoland Congress campaigned in the 1954 election, they received scant support outside a small area around Ho.[7] In the run up to the 1954 election Arden-Clarke and the French were more concerned about the situation which might be created if half the Ewe people were in an independent state and the other half under French colonial tutelage. In fact they worried unnecessarily, for Togo already had a dynamic leader in Sylvanus Olympio, and he was to lead Togo to independence in 1960— far earlier than had been anticiapted in 1954.

Arden-Clarke had been on home leave from February and returned to Accra in May in time for a strenuous tour of the regional capitals before the election. He described his first impressions on returning from leave.

> In fact never before have I returned to the Gold Coast to find a country so peaceful, despite the imminence of the general election. I don't suppose this will last but it is a refreshing and encouraging change. The Service generally seems to have accepted the scheme for retirement with compensation for loss of career as fair and even generous, and morale appears to be good.

On a more personal note he mentioned to the family that the Hungarian

---

[6] Letter to Family 21.1.54.
[7] Eventually in 1956 the UN held a plebisite in the Trust Territories, and although the vote was not decisive the British section was incorporated into the independent Ghana. See D. Austin *Politics in Ghana*, pp. 230 and 310.

artist who had painted his portrait—Mrs Urzenyi, whom the family nicknamed La Belle Hélène—had been to thank him. 'She has accumulated nearly £700 from the sale of her paintings. She said "From the heart of my bottom, Sir Charles, I thank you." One of her better remarks!'[8]

In June Reginald Saloway and his wife came to stay at the Castle before leaving for retirement. He had been Arden-Clarke's closest and most senior colleague, had frequently been Acting Governor and received the KBE, in the New Year Honours list. He came to Accra in 1947 after successful service in the ICS, during the hand over of power in India. Forceful, clear sighted, and with wide experience, he, more than anyone, set up the system of government by consultation, to establish rapport with Nkrumah, Gbedemah and the CPP leaders. Arden-Clarke gave a farewell dinner party where presentations were made to the Saloway's. 'Nkrumah followed with a short sincere little speech which went down very well indeed. It was the first time I had ever heard him speak, apart from reading out some formal statement and I was most favourably impressed.'[9] The occasion finished movingly with the Police Band playing the Hausa Farewell and Auld Lang Syne.

After many months of meticulous preparation, the election took place peacefully in June 1954.[10] The CPP won 72 of the 104 seats, with a clear and absolute majority, and a mandate, it was assumed, to carry the country forward to independence.

---

[8] Letter to Family 29.5.54.
[9] Letter to Family 27.6.54.
[10] For a detailed study of the election see Austin. Chapter V.

CHAPTER TEN

Cocoa and the National Liberation Movement

Swollen Shoot, the virus disease which attacked the cocoa trees, had been a major factor in bringing the CPP to power. The colonial government policy of cutting down and burning diseased trees—the only effective remedy known at the time—had caused bitter resentment among the cocoa farmers, and the CPP had cleverly canalized this into effective political support for their party.[1] Nkrumah's government had to tackle the sensitive and controversial policy of 'cutting-out' within a few weeks of coming to power. They enjoyed one immediate advantage—that the world price for cocoa had doubled since 1948, and by 1954 was to reach £385 per ton. They also inherited two regulations from the old colonial government which they were happy to use. In 1948 the Cocoa Marketing Board had been established in order to protect the cocoa farmer from the violent price fluctuations on the world market. The Board announced a purchase price each year and, should the world price fall below that, then the farmer would still receive the guaranteed price. In practice, successive governments set the price for the farmer at an artificially low level and through the 1950s it averaged only just over 50 per cent of the world price. The powers of the Cocoa Marketing Board were backed up by the Cocoa Export Duty Act which allotted effectively 25 per cent of the export value of cocoa to development projects. Cocoa, thus, produced the major source of the country's export and of its revenue. The CPP saw the cocoa revenue as an almost limitless source of wealth, and cashed in quickly on the popularity which development schemes brought to the different parts of the country. But there still remained the intractable problem of Swollen Shoot.

In March 1951 the Executive Committee met to discuss the issue. It was to prove one of the most important meetings the Committee ever held, and to be a major step towards political independence and responsibility. The Committee, still flushed with the success of their political victory, were also aware that a UN scientific investigation had confirmed that the cutting out of diseased trees was the only effective way to control Swollen Shoot.[2] In this situation, Arden-Clarke, using all his powers of forceful logic, backed up by all the available scientific

[1] See page 85.
[2] See Austin, p. 160.

data, made a powerful case for the continuation of cutting out. The CPP members of the Committee argued that, if that policy was continued, the farmers would no longer trust them. After a lengthy and heated debate, the Committee decided to suspend compulsory cutting out pending an official inquiry.

There is considerable evidence—confirmed as recently as 1978 by Mr Gbedemah—that the CPP members went to this meeting expecting Arden-Clarke to use his veto. Although the decision went against his strongly stated view, he wisely refrained from using the veto. In doing so he proved both to the Committee and to the country that responsible government had really arrived, and that Nkrumah's Cabinet did take the effective decisions. Had he used the veto, the progress towards effective political independence would have been dramatically reversed. His decision proved wise, and after a fairly brief interval the Committee of Inquiry recommended the renewal of cutting out as an urgent necessity if the cocoa industry was to survive. At the same time it criticized the British system for harshness and insensitivity.

Nkrumah, who had violently attacked cutting out, and who had led the Committee against Arden-Clarke's views, and into a decision of weak political expediency, later described the situation as follows:

> Investigations into the matter (swollen shoot) confirmed my former fears, that the only solution was to cut down the affected trees . . . In an effort to arrest the disease I launched what I called 'The New Deal' for cocoa.[3]

In a broadcast he said 'If there was ever a test of our fitness to control our own affairs, this is it.' He added that the cocoa industry could not be jeopardized by a small minority who were unco-operative and in future cutting out would, again, be compulsory.[4] Arden-Clarke's comment on this is not recorded.

Although Nkrumah made light of the opposition to cutting out, it grew steadily and was soon coupled with intense dissatisfaction at the low price paid to the farmers by the Cocoa Marketing Board, and strong feeling, especially in Ashanti, that most of the benefits of the development plans were aimed at Accra and the south, but were paid for largely by Ashanti cocoa. These feelings became the nucleus of an opposition which, before 1957, threatened not only the CPP government but Arden-Clarke himself.

The government normally announced the price of cocoa for the year in April, and because the world price of cocoa had increased to £450 per ton, it was confidently expected that, after the election of 1954, the CPP

---

[3] Nkrumah *Autobiography*, p. 152.
[4] This compulsory cutting out was, in fact, reintroduced in October 1952.

government would announce a substantial increase on the 1953 price of 72 shillings a load. No figure had been quoted but some CPP candidates had spoken in terms of five pounds a load. In August Gbedemah the new Finance Minister announced that the price for 1954, and for the next four years, would be exactly the same as the 1953 price, i.e., 72 shillings a load. This proved to be one of the most critical decisions on the road to independence, for Gbedemah's announcement caused an uproar that led directly to the formation of the NLM. In an interview with the author in 1978 he explained his decision. He had realized that the announcement would cause an explosion whenever it was made, and if it had come just before the election it would have had a disproportionate effect. He, personally, made the decision on the timing, and was prepared to stand by the consequences. The decision was economic, not political—the Government needed the revenue and cocoa happened to be the most substantial source. In addition, the cocoa price was the main factor in Ghana's inflation, and it was deliberately kept low in order to prevent inflation.

Arden-Clarke had been fully involved in the discussions about this important decision. He had called Gbedemah to the Castle early in 1954 and told him that after the election, when the three expatriate ministers would hand over, he would become Finance Minister. Gbedemah asked why it was the Governor who was telling him, and received the reply that the matter had been discussed with Nkrumah, but that it was felt that the Governor should inform him, to make it plain that the British government was fully behind his appointment. Arden-Clarke then added 'Mr Gbedemah, I hope you will not fail, because the Colonial Office needs evidence that you are really able to run things, and this department is crucial.'[5]

In spite of Arden-Clarke's goodwill, the cocoa price incident illustrated quickly and dramatically the changed situation created by the new constitution, and how seriously it curtailed the power of the Governor either to help or to intervene. As the gravity of the NLM crisis increased, both the Governor and the CPP Cabinet were to complain of the limitations on their freedom of action. When Gbedemah decided the cocoa price—August 1954—the Cabinet were already aware of the hostile feelings against them in Ashanti, and a more experienced minister might well, in the circumstances, have compromised with an increase in price to the farmer. The Chief Regional Officer of Ashanti, A. J. Loveridge, as early as May had warned the government about the security situation, and had warned that any provocation could easily stir up Ashanti nationalism and unite the various opposition groups into a powerful and dangerous movement.

[5] Interview 28.12.78.

The CPP very unwisely underrated this strength of feeling. The Ashanti were a proud and warlike people with the Asantehene a proud and symbolic figure at their head. They looked back only to the end of the last century when they had been able to defeat British expeditions sent to take over their country. They remembered, too, the ineptitude of the British in trying to steal the Golden Stool of Ashanti and in deporting the Asantehene to the Seychelles. Now the explosion of feeling when the cocoa price was announced, brought together every element of opposition including the Chiefs and even the Asantehene himself. In September 1954, Loveridge wrote personally to Arden-Clarke expressing his grave fears. He had discussed the situation with the Asantehene and they both considered it to be dangerous and potentially violent.[6] In his Security Reports, Loveridge added more detail:

> I think the whole movement depends upon cocoa, and if the Government could 'explain away' the pegging it might manage to survive the price issue. I am afraid even an explaining away would be hailed as a 'victory' by the movement, but if it removed the reason for the movement's existence the 'victory' would be shortlived and I think it would be worthwhile suffering it.[7]

On 19 September 1954 Loveridge's worst fears were realized, and the National Liberation Movement was formed, with the support of the cocoa farmers; the Asante Youth Association which had formerly supported the CPP; the rich and powerful Ashanti Chiefs who resented the CPP attacks upon them; and at its head, the chief linguist at the court of the Asantehene, Baffuor Akoto, who was a wealthy cocoa farmer and a popular, respected and powerful figure in Ashanti.

The movement soon became a powerful political force demanding a federal form of government prior to independence. It levelled its fiercest initial criticism at the corruption and mismanagement of the Cocoa Marketing Board and the Cocoa Purchasing Company, which had become subsidiary organs of the CPP. As the movement developed many former CPP supporters joined it and were able to testify, from first hand inside knowledge, about the nefarious practices of the Cocoa Purchasing Company.

The NLM took as their motto 'We will hold ourselves apart', and this enabled them to rally to their banner virtually all the discontent throughout the country, which the aggressive and often ignorant activities of the CPP had caused. The Northern Peoples Party, formed in April 1954, had won 12 seats in the election, while the CPP won only eight. They threw in their lot with the NLM, as did the Togoland

[6] Letter Loveridge to Arden-Clarke 17.9.54.
[7] Quoted Rathbone—Thesis p. 223.

Congress and the Muslim Association Party. The NLM also recruited many former members of the CPP who had fallen foul of the centralized party machine in Accra, and who brought to the new organization useful political experience gained within the CPP.

The mounting difficulties throughout Ashanti drew attention to one of the major problems of diarchy. Under the new constitution the powers of the Governor were extremely limited, and, in terms of day to day administrative matters, there was very little he could do. On the other hand he and his expatriate staff still controlled security, which tied the hands of the CPP government. Nkrumah said:

> If the police and the army had been in the hands of my Government, the revolt, disobedience and disregard of law, order and justice in Ashanti would never have happened.[8]

In spite of the crises, Arden-Clarke, in a letter to his family remained remarkably relaxed and light-hearted:

> We have been in the throes of one of our periodical political crises and things have not been helped by the weather . . .

> The Ashantis, who are nearly as difficult and unruly as the Scots once were, have suddenly decided that they don't like the present Government, want Home Rule for Ashanti, and are vociferously demanding a Federal Constitution. They are supporting their demands by occasional brawls, throwing one or two sticks of dynamite about the place, and threatening general disturbance. The Government's first reaction was to deal with all opposition with a sledge-hammer; and it has not been too easy to get them to adopt more restrained and democratic courses. The exercise continues and I am not without hope that we shall get through without any major disturbance. The last thing I want to do is to intervene openly so soon after the new Constitution has come into being, which gives them for all practical purposes full internal self-government. Open intervention on my part would amount to an admission of failure to work the new Constitution. This latest Constitution is more difficult to work than the last, as it involves government by remote control instead of, as before, telling the Cabinet what to do at their weekly meetings and then seeing that they did it.[9]

An effective comment on diarchy!

In an interview in 1979, Daniel Chapman who was Secretary to the Cabinet during the 1950s, recalled Arden-Clarke's favourite adage 'A strong man does not show his power.' In 1954 Chapman was Chairman of the Security Committee which considered reports from all the regions,

[8] *Autobiography* p. 219.
[9] Letter to Family November 1954.

and he confirmed that Arden-Clarke always had a full, detailed and shrewd knowledge of the country, even though Nkrumah tried to keep from him any information detrimental to the CPP. Having witnessed both Nkrumah and Arden-Clarke working at close quarters, Chapman added this interesting anecdote, which he found fascinating and nauseating. Nkrumah would often be talking in the office saying 'I'll do this' or 'I shall tell the Governor to do that', and then Arden-Clarke would telephone, and there would be a sudden change. Nkrumah would become utterly obsequious, suddenly reverent, and would talk through his nose like talking to God.

The formal restrictions of diarchy did not prevent Arden-Clarke continuing to work behind the scenes. During August, the opposition, led by the Northern Peoples Party, stormed out of the Assembly because the Government refused to recognize them as the official opposition. The NPP leader went straight to Arden-Clarke at Christiansborg Castle to complain. Legally and officially he could do nothing, but in practice he had a quiet word with the Speaker (Quist) and Nkrumah, and the next day contrived a solution to the crisis.

> A little act was staged next morning in the Assembly, whereby the Speaker, at the request of the P.M. and the Leader of the Opposition gave his ruling, based on British Parliamentary Practice, and declared that the N.P.P. *was* in fact the official opposition. The P.M. warned the House and the country about the dangers of parties based on regional, sectional or religious differences, and the Opposition Members resumed their seats.[10]

In September Loveridge came to stay at the Castle and followed his visit with a very detailed report on the situation in Ashanti. Feeling, after this, that he was well and fully briefed, Arden-Clarke then had further discussions with Nkrumah, and produced a memorandum which throws an interesting light on his role.

NOTE

I discussed the situation in Ashanti with the Prime Minister, with particular reference to the agitation against the Cocoa price and the demand for a federal form of Government. I suggested to the Prime Minister that he might consider the following courses of action to deal with the situation:-

(a) Propaganda through the Party machine, making it clear that Government had fixed a *minimum* price of 72/- a load for the next four years; and that Government was not precluded from considering an increase in the price to be paid to farmers if next

---

[10] Letter to Family 6.8.54.

year or thereafter the world price of cocoa and the financial position of the country warranted such a course.

(b) It should be made clear that Government took full responsibility for fixing the price of cocoa and that, if necessary, an amendment to the Ordinance would be introduced to make this manifest. In a country whose whole economy is geared to the price of cocoa, no Government could shirk its responsibility by delegating this duty to any other body.

(c) The existing powers of the Cocoa Marketing Board, other than fixing the price of cocoa, would remain unaffected; and there would be no objection to the farmers, if properly organised for the purpose, nominating their representatives on the Board.

(d) The machinery for the issue of loans to the Cocoa Farmers by the C.P.C. should be overhauled, and steps taken to eliminate abuse.

(e) Steps should be taken, as soon as possible, to establish Regional Development Committees on the lines proposed by the Prime Minister.

The reasons for these various steps were discussed at length, with the arguments pro and con. The Prime Minister seemed to find the suggestions as (a), (b), (c) and (e) acceptable, but was doubtful what, if anything further, could be done as regards (d). He promised to send Mr Djin to see me, to explain the working of the C.P.C.

The Prime Minister is considering making a statement on the lines of (a), (b) and (c) at the next big Party Rally to be held at the Arena, after consultation with his ministerial colleagues.

C.N.A.C

5 October, 1954.

All the efforts to play down the Ashanti crisis came to naught in October, when E. Y. Baffoe, an official of the NLM, who had formerly been a CPP member of the Cocoa Marketing Board, was murdered in Kumasi. His murderer, Twumasi-Ankrah, was well known as a violent henchman of the CPP. The murder, which gave the NLM a martyr, immediately started large scale violence between the NLM and CPP throughout Ashanti. Leaders of both parties needed police protection, and any meeting was liable to be broken up by groups of the opposition armed with machetes, dane guns and other weapons. It was widely believed at the time that Baffoe had a detailed list of the peculations of the CPP, and of the CPC loans to CPP members, and that he had been murdered by the orders of the CPP executive. As the violence and bloodshed increased, the young men in Ashanti, who had flocked to the CPP as a way of undermining the overall power of the Chiefs, now returned to their former allegiance and joined the NLM. On the other side, the CPP became increasingly suspicious of the role of the Chief Regional Officer and the Government Agents, and soon began to complain that they were supporting the Chiefs and the NLM. As the CPP criticized the partiality of the administration, the greatly revered and powerful Asanteman Council—the council of Ashanti Chiefs—gave its support to the NLM. Finally the Asantehene, who normally held aloof from political matters, spoke out in favour of federation and supported a petition to the Queen.

These developments set up intense pressure within the administration because Loveridge and his staff in Ashanti felt very considerable sympathy for the NLM. They thought it was fighting a just cause against a crude and hooligan element in the CPP led by a dubious, unreliable and corrupt government. Arden-Clarke, who initially had some sympathy for the NLM, soon came to view it as a dangerous regional splinter group, poorly represented in the Assembly which had just been elected, and the biggest and most unexpected menace to the goal of independence. These developments came all too soon after the settlement of the issue of expatriate compensation, which had seriously stretched people's loyalty, and they set up dangerous tensions between British staff in the field and Arden-Clarke in Accra. Saloway completely supported the Governor's stand. Looking at things with a remarkable degree of clarity and detachment he emphasized that Nkrumah was attempting to weld the nation together, and that sectional interests should be strongly discouraged from stirring up trouble deliberately, in order to secure British intervention. As the volume of criticism from Ashanti grew, Arden-Clarke was increasingly identified with the CPP and now, for the first time, he was personally criticized. Previously, the press had attacked the CPP government and its members, but had never dared to criticize the Governor. Now the *Ashanti Pioneer*, which was to become his most vitriolic critic, led the way by protesting that he had not explained the position fairly to the Secretary of State.

Early in the new year the Secretary of State replied to the NLM petition which had demanded a constituent assembly and a Royal Commission. He closely reflected Saloway's view and stated that in a democracy the will of the majority must prevail. The result of the 1954 election had been clear cut, and now problems had to be solved locally, and not by British intervention which would be unconstitutional. With Arden-Clarke's concurrence, Nkrumah broadcast to the nation and stressed that his democratically elected government had a duty to uphold law and order, and they proposed to do this.[11] The cabinet backed up this policy by extending the Peace Preservation Ordinance.[12]

Arden-Clarke described the events in a family letter. Like Walpole and

[11] 3.1.55.
[12] Cabinet Minutes 7.1.55.

his game keeper's reports, he dealt first with a fishing expedition to Ada, and then continued:

> My chief preoccupation at the moment is the situation in Ashanti where a movement is growing in opposition to the CPP Government, which they distrust, and demanding a Federal form of constitution. They have been refusing to accept Nkrumah's invitation to a round-table conference and the usual bands of thugs are getting busy— throwing gelignite about the place and assaulting their opponents. Extra police have been drafted in and I have just issued a proclamation forbidding the carrying any type of arms or offensive weapons in public places. We may have more trouble before this storm blows itself out. [13]

Dealing with more personal matters, he planned—in order to avoid United Kingdom income tax—to spend some leave in South Africa in 1956 and then to return home on final retirement in May 1957.

This is a particularly significant letter. In it he presents the official CPP line, highly critical of the NLM. The question has to be asked: was he taking this line in order not to alarm the family or was he by this time so critical of the NLM that he no longer realized the very deep, widespread and fundamental opposition in Ashanti, which had been caused very largely by the violent provocation of the CPP, in such incidents as the murder of Baffoe. His view, expressed unguardedly in a private family letter, does lend some credence to the criticism that he was identified too completely with the policy of the CPP and that on the Ashanti problem he no longer had a detached and impartial attitude.

In February 1955 Arden-Clarke and Nkrumah enjoyed a welcome break from the political tensions:

> On Tuesday a party of us, including the P.M. and three other Ministers and the Salkields, carried out an official inspection of the construction works at the Tema Harbour site. We travelled out by special train pulled by one of the new diesel electric locomotives from Achimota Junction and then had explained to us the construction plans and saw the work that was going on. The contractors only got on to the site about two months ago and they have certainly done an impressive amount of work since they got there. It is a terrific streamlined job, which has got to be finished by September 1958 and involves blasting some six million tons of rock at the Shai Hills quarry, transporting it to the harbour site and dumping it between concrete blocks weighing twenty tons each, to form the breakwaters. They propose to run rock trains from the quarry to the breakwater every twenty minutes, working 24 hours each day. It sounded to me impossible but I presume they know what they are talking about. The

[13] Letter to Family 9.1.55.

P.M. and I were asked to set off a blast to signify the initiation of the work on the lee breakwater. We each had to push down hard on two plungers simultaneously which resulted in a most satisfactory bang. At one point the publicity people wanted a photo of the P.M. sitting at the wheel of one of the huge tipper trucks, with myself standing below talking to him. The P.M. had some difficulty clambering up, so I got my two hands under his backside and gave him a heave which shot him into the seat to the considerable amusement of the spectators! Coming down he again got in difficulties and as he seemed in danger of falling I put my shoulder under his behind and lowered him to the ground. An enterprising photographer snapped this and has sent me a copy which I have decreed must not be published! There was a large number of labourers and market women standing by and they all roared with laughter and loud shouts of 'free-dom' were raised. The proceedings ended with a large lunch which began with generous portions of smoked salmon which I had not tasted since I left London.

On Tuesday (15th) we have the State Opening of the new session of the Legislative Assembly, when I have to appear in my thick blue uniform which I wish I had never bought, and read a rather lengthy 'Speech From The Throne'. In the afternoon at 5.30 the P.M. opens the travelling exhibition of the Volta River Project and from that I shall have to dash back to the Castle and get ready to receive nearly 400 guests, including at least 150 Assemblymen and their wives, for the usual Sherry Party.

Meanwhile, Ashanti simmers but the Government is behaving itself and, with luck, we shall avoid an explosion. [14]

The cabinet had become increasingly concerned about the growth of the demand for a federal type of constitution and for a constituent assembly. It was therefore decided, after discussion in the cabinet, that the Governor would refer to these matters in his formal address to the Kibi Durbar on 21 February. This speech later caused Arden-Clarke so much unpopularity, and was referred to so frequently during the next two years as being insulting and provocative to the Ashanti people, that the political section is here quoted in full:

EXTRACT FROM A SPEECH MADE BY HIS EXCELLENCY THE GOVERNOR AT KIBI ON MONDAY, 21st FEBRUARY, 1955.

. . .

I note that you have handed to the Government Agent a formal address which I gather is somewhat lengthy and I can assure you that I shall take it away with me and study it most carefully. In the summary of the address which you have jut read, you have mentioned a number of important questions affecting the constitution and the government

---

[14] Letter to Family 12.2.55.

of this country. As was stated in the speech I read last week at the opening of the Assembly, in the management of its internal affairs, the Gold Coast is now, for all practical purposes, self-governing. I come among you now as the representative of the Crown, one who is bound by the advice he receives from the Ministers of the Crown in the Gold Coast. No longer am I the old-style Governor directly responsible for the day-to-day management of the affairs of this country. It would be most improper and unconstitutional if I were to usurp the functions of my Ministers and make any pronouncements on the important questions which you have raised. It is, however, still open to me to offer advice as well as to receive it. I can assure you that such important matters as the future of Chieftaincy, the question of a Second Chamber, the type of representative organisation that could appropriately be set up in the Regions and the functions and powers that should be attached to such organisations, Local Government, the Native Courts and the other matters you have mentioned, have received and will continue to receive my most earnest consideration and that I shall continue to give to the best of my ability advice and guidance in these matters, based on my 35 years' experience as an Administrator.

I may perhaps be permitted to make one comment which applies not only to the address you have made to me, but to many of the speeches, memoranda and articles that are current in the Gold Coast to-day. It appears to me that all too often terms or expressions are being used which do not convey any clear or precise meaning to the ordinary man. For example, the term 'constituent assembly' is very much to the fore. I have always understood that to mean a representative body, usually elected, empowered and capable of framing and establishing a constitution. The constitution of the Gold Coast is established by an Order made by Her Majesty in Council. It seems to me inappropriate therefore to talk of a 'Constituent Assembly', in the sense which I understand those words to mean, before the Gold Coast has achieved its independence and before it is capable of altering or framing a political constitution without reference to any other authority or power. If it is desired to set up a body to consider matters affecting the constitution of this country, then I think it would be helpful if specific proposals were put forward as to how that body should be constituted, what its membership should be and the questions it should consider. This surely is not the time to throw the *whole* constitution into the melting pot. There is much talk too of 'federalism' and 'regionalism'. As a practical administrator, I am very suspicious of '-isms' and similar generic terms unless they are precisely defined. Frankly I do not know what 'federalism' or 'regionalism' means in terms of practical politics, and I don't believe the ordinary voter or the man in the street does either. The Government has declared its readiness to consider suggestions in regard to the present constitution and to enter into consultations with any responsible body on matters affecting the constitution. It seems to me that it would be a wise thing if those who are concerning themselves with these matters got round a table with the representatives of the Government and tried to find a generally acceptable solution. No difficulties and no questions however controversial are incapable of solution, if those dealing with them are fully determined to find a solution. It would indeed be tragic if the Gold Coast on the threshold of its independence showed itself incapable of settling its own political differences and difficulties in a peaceful and constitutional way and disappointed the high hopes, not only of its own people, but of all Africans and their well-wishers.

His personal comment, prior to the speech, was:

Tomorrow morning I have a Durbar at Kibi and propose to spread myself a bit in my speech which will be addressed more to the country than to the local people. It is time the politicians stopped talking at each other using vague generalities and 'issues' such as 'federalism' and 'regionalism' which nobody understands and got round a table together to work out what it is they really want and how to set about achieving it. I propose to tell them so. [15]

Although this shows that he intended to speak bluntly, it is surprising—considering the actual words of his speech—that it caused such a furore.

The hopes of the Governor and the cabinet that a few blunt words would calm things down and bring both sides together in rational discussion were quickly dashed. In the same month, three young, highly respected and senior members of the CPP—all old Achimotans—formally left the CPP and joined the NLM. They were Joe Appiah, Victor Owusu and R. R. Amponsah. Appiah, a London trained barrister, had been particularly close to Nkrumah, and stated that he had resigned because of the corruption he knew of in the CPP, because of the subservience of CPP members to Nkrumah, and because of the gross abuses within the Cocoa Purchasing Company. [16] He considered the government's refusal to investigate the CPC's activities to be a serious affront to public opinion, and concluded that the CPP threatened 'the Institution of Chieftancy, the very symbol of our culture, tradition and democracy'. [17] Using the information provided by the three recruits, the NLM and the Asanteman Council issued the following statement:

We have examples of the Government's action which can only be described as dictatorship, such as the Government's unyielding attitude to the nationwide protest against its cocoa price policy; its partisan and often misguided appointments to public boards and

[15] Letter to Family 20.2.55.
[16] Austin p. 268. Appiah's father was Secretary of the Asanteman Council.
[17] *Ashanti Pioneer* 4.2.55.

corporations, and its refusal to have the disbursement of public funds by the C.M.B. and the C.P.C. investigated.[18]

General Sir Edward Spears, who was to be closely associated with the NLM visited the Castle at this time. Arden-Clarke after grumbling that a large sherry party had cost him three cases of whisky, described the General's visit:

The General is a great talker and full of stories, and as he gets older he talks more and more. The Chief Justice, Sir Mark Wilson, an Irishman and another great talker was one of the guests and the General completely defeated him. For the first time since I have known him, I watched the Chief Justice sitting silent while someone else did the talkng.

That afternoon I had attended the opening by the Prime Minister of the Volta River Project Travelling Exhibition. It was a delightful change to sit down in the audience and watch someone else on the platform having to do all the work. The Exhibition consists of models and dioramas of the bauxite mines, the huge dam and power house on the River Volta, the smelter plant and its attendant town and a large relief map showing the size of the lake reservoir that the dam will create, 3,200 square miles in extent. The Exhibition is housed in a marquee and is to tour the whole country during the next twelve months. It should do much to make the people understand the vast extent of the project and the benefits it will bring to the people of this country.[19]

Within the next few weeks the situation deteriorated so rapidly that there was an almost total breakdown of trust between the Administration and the NLM. Nkrumah had twice invited the NLM and the Asanteman Council to constitutional talks, but they had refused his offer on the genuine assumption that he intended to silence them. Even the Asantehene said publicly 'We are fighting to restore the lost prestige of the Ashanti nation.'[20] The Security Reports in Ashanti give increasing evidence of violence, lawlessness and a widespread determination to oppose Nkrumah's government by almost any means. Complaints poured in to the Chief Regional Officer that the Governor was no longer unbiased, could not be trusted, and that the Ashantis would therefore have to fight. The NLM had taunted Nkrumah that he was frightened to come to Ashanti, but then Arden-Clarke bravely grasped the nettle and planned a visit to Kumasi on 21 March 1955.

To greet Sir Charles, the *Ashanti Pioneer* produced a special leaflet. It welcomed him but said:

[18] Quoted Rathbone Thesis p. 248.
[19] Letter to Family 20.2.55.
[20] Quoted *Observer* 6.2.55.

We demand
  a) Commission of Inquiry into C.M.B., and C.P.C. affairs.
  b) Nkrumah's government to resign immediately—public opinion
     demands this.
  c) Setting up of Constituency Assembly for Federation.
Are you not aware of
  a) Nkrumah's Dictatorial Tendencies.
  b) Naked Fascism in this Country.
  c) The fact that you should be neutral in LOCAL POLITICS. Why
     take sides with the C.P.P.?
Sir Charles
  Are you for Democracy
              or
        For Dictatorship
  No Federation   No Self Government.

Another leaflet, obviously hitting at Sir Charles, advertised for a
Propaganda Secretary for the CPP, offering an attractive salary, a Rolls
Royce for transport, and accommodation at the Castle. Other
newspapers demanded the Governor's recall. Some Chiefs suggested a
boycott of the visit, but the Asantehene insisted that all the normal
courtesies should be shown to the Queen's representative. The inflamatory leaflets and press attacks, building up since the Governor's
speech at Kibi, had produced a state of dangerous excitement which
exploded when he arrived in Kumasi on 21 March.

He drove first to a meeting with the NLM leaders, and then went to
pay a courtesy call on the Asantehene at his palace. As he went in he was
booed by a menacing and aggressive crowd, and during his visit a
protester actually got into the Rolls Royce. Then as Sir Charles left the
Palace the car was attacked and stoned. The papers in Kumasi, which
largely supported the NLM gave considerable detail of the incident—
some with smug satisfaction—but, generally, the incident was roundly
condemned. The *Ashanti Sentinel* in an editorial represented the
majority view.

> All sane elements in Ashanti join us in vehemently condemning the
> way the N.L.M. organized crowd acted towards the Governor Sir
> Charles Arden-Clarke when he visited Otumfuo the Asantehene at his
> palace.[21]

Another view came from the *Daily Echo*:

> While we do not praise the doers of the act, we hasten to say that the
> incident is a natural sequence to the train of events which have gripped
> this country since the formation of the N.L.M. . . . We say that if Sir

[21] *Ashanti Sentinel* 24.3.55.

Charles had been more discreet in his speech at Kibi he might well have played the role of the twins' father in the dispute. That unfortunate incident is one of the contributors to the stone and bottle throwing reception H.E. had at Kumasi. . . . The blame is the Government's and to some extent H.E. himself for making the Ashantis feel snubbed and slighted.[22]

Nkrumah's own reaction—recalled years aftewards by Gbedemah, was 'Well Sir Charles I can only apologize for the immaturity of our people.'

The Governor spent a further five days touring Ashanti, and when he returned to Accra sent a detailed description of the whole tour to the family:

Dear Family,

I have just returned from my six days' tour of Ashanti which was not uneventful. About six months ago, a political party calling itself the National Liberation Movement was started in Ashanti. It pretends to be a democratic organisation but is, in fact, backed and led by the Chiefs with the Asantehene (the King of the Ashantis) at their head. It represents the resistance of the Chiefs to the curtailment of their own powers under the present democratic system and their attempt to reassert their authority by appeals to Ashanti tribal feeling which is strong. They have for the present gained a considerable following. The movement demands the setting up of a Constituent Assembly to devise a federal form of government for the country. In fact, they don't know what they mean either by 'Constituent Assembly' or 'Federal form of government'. They hate the C.P.P. (the Government Party) and are quite determined that they will not have independence under a C.P.P. Government and seem prepared to go to almost any lengths to cause the present constitution to break down. The P.M. has twice invited them to round-table talks which they have refused. There have been long-range exchanges of memoranda and a lot of inflamatory speeches on public platforms on both sides and this was getting the country nowhere. I went up to Ashanti to see what it was all about and try to break the deadlock. Some little time ago, I made a speech at Kibi in which I told all the political parties they had better stop using terms such as 'Constituent Assembly', 'Federalism', 'Regionalism', which they did not understand and which did not represent what they really wanted and said that they had better all get round a table to try and settle their differences. This speech was bitterly resented by the N.L.M.

When I got to Kumasi on Monday, the first thing I did was to send for the leaders of the N.L.M. and have a talk with them to try and get them to clarify what exactly it was they wanted. As I expected, I found that it was not a Constituent Assembly in the ordinary sense of the term they were seeking and that they had not the slightest idea what

[22] *Daily Echo* 25.3.55.

they meant by a federal form of government. The talk was quite friendly. After tea, I went off to pay my customary courtesy call on the Asantehene whom I like and with whom I have always been very friendly. The N.L.M. had selected this occasion to arrange a demonstration which took the form of a number of placards carried by women and children with slogans such as 'The Governor must go' and other derogatory remarks. A large crowd had collected and there was a lot of booing and hooting and screaming but we got through without any trouble to the Asantehene's Palace. While I was talking to him the crowd worked itself up into a state of hysteria and when I came to leave they were beginning to get a little out of hand. As I drove out of the gates, the Police had some difficulty in clearing the way for the car, while the screaming and booing rose to a frenzy. Then some people at the back of the crowd started throwing gravel and mud and stones. The Rolls received a few dents, lost a few chips of paint, but no other damage was done except to two of the stone-throwers whom the Police got at with their truncheons. We were soon through the crowd and motored peacefully back to the Residency. Johnny Loveridge, the C.R.O., was with me in the car. The whole incident was singularly stupid and merely showed how quickly an hysterical mob could get out of hand. It obviously was going to do a great deal of harm to the N.L.M. who had never intended that things should go so far because the people are still loyal to the British Crown and were disgusted that the Queen's Representative should be treated in such a fashion. Immediately after the incident the crowds dispersed and Kumasi remained extremely quiet for the whole of my time in Ashanti.

Later a Police Constable was asked if he was the man who had truncheoned one of the stone-throwers who was in hospital with four broken ribs. He replied 'Is the man dead?' 'No.' 'Is he dying?' 'No.' Then with a broad grin and the greatest possible emphasis—'Yes, sir.' It is fortunate that the Police discipline was good or there might have been a lot of casualties among the crowd.

I decided to deal with this when I got back to Kumasi and continued with my tour as arranged to Mapong, Ejura, Sunyani, Berekum, etc. The opportunity of my visit was taken to have political demonstrations, both by the N.L.M. and the C.P.P. but they were all quite peaceful. In fact, conditions were very similar to the time when I first arrived in the Gold Coast except that then no-one was feeling friendly towards me and this time the C.P.P. regarded me favourably. After the Kumasi incident, I was followed wherever I went by three lorry loads of Police but the only really hard work they had to do was when we were travelling from Sunyani to Berekum in a heavy storm and a big tree was blown across the road in front of us. All my meetings and speeches went off quite peacefully except at two places where, when I went to pay the usual courtesy visit to the Chief, I found a political demonstration had been arranged whereupon I sent a message to the Chief saying that I was not being greeted in a manner befitting my office. I refused to meet him and turned my back and walked out. When I got back to Kumasi, I summoned N.L.M. leaders and dealt very faithfully with them for an hour. I also saw the Asantehene who was very upset at what had happened and had written expressing his very sincere regret and I warned him of the consequences if the movement with which he had identified himself continued on its present way. I think the visit has served a useful purpose and has helped to clear the air. Certainly, the N.L.M. are in no doubt as to what is going to happen to them if they try and break the Queen's peace. I gave them the same warning I gave the C.P.P. leaders in 1949 and told them I would hold them personally responsible for any act of violence by their followers and that they would finish up in prison as the C.P.P. leaders did in 1950 unless they mended their ways. My chief difficulty throughout the visit was trying to keep my temper and that is no easy thing to do when one is under continuous provocation for five days. I should think my blood pressure is now considerably higher than it was before I left on the tour!

There was a final Gilbertian touch towards the end. Throughout the tour, there had been rumours of trees felled across the road and ambushes being laid, all of which was rubbish. Motoring back to Accra yesterday afternoon with everything extremely peaceful, I suddenly saw a huge tree fall across the road just in front of the Police jeep which was leading the way. This, however, was not a political demonstration but turned out to be the P.W.D. felling trees and, as the headman of the P.W.D. gang explained, the tree was meant to fall the other way into the forest but Allah had decided that it should fall across the road! We had to wait twenty minutes until that obstruction was shifted.[23]

During his visit he met both CPP and NLM supporters, but both sides tended to interpret his remarks differently. In the Brong area of Western Ashanti, which had long resented the domination of the Ashantis, his sympathetic hearing appeared to give encouragement to their separatist demands. This in turn incensed the Ashantis. The NLM and the Chiefs certainly believed that, after the visit, the Governor would control the CPP more firmly, but failed to realize how limited his powers were. His visit seemed to give a breathing space for a few weeks, but then the lull was terminated by the absurdly provocative action of the CPP allotting over £1M for improvements in Accra and for building a new house for the Prime Minister.

The Kumasi visit did no good in the long run, and it certainly did not prevent the NLM pursuing the controversial issue of CPP corruption. Early in March Busia had presented a well reasoned case in the Assembly for an inquiry into the activities of the Cocoa Marketing Board.[24] The

[23] Letter to Family 27.3.55.
[24] Assembly 4.3.55.

debate produced overwhelming evidence of malpractices, but Arden-Clarke again had to emphasize that, under the new constitution, he had no power to appoint a commission of inquiry unless advised to do so by the Cabinet.

Still concerned about the growing demand for federation, Arden-Clarke flew to Tamale.

> The main purpose of my visit to the north was to have a talk with the Standing Committee of the Northern Territories Council, and for two and a half hours I tried to bang some common-sense into some very stupid heads. I also drove out by car the eighty miles to Damongo to see what progress was being made in the big scheme of mechanized agriculture which is going on there. Nowhere in Africa has mechanization proved an economic proposition but Damongo gets as near to it as any. [25]

During these excitements, Arden-Clarke, whenever he was in Accra, had to spend considerable time sitting for his portrait. The portrait was required for the new luxury hotel in Accra which the Government wished to name after him. He refused to give his name to the hotel—it was subsequently called the Ambassador—but allowed the banqueting hall to be called Arden Hall. Both names are still used. The artist, Mrs Urszenyi, proposed a portrait in full blue ceremonial uniform against a sumptuous background of dark crimson. She put this idea to Nkrumah who strongly opposed any presentation of imperialist pomp and panoply and wanted HE to be painted in a civilian suit 'as a friend of the African'. Arden-Clarke continues:

> They then had a wonderful argument which both of them have described to me—Helena talking of the pageant of history, the magnificence of the Hapsburg Court, and how popular pictures of that period now are in Vienna etc., while Nkrumah spoke of the iniquities of imperialism and the danger that the picture would be removed by some subsequent government if it represented an imperialist Governor instead of a friend of Africa. [25]

Arden-Clarke eventually intervened, decided on the white suit, and said that anyway he was going to sit in shirt sleeves.

The stress of the early months of 1955 eventually took their toll, and the Governor was laid low by a fever which prevented him taking the Queen's Birthday Parade, but he recovered just before going home on leave in April.

[25] Letter to Family 7.3.55.

CHAPTER ELEVEN
The Final Struggle

During his leave the Ashanti crisis simmered on. The CPP gave more serious consideration to the claims of the Brong people to be released from the domination of Ashanti. This had obvious and immediate political significance, but reflected a serious and long standing movement, which substantially pre-dated the rise of the CPP.[1] At the same time Sir Edward Spears threw his weight more openly behind the NLM. Speaking to the shareholders of the Ashanti Goldfields Company, he maintained—quite inaccurately—that the whole of Ashanti was opposed to the CPP. Again the *Daily Telegraph* followed his lead and, from then onwards, it becomes clear that the NLM—powerfully backed by Spears—realized that they might oppose the CPP more effectively in London than in Accra. Mounting a propaganda campaign to influence both Westminster and the City, they were soon joined by expatriate business interests, which were apprehensive about their future in an independent Ghana dominated by Nkrumah.

During his leave, Arden-Clarke did his best to convince the Colonial Office that they should give maximum support to the Gold Coast government and should not in any way encourage the opposition. The warning was necessary because Dr Busia was in London at the same time, lobbying vigorously for the NLM and using every available contact provided by Spears. Arden-Clarke showed the Secretary of State the Assembly's report on Federation, before it was published. It rejected a federal form of government but recommended Regional Councils with certain delegated powers, in order to ensure full co-operation between the central government and the regions. This appeared to be a very sensible compromise, and he emphasized that the CPP fully accepted the report, and had also accepted and backed up the recent establishment of the Public Service and Judicial Commissions, which went a long way to ensure the independence of the executive and the judiciary.

During May, when Sir Gordon Hadow was acting Governor, a new development took place. A CPP member of the Assembly for an Ashanti constituency was killed in a traffic accident. As a precautionary measure,

[1] The Brong issue is dealt with in two books published in the 1960s: Meyerowitz, E. *At the Court of an African King*. London 1962. Tordoff, W. *Ashanti under the Prempehs*. London 1965. In 1960 Brong-Ahafo became a separate region.

the Chief Regional Officer imposed a dusk to dawn curfew in Kumasi and drafted in a battalion of the Gold Coast Regiment. This action provoked the NLM and its supporting organizations, which sent telegrams to the Queen, to the Secretary of State and to the Governor. In spite of the brief rise in tension the resulting by-election took place in a peaceful and co-operative atmosphere. The NLM candidate won by a large majority, and the government hoped that this would contribute to the establishment of the NLM as the formal constitutional opposition which the country badly needed.

At the end of his leave, spent largely at Syleham House, Arden-Clarke wrote to his mother in Exeter:

> I go off by early train tomorrow morning to London to give myself time for a final passage-at-arms with the pundits of Whitehall . . . I do not relish the thought of leaving all this peace and beauty and happy family life for the strains and responsibilities and political turbulence of the Gold Coast, though I shall doubtless be happy enough when I get there.[2]

On his return to Accra, he left almost immediately for Kumasi. He described his visit in a relaxed and confident letter to the family, letting them know that he had told the Ashantis about his visit to the Queen:

> Dear Family,
>
> I spent an enjoyable and useful weekend in Kumasi, travelling up on Saturday morning by one of our new Heron aircraft and returning on Monday. My objective was to get into contact with the Asantehene and the leaders of the N.L.M. and try and talk some sense into them. I certainly had plenty of full and useful talks but whether anyone is going to be any more sensible as a result remains to be seen.
>
> On Saturday afternoon, I went to the Kumasi Races to which I had never been before. Races bore me to extinction but I felt it was a good thing to see and be seen by the local V.I.Ps. in Kumasi. It was a very friendly and cheerful affair. I was tipped three allegedly certain winners and duly put my money on them, only to watch them come in unplaced.
>
> On Sunday afternoon I played golf with the Asantehene. To call it golf is a euphemism because he is even worse than I am and as it is the only time that he and I can be alone together, we are apt to discuss matters of state and not concentrate on the game. He gave me a wonderful lesson in Ashanti arithmetic. With a beaming smile Nana turned to me on the last green and said, 'A half—that makes you one down on the match'. According to my reckoning I had won the match by two and one, and for half a second was taken aback. Then I laughed and said, 'How right you are, Nana, you are much too good

for me'.—it was his arithmetic not his golf to which I was referring! Anyhow it was a satisfactory ending, as each of us was satisfied that he had won.

I had another lesson in the Ashanti idea of negotiation when I was talking to Bafuor Akoto, the leader of the N.L.M. In the course of our conversation, he said, 'I am ready to compromise if they give me what I want'. I questioned whether this was, in fact, a compromise. 'Oh yes', said he, 'If I ask you for cigarettes and you give them to me, that is a compromise'.

Both the Asantehene and the N.L.M. leaders were anxious to hear about my interview with the Queen. This gave me my opportunity and I told them, among other things, that Her Majesty was extremely well informed and had heard of the reception accorded to me when I had last visited Kumasi. This made them look down their noses and feel ashamed. I added that I had nevertheless been able to assure Her Majesty that she had no more loyal and devoted subjects than all her people in the Gold Coast, including the Ashantis. In fact, before throwing stones at me they had been careful to hold up a placard reading 'We have no quarrel with the Queen, God Bless Her'. This had made the Queen laugh but I pointed out that neither the Queen nor her representative would regard it lightly if anything like that ever happened again. This brought forth fervid assurances that it never would. [3]

In Kumasi, Arden-Clarke had serious discussions with the CRO and senior staff including police and army representatives, and they agreed that, although there were still some sporadic outbreaks of violence, the overall tension had been greatly reduced. They therefore decided to return to normal security arrangements, and the NLM appeared to respond to this move.

The Government report on Federation, which Arden-Clarke had shown to Lennox-Boyd, was debated in the Assembly at the end of July. The NLM boycotted the debate, and, instead, kept up their pressure in London. Busia—much to Arden-Clarke's disgust—was given an interview by Lennox-Boyd, but, as a result of the interview, Lennox-Boyd cabled that he could accept none of Busia's suggestions unless they were put formally through the Governor. The cable added that the NLM had failed to discuss their views with the Government or to attend the select committee, and it urged Busia and the NLM to be more co-operative. [4] The House of Lords debated the Gold Coast situation at this time and the Government spokesman Lord Lloyd backed up the stern line taken by Lennox-Boyd.

[3] Letter to Family 27.7.55.
[4] Cabinet Minutes 12.7.55.

The NLM then published their 'Proposals for a Federal Constitution', which suggested a Governor-General, under the Queen, as Head of State, with either a Governor, or a traditional ruler like the Asantehene, in each region. The Federal Government would have two houses with a prime minister, as would each region. Such a constitution would have been vastly expensive and top-heavy for a country of five million people, and the Select Committee rejected it.[5] Their reasoned reply did little to convince the NLM, which regarded the committee as a group of CPP stooges, but at least the two opposing views had now been publicly stated. In September, Lennox-Boyd—prompted by Arden-Clarke during his recent leave—sent out a distinguished constitutional lawyer, Sir Frederick Bourne, to consider every aspect of the new constitution. Bourne had clearly not been briefed on the urgency or delicacy of his position. Interviewed on his arrival, he said that he did not know his terms of reference and that the Prime Minister would decide the method his inquiry would adopt. He was also misquoted as saying he represented the Gold Coast government. His remarks had an immediate and disastrous effect. The NLM assumed that Bourne would be as biased as the Select Committee had been, and that he had merely been appointed to set up the regional councils, which they rejected.[6] The *Ashanti Pioneer* which normally took an aggressive view, proposed that the NLM should boycott the Bourne Mission altogether, but the more mature leaders like the Asantehene and Busia realized that they would damage their cause if they appeared too intransigent. The NLM then made a shrewd move, demanding that Bourne's terms of reference should be published in the *Gold Coast Gazette* before they would decide whether to co-operate. The CPP responded reasonably to this and published the required statement.[7] Bourne also gave a press conference and assured the country that he was a completely free agent.

In this delicate and sensitive situation, the CPP now made a major blunder—both of tact and of timing. They had given notice earlier in the year that they were going to pass a Bill giving chiefs the right to appeal to the Governor in constitutional disputes. This may have been part of their declared policy of making the chiefdoms more democratic, but it appeared—especially at this time—as a crude and deliberate ruse of the CPP to undermine the paramount chiefs in Ashanti by encouraging chiefs to join the CPP and to break away from the Asanteman Council. For the CPP it has to be said the Bill was based on factual evidence that the Asanteman Council was coercing lesser chiefs into joining the NLM.

[5] Report of the Select Committee on a Federal System of Government and a Second Chamber for the Gold Coast, 1955.
[6] *The Times* 27.9.55. Further detail is given in Austin p. 301.
[7] *Gold Coast Gazette* 15.10.55.

In one case, Bechem, the Asanteman Council had de-stooled the Chief for refusing to support the NLM. The initial mention of this Bill had caused strong protest but in October 1955, just before Bourne was due to visit Kumasi, and when discussion about his mission was at its most sensitive stage, the Bill was published as The States Council (Ashanti) Bill. This inept and badly timed action of the CPP government, made it certain that the NLM would boycott the Bourne Mission, and created another major constitutional crisis. For Arden-Clarke, instead of a joyful final progress towards independence, it meant a year of fierce tension and perpetual crisis, upheavals both in London and Accra, attacks on his probity, and the intervention of the Secretary of State.

In September 1955 A. C. Russell replaced Loveridge as CRO Ashanti, and he quickly became embroiled in the fight over the States Council Bill. In October he stated that if the Bill was passed, the fairly reasonable hope of the NLM accepting a compromise constitution would have vanished.[8] He forecast accurately that the Bill would be considered discriminatory, and that if it passed it would cause violence. In the weeks before the passing of the Act, petitions and resolutions poured into Christiansborg Castle. Early in November the NLM had formally stated to Arden-Clarke that they would boycott the Bourne inquiry if the Bill passed. The vocal and active Asante Youth Association cabled the Governor demanding that he should do his duty, in the interests of peace, adding 'Britain expects you to do your duty. This is your finest hour.'[9] Bafuor Akoto, the NLM leader, in a serious and reasoned statement, warned not only that the role of chiefs and the whole apparatus of Chieftaincy were threatened by the Bill, but that it would be the prelude to communist inspired People's Courts. The left wing clichés bandied about in the exciting days of 1950 gave powerful ammunition to the increasingly formidable opposition, and to a world press growing more alarmed at the performance of the CPP. Mounting criticism was now directed at Arden-Clarke himself. The press frequently referred to his speech at Kibi, and when he failed to prevent the passage of the Bill in November the Ashantis became convinced that he was in the pocket of the CPP.

Russell, during these very difficult weeks, waged an active personal campaign to prevent the Government from passing the Bill, because he believed—correctly—that the NLM would permanently boycott Bourne's visit if it passed. Bourne went to Kumasi on 24 October for a four day visit and Russell arranged a sherry party for him to meet the local leaders. All the NLM leaders and all members of the Asanteman Council refused his invitation, though some of their representatives met

[8] Security Appreciation Ashanti 23.10.55.
[9] Ashanti Pioneer 3.11.55.

Bourne informally the next day. They explained that they refused to meet him formally because of the States Council Bill, the passing of which would prejudge his mission. Feeling was now running so high in Ashanti that the Asantehene threatened to leave the NLM if they did not attempt to curb the violence of their supporters; but in a meeting which was eventually arranged between Bourne and the Asanteman Council, the Asantehene told Bourne that they had nothing to tell him and he could tell them nothing.[10] When the States Council (Ashanti) Bill passed by a large majority on 16 November, Russell wrote angrily to Arden-Clarke 'After several months calm, the cautions expressed in my security appreciations unfortunately proved to be true and a nasty situation again prevails in Ashanti.'[11] The Government's view of this incident is given in Nkrumah's autobiography:

> Sir Frederick, along with many others, felt that the state Councils Ordinance was ill-timed and that it should have been postponed until a later date. But it should be appreciated that the circumstances in the country at that particular time warranted passing into law an ordinance of that nature, when chiefs were being unjustly de-stooled for not supporting the federalist idea. They had no right of appeal and it was high time the Government took measures to protect them from such unfair treatment. If the Bill had been withdrawn, it would have weakened the Assembly, and the chiefs for whose benefit it was being put through, would have suffered at the hands of those who dealt in corruption, violence and injustice.[12]

Bourne paid a second visit to Kumasi at the end of November when, although he was formally boycotted, another private meeting was arranged. At this meeting Akoto introduced a new dimension to the problem. He stated that if there was another election and the NLM gained a majority in Ashanti, even though the CPP gained a majority in the country as a whole, Ashanti would secede.[13]

During these months Arden-Clarke was made aware—both formally and in private letters—of the growing anxiety felt by his staff in Ashanti. Officers serving there, including the most senior, gave very strong backing to the NLM attitudes, and did their best to convince him that the States Council Bill must be repealed. All the heat and venom in the exchanges centred on this Bill, and Russell assured the Governor that as long as it remained there would never be peace in Ashanti. Russell certainly believed that his views and his appreciations of the Ashanti situation were not received sympathetically either by Arden-Clarke or

[10] Rathbone Thesis p. 305.
[11] Letter Russell to Arden-Clarke 22.11.55.
[12] *Autobiography* p. 243.
[13] Security Appreciation 30.11.55.

Nkrumah, and consequently there developed a dangerous rift between the field officers in Ashanti and the Secretariat in Accra.

Lennox-Boyd supported Arden-Clarke, but in a statement in the House of Commons at the end of 1955, in attempting to give a balanced and rounded picture, he gave considerable encouragement to the NLM. He said he had had some sympathy with their past situation, and they knew that Her Majesty's Government wished to be satisfied that the independence constitution would be generally acceptable throughout the country.[14] He used this as an argument to get both sides to co-operate with the Bourne inquiry, but the Ashantis interpreted it very differently, judging correctly that their protest had by-passed Arden-Clarke and had influenced the British Government. On the same day as the Commons debate, *The Times* put forward the suggestion that there should be another election before independence.[15] The Commons debate and the comments of *The Times* deepened the rift between Arden-Clarke and his Ashanti staff. He and Nkrumah had clearly anticipated independence in 1956, and they now began to realize that the NLM had gained sufficient support in the country and in London to make this impossible. The intensity of Arden-Clarke's frustration at the delay in the independence programme clearly accounts for his apparently unsympathetic attitude towards the NLM and towards his own staff in Kumasi. It is matched by the almost desperate attempts of Russell and his deputy Michael Gass[16] to get him to have the States Council Bill repealed. Richard Rathbone quotes a private letter which said:

> Arden-Clarke of course was against the N.L.M. (because he was pro-Nkrumah who couldn't stand anyone to have thoughts) and A-C had a couple of 'yes-men' in Accra, but I would say that the bulk of the service had great sympathy for the N.L.M.[17]

Since 1954 the NLM had demanded an inquiry by an impartial outside observer into the affairs of the Cocoa Marketing Board and the Cocoa Purchasing Company. Arden-Clarke had advised this too, but the CPP—knowing the NLM had damaging inside information—stoutly resisted the demand. For many months, Busia, the NLM's most eloquent leader, had been in England lobbying support. In Whitehall and Westminster, in London, Oxford and the City he used all his contacts and opportunities to publicize his cause. Eventually, and largely because of Busia's efforts, Lennox-Boyd added his backing to Arden-Clarke's and this ensured that an outside inquiry would be held. Nkrumah,

---

[14] Hansard 7.12.55.
[15] *The Times* 7.12.55.
[16] Later Sir Michael Gass, KCMG.
[17] Quoted Rathbone, Thesis, p. 308.

realizing the need to repair his public image, grudgingly agreed though he delayed for several months before making the appointment. In the end Mr Justice Jibowu a distinguished Nigerian lawyer headed the inquiry, but his appointment proved that the NLM had won a significant victory.

Some of the tension of the times, as well as Arden-Clarke's positive and mature leadership, are illustrated when at the Caledonian Society's Dinner, he again proposed the toast 'The Land we live in'. After congratulating the Society on the chivalrous precedent they had set by also inviting Nkrumah, he continued: ·

As Senior *Amateur* Expatriate[18] then let me say this. There seems to be too much of an 'end-of-an-era' mood about these days. Too many of us seem to be working out here as if we were closing down an old family concern and selling up. If this is indeed our mood, I think it is all wrong . . . I am sure if we could regard ourselves as pioneers in helping to establish a new branch of an old family concern, we should feel much happier in our work. It is hard work, I know, but it is well worth the doing . . .

There are plenty of clouds about in the Gold Coast today, and all of us who love 'the land we live in' are surely praying that they will rapidly disperse and allow the Gold Coast sunshine to radiate its warmth all over Africa. No one who has worked in this country for any length of time can have failed to be impressed by the sound common-sense of the man-in-the-street—in which term I include the man-in-the-bush. One of his virtues is also tolerance, that hall-mark of all civilized living. It is a virtue that has not been shining much in recent months. But I am convinced that it is still there waiting to be evoked in all its strength. We must all devoutly wish that it will be evoked quickly, so that the Gold Coast can continue to be the beacon light it has been in the past for all those countries in Africa who are having to pass through the jungle of racial disharmony. [19]

He referred, more light heartedly, to racial disharmony in a letter to his mother describing a visit from Garfield Todd, the Prime Minister of Southern Rhodesia:

He is a liberal minded man, an ex-missionary, and I liked him, and I think he liked what we are trying to do here and wishes us well. I want to get as many South Africans as possible to visit us but so far have not managed to get any Nationalist politicians to come—they fear it would cost them their seats if they were photographed shaking hands with Africans! [20]

In spite of the total boycott by the opposition parties, Bourne issued

---

[18] He regarded the Scots as the professional expatriates.
[19] 30.11.55
[20] Letter 19.9.55.

his report in December 1955. The report rejected the idea of a constituent assembly, since responsibility for the constitution was vested in the cabinet under the Governor and the Secretary of State. It argued that the fragmentation, which would be caused by the NLM proposals, would be a serious mistake, but empowered any of the regions to set up regional assemblies if they wished to do so. The existing regions were East and West Province, the Northern Territories and Ashanti; it was likely that Trans-Volta-Togoland would be added. Bourne made no comment on the more controversial question of the Brong area seceding from Ashanti. He proposed to give delegated powers to the regions with residual powers to the centre, and his report also included a 10 year plan for the development of the Northern Territories.

The Bourne Report proved to be a major disappointment—it achieved nothing and pleased neither side. In the discussions that followed, it emerged fairly clearly that Arden-Clarke's powers were severely circumscribed and that the general initiative had passed to the NLM. After a Christmas lull Nkrumah broadcast to the country on New Year's Day. It was a quietly impressive performance but totally failed to influence the NLM. He said:

> In any democratic country the final decision in national affairs remains with the elected representatives of the people assembled in the national legislature. Similarly, in a fundamental matter such as that of our constitution at independence, the final decision of a fully representative legislature is accepted as having the general agreement of the people and must prevail. Racialism and violence must be completely rejected as an instrument of policy.[21]

At this time Nkrumah also came under pressure from his own party to take more effective action against the NLM. In a speech to the party at Saltpond just before Christmas he had made it plain that if he had controlled the police he could have smashed the NLM, but he added 'that would not be a good step towards our objective of self government which will be granted next year or early in 1957'.[22]

How far the political initiative had passed to the NLM is shown by their reply to Nkrumah's broadcast. Before agreeing to a conference they demanded that it should consider all the constitutional questions and not only the Bourne Report; that an election should be held after the conference and before independence; and that the Secretary of State should guarantee this. They hoped there would be a spirit of compromise and that, as a gesture towards this, the government would repeal the States Council Bill.

In the next few months the situation deteriorated still further. Nkrumah appeared determined to go ahead with the discussion of the Bourne Report and called a conference at Achimota in spite of the total opposition of Ashanti and the North. At the same time he stalled over the appointment of the commission to investigate corruption in the CPC. The Asanteman Council once again demanded a national conference to look into the whole constitutional position prior to independence, and asked Nkrumah how he could claim to represent the whole country when it was more than 18 months since he had dared to come to Ashanti. His reiteration that the final constitutional decisions had to be made by the elected representatives of the people carried little conviction in Ashanti where, they were convinced, the CPP would be completely trounced if there was another election. Nkrumah's reference to the Council as 'feudal tribalists' merely deepened the division. As, with increasing violence spreading across the territory, both sides entrenched their positions, the Asantehene welcomed back the Ashanti Ex-Servicemen's Organization, which apologized for supporting the CPP and repented for their action against the Golden Stool—the symbol of Ashanti nationhood. While there were deep and serious divisions between the two sides, further trouble was caused by unnecessary tactlessness. Just a few days before the Achimota Conference, which was to be boycotted by the whole opposition, Nkrumah appointed a commission made up entirely of CPP members to plan the independence celebrations.

At the Achimota Conference, which started in the Aggrey Memorial Hall on 17 February 1956, the Government was making its final attempt to obtain agreement to the constitutional proposals for independence. Fourteen organizations had been invited but only seven accepted. Some individuals representing the Ex-Servicemen and some Northern Territories Councils did attend the conference, but were immediately disowned by their parent organizations. Floods of protests arrived at Christiansborg Castle, at the Achimota Conference, and at the Colonial Office in London. The strength of these petitions caused further questions in the Commons together with the bland reply that 'Her Majesty's Government hopes the Conference will accept the progress of the Gold Coast towards the attainment of full self-government within the Commonwealth.' Arden-Clarke, although he was on leave at the time, was becoming increasingly enmeshed in the toils of the NLM dispute and, increasingly, losing credibility in the eyes of the Ashanti. During the Conference the Asanteman Council again petitioned him directly, pointing out that Ashanti and the Northern Territories were wholly unrepresented and 'the conclusions of this farcical conference will be unacceptable, and the NLM would not be bound by its decisions.'

At the same time as the Achimota Conference, Arden-Clarke faced another very tricky and potentially dangerous decision. A minor council, prompted by the CPP, had threatened to secede from the Asanteman Council, and the Asantehene himself posed the question whether the Governor would be party to a completely anarchical precedent which would hit at the very foundations of Ashanti society. The lack of a clear answer to this challenge, and the intensity of feeling over the Achimota Conference, were shown in an editorial in the *Ashanti Pioneer* referring to 'the lies told to the Secretary of State about the Achimota buffoonery.'[23]

The deep and genuine fears of the Ashanti people and those of the Northern Territories, that they were being handed over to a government which they had every reason to despise and distrust, and that the Governor himself was conniving at this process, caused almost unbearable tensions and resentment. Gbedemah—Nkrumah's second in command and Finance Minister in the CPP government—increased the tension still further by a speech at Koforidua saying that if Britain did not hand over independence to the Gold Coast, the people of the Gold Coast might be forced to declare themselves independent as the people of the Sudan had recently done. Such remarks, coupled with the blowing up of the Ashanti Royal Mausoleum at Breman, by CPP agents, convinced the Ashantis of what they could expect at independence. This period illustrates a people with sincere, competent and genuine leaders, driven to desperation because there appeared no legal way of getting a fair hearing. Their alarm was now deepened by the belief that the CPP, by depressing the salaries of judges, were deliberately trying to get rid of trustworthy and impartial ex-patriate British Judges—including the Chief Justice, Sir Mark Wilson—and to replace them with CPP nominees. In this highly charged situation Sir Mark managed, inadvertently, to bring a moment of light relief, by making what must be the most dramatic court entrance in history. He was inspecting a new ventilation system in the roof of the High Court Building, when he stepped on a piece of plaster board. He fell through the high ceiling, into the Court below, where fortunately his fall was broken by the canopy over the Judge's chair. The court was in session at the time, but what the prisoner in the dock thought when the Chief Justice descended from on high is not recorded.

The political temperature in Ghana can often be assessed by the amount of interest shown by the British and world press, and early in 1956 an ominous number of articles appeared. Professor Carrington, the distinguished Commonwealth historian, put Ghana's case in wider perspective. He reminded Ghanaians that the road to independence was

[23] 1.3.56.

well-trodden but rather crowded. They were not alone in their difficulties and complications. Malta wanted union with Britain; Cyprus sought union with Greece; Western Nigeria wanted self-government within a federation; the West Indies were forming a federation; and Singapore, Somaliland and Northern Rhodesia all had their urgent problems.

The British press gave increasing detail about the tide of violence in Ashanti, and generally sympathized with the Ashanti uprising under the powerful leadership of the Asantehene, Prempeh II. Kumasi was compared with Chicago, because gunmen in fast cars roamed with impunity, with bombs, bullets, and knives—gelignite was tossed about like confetti. In the wave of violence 13 CPP supporters had been murdered in Kumasi and a similar number of their opponents. The British press echoed the Ghanaian criticism of Nkrumah's new fangled doctrine of democratic centralism. The correspondents maintained that the NLM was gaining increasing support from the Chiefs and their followers, from CPP refugees, from most of the country's intellectuals and, finally, from 'honest men who are sick of the corruption nepotism and patronage that besmirch the government's record.'[24]

Because the opposition had completely boycotted the Achimota Conference, a British parliamentary delegation came out to Kumasi in March. Led by Creech-Jones, the former Labour Colonial Secretary, they invited the NLM to put its case. Dr Kurankyi Taylor presented the case, arguing that the CPP government was corrupt and inefficient, and was attempting to impose a foreign system on the country. Before 1951, the country had been administered on a regional basis but now the central government had too much power and there was insufficient public opinion at a national level to prevent abuse of power. For all these reasons the NLM demanded a federal type of government, and demanded that the people of the Gold Coast should have the right to decide what type of government they were to have at independence.

Joe Appiah a Kumasi barrister,[25] who was to have a long and stormy political life in Ghana, explained to the delegation that as a former CPP leader he knew that the Central Committee of the CPP and not the Cabinet was the real ruler of the country. He alleged that Nkrumah had been trained as a communist by the sister of Sir Alan Burns, the former governor. Appiah also refuted the CPP allegation that the chiefs were feudal reactionaries, maintaining that throughout the Gold Coast the land of the tribes was vested in the stool and not in the Chief, who could be, and often was, removed from the stool. The people were not

---

[24] *News Chronicle* 28.2.56.
[25] Almost an Ashanti Vicar of Bray, he embraced not only the CPP and NLM but after many vicissitudes became a henchman of the detested Acheampong and suffered eclipse with him in 1978.

feudatories of the chiefs. The people respected the Chief because he provided stability, dignity and a sense of continuity, and they rejected Nkrumah's phrase 'We will make the Chiefs run away and leave their sandals behind them.' Representatives of the Northern Territories also put their views to the visiting MPs and claimed that having made legal treaties with the British to establish protectorate status, they required clarification of their status before independence, and an assurance that Britain would not unilaterally alter their treaty relationship.

At the end of their stay Creech-Jones thanked the NLM for presenting their case so competently. The effect of this visit was to step up the pressure against the Accra government and also against Arden-Clarke. Before this the press had been reticent about mentioning him personally but now such restraint disappeared. In April 1956, when Arden-Clarke returned from London, he was fiercely belaboured by NLM supporters for his part in handing on incorrect information to the Colonial Office about the number of groups attending the Achimota Conference. The press, realizing perhaps that this was their last chance to influence opinion in London, dragged up again the indiscreet speech which the Governor had made in 1955 when he condemned the Ashanti interest in a federal type of solution. 'The unfortunate results of his indiscretion are well known and one could not help trusting that Sir Charles had learnt a lesson from this incident . . . A clear answer by Sir Charles as to who misinformed the Colonial Office about those attending the Achimota Conference will help resolve the present tortuous deadlock.'[26]

Arden-Clarke's isolation from Ashanti, and the deep division between him and his senior staff in Kumasi, seemed to be emphasized by the opening of the Ashanti Cultural Centre in Kumasi. This remarkable centre had been built up by a distinguished Ashanti scholar, Alex Kyerematen, who had studied at Keble College Oxford in the late 1940s. The Asantehene and Colin Russell, the Chief Regional Officer for Ashanti, spoke at the opening ceremony and emphasized the achievements, the traditions and the dignity of the proud Ashanti nation. The Governor, significantly, was not present.

Again the London press provided advice for the Governor and expressed concern at the deteriorating situation. *The Economist* in an article headed 'War Drums on the Gold Coast', while suggesting that an election must be held before independence, posed the cruicial—and, as it turned out, accurate—question: 'what would happen if the CPP gained an overall majority in the country, while the NLM gained a majority in Ashanti?'[27] At about the same time *The Observer,* criticizing the eighteenth century partisan virulence of the CPP, also gave warning of

[26] *Ashanti Pioneer* 4.4.56.
[27] *Economist* 14.4.56.

its plans for a one party state and people's courts.[28] It continued in a further article 'It is probably true that the NLM and its allies, united into a national political party will one day provide the Gold Coast with a government more stable, more intelligent and more honest than the one that has brought the country through transition from colonial rule to independence.'[29]

While the Press waged its wordy warfare, the critical decision—whether or not to hold an election—was being handled by Arden-Clarke in London. Ostensibly on leave, he made many visits to Lennox-Boyd and to the Colonial Office, and he was also contacted by Kojo Botsio. Nkrumah had sent Botsio to London to see Lennox-Boyd and to emphasize his strong opposition to the idea of another election. In his autobiography[30] he describes in detail how he instructed Botsio to inform the British Government that he could not in any circumstances agree to an election.

By this time it is clear that Arden-Clarke had made up his mind that another election was the only answer. When he arrived home in February, Norfolk was covered with a deep blanket of snow, but after a week's relaxation he spent the following week in London. He wrote:

> I had a very busy four days in London last week and my efforts were not unproductive. My advice about the action to be taken in the Gold Coast was largely accepted and a memorandum should shortly be going to the (British) Cabinet seeking approval of the courses I have advocated. Then it will be my job to make my Gold Coast Ministers toe the line and do what I think should be done.[31]

In another letter written to his mother at the end of his leave in March he wrote:

> This is my last day at Syleham, a gorgeous spring day with the sun blazing, which makes me hate all the more the thought of returning to the turbulent Gold Coast. Perhaps if all goes well and according to plan, when I return next year it will be for good.[32]

He flew back to Accra with Kojo Botsio, and spent the Easter weekend with Nkrumah and Hadow—who had been Acting-Governor—discussing the implications of the decision to hold an election before independence. Nkrumah, sensing there was no real alternative, accepted it. This decision now involved both Arden-Clarke and Nkrumah in

[28] *Observer* 8.4.56.
[29] *Observer* 15.4.56.
[30] *Autobiography* p. 249.
[31] Letter to Family 25.2.56.
[32] Letter to Mother 26.3.56.

lengthy battles to gain the agreement of the Cabinet. In a personal letter to his wife he vividly described his relationship with Nkrumah:

> What a day it has been—I have had a continuous stream of people since 8.30 a.m. finishing up with a rather overwrought and tired Prime Minister who has just left me (6.30 p.m.) to go and deal with a difficult meeting of his party exeuctive and Ministers. He is going to break the news to them that there is to be a general election and he expects trouble. I think he went off encouraged and fortified: he feels thwarted and frustrated, never able to do what he wants to do as and when he would like and he has not yet developed the quality of patience. At least I can come back to a whisky and a quiet talk with you: he, poor devil, will be dealing with emotional stupidities until the small hours.[33]

The following day, when Nkrumah had failed to carry his cabinet with him, he came back to the Governor, who again wrote vividly to his wife:

> Yesterday was another of those days. The P.M. rang up and asked if I could see his whole cabinet at 10 a.m. I cancelled my appointment for 10 a.m. and up they all trooped and for two hours I wrestled with them. First they did not want a general election or, if there had to be one, let it be in October or later. After much excited debate among themselves and some fairly forceful interpositions by me, it was agreed that there must be a general election and that it should be held as early as possible. Then it had to be decided whether the initiative for this decision should seem to come from the P.M., as the P.M., the Secretary of State and I had arranged, with the P.M. getting all the kudos for a statesmanlike and democratic decision, or whether the Secretary of State should first make it clear that there could be no independence without first holding a general election on the constitutional issue and then the P.M. announcing he would have one. Despite its manifest disadvantages and the resultant loss of kudos to the P.M. they all agreed that things would be easier for them with their supporters and back benchers if the second alternative was adopted. So I drafted and sent off a long telegram to the Secretary of State explaining the position and asking him to make an appropriate statement on the 10th or 11th, i.e., after the (Togoland) plebiscite and before the Assembly meets on 15th.

In the afternoon Professor Busia came to the Castle to say that he and the Asantehene might persuade the NLM to compromise on the constitutuional issue provided another conference was called and was followed immediately by a general election. Arden-Clarke told him he had left it too late, and concluded:

[33] Letter to Lady Arden-Clarke 1.5.56.

I wonder how many wriggles and shifts I shall have to deal with. [34]

During the weeks between his return from leave and the general election of July 1956, Arden-Clarke once again showed his unerring grasp of affairs and gave that firm and confident leadership which prevented a highly dangerous situation developing. In a general letter to his family he gave an admirably lucid description of the whole complex series of negotiations. The letter also shows how totally he was committed to the legislative programme leading to independence in 1957:

Since my last letter there has been considerable activity on the Gold Coast political front. As I think you know, I had to spend a considerable part of my leave battling with the politicians in Westminster and the officials in Whitehall to make them see that an early General Election on the issue of the form of constitution under which the Gold Coast should become independent was the only way to break the deadlock between the political parties in the Gold Coast and that the British Government must abide by the result of such an election without attaching conditions regarding the size of the majority in each region, etc., etc. Eventually this was approved by the U.K. Cabinet, and the Secretary of State agreed to make a statement in the House of Commons about this at the appropriate time. When I came back here I had to join battle with my Cabinet who were all strongly opposed to having a General Election. After a long tussle I got their agreement to a General Election if the Secretary of State would first make his statement in the House. This statement he made on Thursday last (10th). He stuck to the text he had been given and it was well received by all parties in the House. Yesterday Saturday 12th the Cabinet here approved the draft which I had prepared for them of the 'Speech from the Throne' which I read when I open the meeting of the Assembly on Tuesday the 15th. In it I announce that the Assembly will be dissolved and a General Election will be held on July 19th and 24th. As the Speech sets out briefly what has been happening on the political front here during the past 18 months, you may be interested to have a copy. The C.P.P. who at present have an overwhelming majority in the Legislative Assembly and have two more years to go before their statutory term of office expires naturally hate the idea of putting their seats in jeopardy before they have to and will be very angry with me for forcing a General Election on them. However, that can't be helped.

The next round in the battle will be when I go to the Northern Territories and hold a big durbar for all the Northern Chiefs on the 29th May. The Chiefs do not want to lose their protectorate status and rather than lose it they would like the independence of this country deferred. I shall have to tell them that they have no future except as an

[34] Letter to Lady Arden-Clarke 3.5.56.

integral part of an independent Gold Coast, that the country will soon be independent and that they will then lose their protectorate status. This they will not like.

I never realised what a prolonged battle I would have with the politicians and chiefs and people of this country in order to give them the independence for which they have been clamouring all these years. Now they are going to have it whether they like it or not!

Last Tuesday 8th, I went off to Ho for three nights to watch the conduct of the Togoland Plebiscite. This went off extremely well. It was extremely well organised and run and the people behaved with the greatest restraint and showed a real sense of responsibility. In fact, such was the sense of decorum, that when visiting some of the polling stations, it was like going into a Church and I felt I ought to take my hat off and whisper. There was a heavy poll of over 80% of the registered voters and out of the 160,000 votes cast throughout Togoland as a whole, there was a majority of 25,000 for union with the Gold Coast. The North was solid for union but in the South there was an overall majority for separation from the Gold Coast. This will cause a lot of fun and games in the United Nations Assembly when they meet to decide the future of British Togoland in December next. There is, of course, only one practical solution—that is for the whole of British Togoland to be joined with the Gold Coast but that will not stop a lot of the anti-colonial representatives in the United Nations putting forward idiotic schemes for administering the Southern part of Togoland as a separate unit.

On my way back from Ho on Friday the 11th, I visited the site of the Volta Bridge. The arms of the huge steel arch which is to span the river are being built out from each bank simultaneously and they hope to get the arch completed about the middle of July. They have promised to let me know the day the two arms will join and Gina and I will go and watch the operation.

I am afraid this is a very political letter. As a tail-piece, here is the description given by young Cumming-Bruce, aged four, to his mother of the Queen's Birthday Parade—he knows me as he comes bathing with us sometimes on Sundays—'That nice uncle wore a fevver in his hat and looked at the soldiers to see if their buttons were sewn on right.'[35]

Intense pressure from the NLM had forced the governments both in London and Accra to agree to a general election prior to independence, but when the date of the election was announced they soon began to realize that their position was not strong, and once again they proved inept and ineffective in the practical work of running an election campaign. Their election forecasts proved to be wildly inaccurate and far too optimistic. There had been talk of secession and, if the NLM had swept

[35] Letter to Family 13.5.56

the board in Ashanti, Arden-Clarke would have faced another serious crisis. Their over confidence prompted them to write to the Governor demanding that, if they and their political allies gained 52 seats or more (i.e., in a majority of one), they would expect him to call on Dr Busia to form a government. This letter—published in the *Daily Graphic*—later restricted their political manoeuvres. At the same time the Asantehene expressed concern to Colin Russell that if the CPP won the election they might send the army in to Ashanti and deport him, as the British had done to his predecessor in 1896. Russell, with wry humour, said he found it difficult to reassure the Asantehene since one of the CPP Ministers had discussed that very issue the previous week.[36]

Although the NLM had gained considerable support in London in the previous months, they lacked any political support for further action. On 11 May 1956 Lennox-Boyd had announced in the House of Commons that 'The British Government will be willing to accept a motion calling for the independence of the Gold Coast, backed by a reasonable majority in the newly elected Gold Coast Assembly, and will then declare a firm date for this purpose.'[37] Creech-Jones immediately associated the opposition with this statement and in doing so made it plain that as far as Westminster was concerned there was little point in any further discussion of the major issues.

On 15 May Arden-Clarke opened the new session of the Legislative Assembly with full ceremonials, a Lancer escort, guard of honour and fanfare of trumpets. It was a tense moment, for the CPP—both ministers and members—had been strongly opposed to another election. The Governor quickly sketched in the constitutional background and then announced that the Assembly would be dissolved and an election held. He wrote:

> I had expected that the speech would be received in disapproving silence by the Government backbenchers. On the contrary, it met with uproarious applause from them and it was the ranks of the opposition that looked glum and disconsolate . . . any stranger going into the House during the speech would have gained the impression that a General Election was the dearest wish of all the Government backbenchers.[38]

Almost immediately after the formal opening of the legislature, Arden-Clarke took on the difficult task of formally telling the Chiefs of the Northern Territories that they would have to accept a centralized independent Ghana, and that their protectorate treaty rights with Britain

[36] Rathbone. Thesis p. 339.
[37] Hansard 11.5.56.
[38] Letter to Family 27.5.56.

would not be continued. His own comment was 'The Speech itself is couched in reasonably diplomatic language, and the pill is concealed in a lot of verbal jam.'[39] The chiefs took a clear, firm and honest stand on their treaty rights with Great Britain, and Arden-Clarke had only one really effective argument—that it was unthinkable to leave the Northern Territories in tutelage while the rest of the country became independent. He embroidered and elaborated this argument in a dozen different ways and mixed it with joviality, bonhomie and pure bluff, and in achieving a measure of success, he made a vital personal contribution to solving this intractable problem.

The formal Durbar in Tamale took place on Tuesday 29 May but it was followed on the Wednesday by less formal meetings with the Chiefs. Arden-Clarke writing to his wife said:

> It was really very satisfactory and I think at last they have begun to grasp the elementary facts of life, that the North must remain an integral part of the Gold Coast, and that when independence is granted it automatically and inevitably loses its Protectorate status . . . The most difficult part of a meeting like that is to sit patiently for hours and listen to a lot of foolishness endlessly repeated and then at the end refrain from saying a lot of things one would like to say.[40]

Later he gave a more detailed description of this very important occasion, in a letter to the family:

> The Durbar at Tamale was a terrific affair—the biggest they had ever had in the North. Everything was done with the greatest pomp and ceremony. They had built a circle of stands and grass shelters about quarter of a mile in circumference to accommodate the Chiefs and their retinues and the spectators. It was estimated that there were about 25,000 people present. I wore my blue uniform for the occasion and arrived at the Durbar Ground escorted by my colourful lancers. The soldiers had mounted a Guard of Honour and the Regimental Band was present. I mounted my special dais, took the Royal Salute, inspected the Guard of Honour and then took the Salute as the troops marched off. Then I went to walk slowly round the stands to greet and shake hands with all the Chiefs. This was when I got really hot as there was a strong sun and I was cut off from the breeze and surrounded by people. It took quite a time before I could get back to the dais. Then it was the Chiefs' turn, and each Chief came up under his umbrella with his retinue, preceded in some cases by drummers and dancers, to return my greetings and shake hands again with me as I stood in front of my dais. After that I could at last sit down and listen to a short

---

[39] *Ibid.*
[40] Letter to Lady Arden-Clarke 31.5.56.

speech of welcome read by the Chairman of the Northern Territories
Council. As I sat I got the full benefit of the breeze and soon began to
cool off. I then delivered my own speech and read it sitting. This took
quite a time as it had to be translated sentence by sentence into
Dagbani. The end of my speech marked the end of the Durbar. The
band played The Queen and I drove off with my escort. The speech
had contained a lot of very unpalatable information but there was no
reaction to it at the Durbar itself. I think everyone was too impressed
with all the ceremonial and I was glad to see that all the Chiefs were
also dressed in all their finery and had put on all their robes and were
in many cases even hotter than I was. The whole show took about two
hours. Within a few minutes of getting back to the Residency I was
wallowing in the swimming pool there. I expected trouble next day
when I had an informal meeting with the Chiefs which lasted three
hours but on the whole, they had taken their medicine well and the
general opinion was they would have to accept the advice I had given
them on behalf of the British Government. One or two rude speeches
were made by young politicians ostensibly speaking on behalf of their
Chiefs but the Chiefs themselves seemed to accept as inevitable what
had been said. The best thing was that they made it quite clear that
they had dropped all idea that the North should secede from the Gold
Coast, an idea that was uppermost in their minds when I was last in
the North.

The broadcast I made last Tuesday telling the country that everyone
had got to behave themselves properly and that the General Election
must be peaceful and orderly seems to have gone down quite well.
Musa, my boy, who is an illiterate and whose knowledge of English is
fragmentary, said that he was going to listen. When I got back from
Broadcasting House I asked him what he had heard. He said 'Master,
he speak fine—he say no one fit go make palaver for this election. He
tell Chiefs and everyone what they do. If they no do, they catch
trouble.' I thought that was an admirable summary of what I was
trying to get across and I only hope that that is what the ordinary man
in the street understood.[41]

While the Governor was in Tamale the Assembly debated the new constitutional proposals, which were very close to the recommendations of
the Bourne Report, and included the division of the country into six
regions, and the constitutional safeguard of a two thirds majority before
the Assembly could be dissolved. At independence there would be a
Governor General appointed by the Queen. Gbedemah had been asked if
Arden-Clarke would be the first, and had answered 'No, that would not
do, as people would not realize there had been a change'. At this time
Lady Arden-Clarke found the climate very trying and her stays in Accra

---

[41] Letter to Family 9.6.56.

were usually limited to about four months, and the Governor was certainly looking forward to retirement after independence. Commenting on Gbedemah's remarks he said 'This is what I have told ministers here more than once and you will be relieved to notice that it seems to have sunk home.'[42]

On Tuesday 5 June 1956, the Governor dissolved the Assembly, announced the date of the election—17 July, with an additional day, 12 July, for the Northern Territories—and broadcast to the nation. In addition he spent much of the day intervening in a violent dispute over whether the NLM could use the cocoa tree as an election symbol. He commented that under the pressures of an election his Ministers were going more lunatic than ever, and concluded 'I feel like a schoolmaster dealing with a bunch of naughty and truculent schoolboys: I wish I could use the cane on them.'[43]

In the period before the election on 17 July most of the country remained calm though, as expected, Ashanti did not. There were a number of murders and ambushes carried out by Action Troopers, whom Arden-Clarke had specifically condemned in his broadcast. He realized that there might be some trouble in Ashanti after the election if some die-hard Chiefs decided to go down fighting, but in describing the pre-election situation, he preserved his good-humoured and unruffled calm.

There is plenty of loud flamboyant talk but I anticipate the bark will prove much worse than the bite. There are cases of gangs of toughs and hooligans being collected and of Ju-Ju ceremonies being performed, which will make them invulnerable, by turning bullets aimed at them to water, and cutlasses and bayonets used against them to paper. Two of them were so impressed by the efficacy of these rites that they invited a friend to shoot at them with a shot gun. He did so and they are both in Kumasi hospital having pellets extracted.[44]

[42] Letter to Family 25.5.56.
[43] Letter to Family 5.6.56.
[44] Letter to Family 15.7.56.

CHAPTER TWELVE
Independence

The election on 17 July passed off peacefully enough even in Ashanti, and the results left little doubt that the CPP would demand a clear run to independence. Once again, in spite of all the criticism of their corruption and incompetence, and in spite of the active campaigning of the opposition parties in Ashanti and the North, the CPP had shown that they were the only countrywide party. Gaining 57 per cent of seats overall, they polled 43 per cent in Ashanti against the NLMs 57 per cent, and in the Northern Territories they even increased their vote to 44 per cent. *The Times* in an editorial, which generally reflected outside opinion, felt it was reasonable for Lennox-Boyd and Arden-Clarke to go ahead with a programme for independence. Not unexpectedly, Busia, the NLM leader, believed that the election had given a clear mandate for a federal form of government. Arden-Clarke's own view was:

> The result was not all I had hoped for. I had expected the CPP to get back, but with a reduced majority. Instead they are back with a dangerously large majority which in the absence of a strong and effective opposition may lead them to do foolish things. The new opposition is much superior to the last in the quality of intellect and debating power. Despite its numerical inferiority, 32 against the C.P.P.'s 72 it could still play a potent and effective role. [1]

By mid July the Cabinet had resigned and Arden-Clarke had reappointed Nkrumah as Prime Minister. With few changes, the new Cabinet tackled the independence issue with vigour and determination, but the opposition had still not given up the fight. The Ejisuhene wrote to Arden-Clarke and demanded, on behalf of his people, a conference to decide on an acceptable constitution. The Asante Youth Association cabled both to Arden-Clarke and the Secretary of State demanding a federal constitution. The Muslim Association Party, which in early 1955 had requested Arden-Clarke's recall because it was impossible to trust his judgement, kept up the demand for a federal solution.

On 1 August 1956 the Governor opened the new Assembly, and the occasion produced a major blunder by the opposition. During the previous session they had frequently boycotted the Assembly and had

[1] Letter to Family 12.8.56.

gained a reputation for acting irresponsibly. Now at the ceremonial opening of the new session of the Assembly, only two of the opposition were present. The explanation was not some major constitutional strategy, but they had been prevented by the dense crowds from reaching Parliament House in time. They maintained that they were afraid to leave their cars and walk, through fear of violence. Busia personally apologized to Arden-Clarke, but the incident made them a laughing stock in Accra and did nothing to improve their image. In the debate on the motion for independence, Braimah—not a major opposition spokesman—moved an amendment regretting the motion for independence, because there was not an agreed constitution, because the government had failed to publish the Jibowu report, and because the government had failed to take action against widespread corruption in the public service. The CPP government comfortably defeated the amendment by 69—32. Although they were defeated, the opposition kept up their claims for further constitutional discussions and compared the CPP action—backed by Arden-Clarke—to the early days of Hitler and Hindenburg.

Having successfully completed the election and started the new session of the Assembly, the Governor and Nkrumah were clearly taken aback at the continuing and intensified opposition by the NLM. It took its first stand at a monster meeting in Kumasi, attended by every opposition member of the Assembly, and was addressed in sombre tones by its leaders. Amponsah declared that nothing short of federation would satisfy them—arguing that three out of the four regions in the country favoured federation. Members of the Assembly gave examples of how they had been jostled and stoned by the crowds in Accra, and told to go back home; this sort of treatment did not encourage them to place their destiny in the hands of the CPP. At the same time, in the Assembly, the government were charged with changing the electoral registers in order to prevent people voting. Gbedemah, answering for the government, gave a weak and evasive reply, which totally failed to satisfy the house, and gave a clear indication that malpractices were being openly condoned.

Arden-Clarke again became involved in fierce personal criticism. The NLM in August 1956 sent an impressive delegation to London to see the Secretary of State to explain 'their serious lack of confidence in the role of His Excellency the Governor.' They were convinced that Busia's previous visit to Lennox-Boyd had been successful, and they were further encouraged when in August *The Times* took up their cause, demanding that the CPP should grasp the opportunity to settle the constitutional differences prior to independence.[2] At this stage Arden-Clarke's reaction was blunt and categoric:

[2] *The Times* 9.8.56.

I am telling the Secretary of State what I expect him to do with the delegation from the Opposition Parties which is to visit London in the near future. The delegation proposes to make their case that a constitution on a federal basis must be agreed before independence is granted. I hope the Secretary of State will tell them plainly and categorically that the results of the Election have given a mandate for the immediate grant of independence under a unitary form of constitution and that they had better go and discuss with their own government their constitutional proposals in a spirit of compromise.[3]

Later in the month came the most serious criticism of Arden-Clarke. The *Ashanti Pioneer* maintained that he had failed because he was guided by sheer optimism rather than experience. It added 'Senile decay to be more precise. A canker is eating into the opposition's confidence in the role of the Governor, with his fanatical support of Nkrumah.'[4]

Instead of clearing the air the election seemed to increase the oppressiveness of the torrid August humidity in Accra. Joe Appiah now took up the cudgels on another issue. The investigation into corruption and malpractices in the Cocoa Marketing Board and the Cocoa Purchasing Company had been conducted by Mr Justice Jibowu. The opposition became suspicious when in August 1956, and before the report was published, the *Accra Evening News*—the organ of the CPP—began to heap abuse on Mr Jibowu. Appiah voiced the general feeling that the CPP abuse was deplorable, and that Arden-Clarke should restrain them from insulting Mr Jibowu.

The Jibowu Report, published on 1 September 1956 gave powerful ammunition to the NLM. It found that the Government could not escape the charge of conniving at and condoning irregularities, both in the Cocoa Marketing Board and in the Cocoa Purchasing Company. It also found that Mr Djin, who had employed vast numbers of his relatives and friends in these organizations, was not a suitable person to hold high office. Djin almost immediately admitted that he had defrauded the CPC, and the NLM made the most of the uproar that this caused, demanding that Arden-Clarke should take action and enforce the resignation of Nkrumah and Gbedemah, because of their involvement in the case. The CPP sat tight and let the storm pass, but their image suffered severely, and much of the London press—notably the *Daily Express* and the *Daily Telegraph*—ran articles highly critical of Arden-Clarke, for hustling the Gold Coast to independence while corruption was tolerated at the highest level.

While the press showed genuine concern at the trend of events in the Gold Coast, the flurry of interest was caused in part by the vigorous and

---

[3] Letter to Lady Arden-Clarke 26.8.56.
[4] *Ashanti Pioneer* 25.8.56.

powerful lobbying of the NLM and its allies in London. Busia visited Lennox-Boyd in mid September and also, in a letter to *The Times* on 11 September, presented a dignified appeal for differences to be settled before independence. At the same time it appears likely that the harsh criticism of the *Daily Telegraph* stemmed from the influence of General Spears. A right wing Tory and former MP for Carlisle, he wielded tremendous power in the Ashanti Goldfields and used his substantial influence to thwart the whole move towards independence. His total failure to move with the times and his arrogant and reactionary attitude towards Africans, illustrates one, at least, of the attitudes with which Arden-Clarke had to cope. On one occasion when Arden-Clarke had received a high level deputation of TUC and Labour party representatives from Britain, and a visit to the mines had been arranged, Spears stepped in and forbade them to set foot in the mines area. Arden-Clarke contacted another mines representative, Colonel Bean, and said 'For God's sake can't you put some sense into him.' Spears, with Ashanti Goldfields money ran the *Ashanti Times*, and hoped through his activities to save the colony for the British Empire. He is still remembered in Ghana as a cantankerous reactionary eccentric.

Throughout their long association Arden-Clarke had always been Nkrumah's mentor, and had provided the firmness and stability that Nkrumah so signally lacked. In April he had had to redraft Nkrumah's reply to Lennox-Boyd pledging in writing that another election would be held. Arden-Clarke added 'he is now committed too deeply to do any last minute wriggle.' Nkrumah had also drafted a Speech from the Throne but Arden-Clarke thought it was quite hopeless and rewrote it. The role of master and pupil continued virtually to the end, but their close and trusting relationship, which had endured for five years and had achieved so much for the country, in September 1956 reached a moment of supreme triumph—indeed a moment of the greatest significance in the history of Africa.

Lady Arden-Clarke had returned to Norfolk in mid September, and the details of these triumphant days are told vividly and unforgettably in letters which the Governor wrote to her at 6 o'clock every morning.

Sunday 16.9.56

I have been having a hectic time since you left, with 'immediate' and 'emergency' telegrams flashing to and from the Secretary of State, with Nkrumah in a flat spin and ready to do foolish things. The S. of S. (Secretary of State) was doing a wobble and wanting to defer announcing a firm date for Independence, while I was insisting that the announcement must be made before the Assembly rises on Tuesday next (18th). Yesterday the S. of S. surrendered with the words 'I feel you have left me no alternative'—he was right, I hadn't! So listen to the B.B.C. news on Tuesday and you should hear a bit about the Gold Coast.

Later. I got interrupted there darling and now it's 6.p.m. We had a pleasant beach party with Sue, Snappy, Anne and the Cumming-Bruces with their two delightful kids. When I got back to the Castle Hammy (Mr Eric Hamilton, A.D.C. to the Governor) suddenly remarked that there was an official envelope marked 'Immediate' for me which he had forgotten to bring with him, and he went off to fetch it. I knew what it was—the text of the S. of S.'s despatch fixing a firm date for independence—and I put it unopened into my pocket, much to the disgust of Frame-Smith who was bursting with curiosity. After curry I read it alone in my dressing-room. I wish you could have been there, darling—it is the culmination of seven years hard, anxious and exciting work and I couldn't help a thrill of triumph and achievement. If I could feel like that, I wonder how Nkrumah will feel when I tell him tomorrow afternoon and how the Assembly members will behave when the announcement is made in the House on Tuesday morning. A cool head will be needed at the top, so after tea I went for a strenuous solitary walk to look at State House, the P.M.'s Residence, the new Stadium buildings and the beginnings of the Independence Memorial Archway—all being built to celebrate the telegram in my trouser pocket. I shall have to see to it that my children do not smirch the record or throw their 'freedom' away between now and Independence Day. [5]

The next letter, which is quoted in full, illustrates not only the details of dramatic historical events but something else, which played a very significant part in Arden-Clarke's career and in his success—his love and devotion to his wife, and the happy marriage which sustained and fortified him throughout these tempestuous years.

Accra
Tuesday 18th September

My own darling,

I am adopting my former habit of writing to you as soon as I get up in the morning—it seems the only hour of the day when one can be sure of not being interrupted.

Today we make history in Ghana—at noon the P.M. will ask the Speaker's leave to interrupt the debate in the Assembly in order to make an important statement. He will then say that the publication has been authorised of two despatches, the Governor's despatch asking that a firm date for the independence of Ghana be fixed, and the S. of S's reply. He will then read the S. of S's despatch which promises independence to Ghana on 6th March 1957. He will then move the adjournment of the House to give time for serious reflection, 'At this turning point in the history of this country', and promise a further

[5] Letter 16.9.56.

statement about the Government's plans when the House resumes tomorrow.

I had the P.M. up to my office yesterday afternoon after the debate on the Jibowu Commission's Report had been concluded in the Assembly, and showed him the text of the S. of S's despatch which had been telegraphed to me on Sunday and which he had not seen.

It came as a surprise to him as he had never really believed that an announcement would be made so soon, though he knew I was battling with the S. of S. to get it. After he had read the text of the despatch he looked up and said in a rather awed voice 'H.E. that's nice'. I reminded him of our first meeting alone together after he came out of prison, when I had said that there were two men who could break this experiment in five minutes, he and I, and there were two men who could make it a success, he and I, though I thought it would take a bit longer than five minutes—now here was the result and it had taken us five years. 'We must have a party to celebrate this' said he. 'Not yet' I replied 'we have got to plan how this situation is to be handled.' So I called Hadow in and we made our plan, and while Hadow went off to draft a telegram to the S. of S. I dictated the outline of what the P.M. should say in the House at noon today. It was rather a solemn and subdued little man that left my office. He promised that he would not divulge the contents of the despatch to anyone—I wonder if he has managed to keep his promise. He took no copy of the despatch away with him. He comes to me again at 11 o'clock this morning to collect the copies of the two despatches for distribution to the M.L.As (Members of the Legislative Assembly) after he has made his statement, and to make final arrangements for a press release and wireless bulletin, and then he goes down to the House for his great moment, which in his own words is 'going to come as a shock to all of us.'

I wish you could have been here for this, belovedest,

All love my precious
Your Charles.

The dramatic story continues in another letter written the following morning:

I wonder if you listened to the B.B.C. news at one o'clock yesterday when the Gold Coast took precedence even of Suez.

Everything went according to plan. The Assembly was debating the Opposition's Motion demanding the resignation or dismissal of the P. M., Gbedemah and Ako Adjei, and the Government Amendment expressing complete confidence in them, when at 11 o'clock the P.M. slipped out of the House and came up to the Castle with Daniel Chapman and Moxon. The last two, of course, had not got a clue what all this was about. I explained the position to them, told them what had to be done, and gave them copies of the despatches, 120 to

Chapman for distribution to the M.L.A.'s and 350 to Moxon for the press, broadcasting and general publicity. As Moxon rose to go he turned to the P.M. and to me and said 'May I offer you my congratulations' and shook hands with us—later he told Frame-Smith 'I was the first to shake their hands and that is going into my book': the number of people who are going to write their reminiscences of the Gold Coast is legion.[6] The P.M. got back to the House at about ten to twelve. I could not of course be there but I had sent Hindle and Frame-Smith to watch and report, and the latter has promised to write a description which I will send you. On the stroke of noon the P.M. rose from his seat—the Member speaking sat down—and he asked the Speaker's leave to make an important announcement. He went slowly to the Despatch Box and, looking up at the clock began, as I had suggested, 'With effect from mid-day today the publication has been authorized of two despatches' etc. Not a soul knew what was coming and the House was silent until the impact of what was being said hit them, and when the date was announced, 6th March 1957, the Government benches went mad, while the Opposition sat in shocked silence. The best thing happened at the end, when Dombo, the Deputy Leader of the Opposition, rose and offered his congratulations—I didn't think he had it in him—and added that he hoped there would be an agreed constitution by 5th March. If he meant what he said—and it was completely spontaneous and unrehearsed—this is hopeful.

In the afternoon the P.M. rang up and asked if he could bring the whole Cabinet up to see me 'and perform a Custom'. They all turned up about five. Archie (Casely-Hayford) made a laudatory speech and I replied, and then we repaired outside under the tower and stood in a cluster while a bottle of whisky was opened, a tumbler of neat spirit was filled, and Gbedemah poured a libation to the Gods of Ghana while making a long recitative in Twi. This over, I gave them all champagne and we laughed and chatted for a while until they left just before six.[7]

This description, written within hours of the events has a freshness and immediacy that is lacking from Nkrumah's description which appeared some time later in his autobiography, in the chapter 'The Hour of Triumph'.

Congratulations both to Arden-Clarke and Nkrumah poured into Accra from all over the world. He particularly cherished two of these. James Griffiths—Colonial Secretary when he was appointed Governor in 1949—wrote 'On reading the news of the conferment of independence on the Gold Coast my first thought is of you. Permit me to offer you my sincere congratulations on this very great achievement. You have shown

---

[6] In fact there are pitifully few reminiscences of these historic days, although James Moxon remained in Ghana until 1979 and wrote a book on the Volta Lake.
[7] Letter 19.9.56.

qualities of statesmanship which will earn a niche of its own in the history of our Commonwealth.'[8] The second came from Malcolm MacDonald, who had been involved in Arden-Clarke's appointment to Bechuanaland in 1936, and had been Governor General of Malaya and British Borneo when he was in Sarawak:

> My Dear Charles,
>   I meant to write to you before this to congratulate you very warmly on the wonderful culmination of all your statesmanship in the Gold Coast, in the decision that the country shall become independent in the Commonwealth early next year. I remember so well the frightful state of affairs there when you were torn from us in Sarawak and sent to West Africa. Your achievement since is so remarkable that it has a touch of the miraculous. One of the things that I like is the way in which you yourself have kept in the background, so far as publicity is concerned, though you have been in the very forefront of the work. I need not write at length about the various good aspects of your efforts, but merely express the deep gratitude of one British citizen, and an old colleague, to a great Governor who has performed a historic task. You have really shed some light into the dark continent and I hope that it may spread . . . I hope you have enjoyed it all and also that you will continue to preside over the destiny of Ghana during its earliest period as an independent state. They will need you badly . . .
>   Warmest regards to you and your wife,
>   and every good wish
>   Yours ever
>   Malcolm[9]

The period of joy and elation at the announcement of independence was shortlived, and the Opposition quickly turned to fierce and violent measures to prevent or at least delay independence under a CPP government. The NLM leaders, turning to desperate measures while there was time, resolved to prepare for a completely separate government at independence. They put forward the telling argument that if Lennox-Boyd could consider the partition of Cyprus—less than one tenth the size of Ghana—on ethnic grounds, he should consider the equally strong ethnic divisions in Ghana.

In addition to the formidable and growing problems presented by the intransigent opposition of the NLM, Arden-Clarke now had the daunting responsibility of preparing the constitutional instruments for independence and at the same time making the detailed preparations for the independence celebrations. The true relationship he had with Nkrumah and the CPP is vividly portrayed during these weeks. Within days of the independence announcement he wrote:

[8] Letter 19.9.56.
[9] Letter 1.10.56.

I settled down with the P.M., three other Ministers, Hadow and the Attorney-General to tackle the details of the constitution . . . For three hours we disposed of one bit of lunacy after another and got precisely nowhere with the real job. In the end they decided to go and tackle the job by themselves over the weekend and God knows what sort of nonsense they are going to make of it. As the party broke up we got an account of a Press Conference held by Dombo, the Deputy Leader of the Opposition, which annoyed everyone by its stupidity and truculence. The Ministers wanted to reply in kind but I told them to ignore it and to carry on in the manner agreed. [10]

Early in 1956, realizing that the Jibowu Report would be critical of the CPP Arden-Clarke advised Nkrumah to get hold of an able lawyer to handle the case. Nkrumah accepted this advice, and shortly afterwards Geoffrey Bing came out as his legal adviser. He was ultimately to wield great influence over Nkrumah but at this time he was not well known. Arden-Clarke's comments show that he did not altogether approve of him:

Yesterday afternoon was taken up with yet another long constitutional excercise, when with Hadow and Patterson, I worked through the draft of a model constitution which Nkrumah has produced with the aid of his personal constitutional adviser, Bing. Bing, half Irish, half Chinese, is an ex-Bevanite Labour M.P. and a clever lawyer. There did not seem to be much wrong with his draft constitution except that nearly all the difficult and controversial points were left to be dealt with by subsequent acts of the Ghana Parliament. I expect the legal advisers of the Colonial Office will have a fit when they see it as it departs from the stereotyped form. [11]

His prognostication proved right. Within two weeks the Colonial Office rejected the constitution which Nkrumah and Bing had prepared, with its high flown aphorisms about fundamental human rights, and simply announced that they would amend the existing constitution to make Ghana independent.

The virulent opposition of the NLM tended to throw the CPP and the Governor together, but he still had major disagreements with the Cabinet over some important issues. A Salaries Revision Commission had been appointed to deal with the Civil Service salaries at independence, but suddenly the Cabinet decided to cancel it. Arden-Clarke felt strongly about this and feared that there might be few expatriate civil servants left at independence. He wrote:

Now, for no comprehensible reason the Cabinet decide to go back on their word and cancel the whole thing. It's just heart breaking. I can

[10] Letter to Lady Arden-Clarke 25.9.56.
[11] Letter to Family 27.9.56.

probably bully them into changing their minds—but what of the future?[12]

Concern for the future features also in his next letter:

In the afternoon I had to read the riot act to the P.M. The P.M. is getting a very tired man and is having a lot of difficulty with his colleagues. I have told him that if he cannot carry his colleagues with him over the Salaries Commission I shall want to see them all myself. What an endless battle it is trying to stop them doing the wrong things! As the P.M. said at the end—'H.E., I am worried about the future. I can come and talk to you about these things but what is to happen when you have gone?'[13]

The issue of the Salaries commission was finally dealt with the following day when the Governor had a meeting with the whole Cabinet.

The P.M. could not persuade them to change their minds about cancelling the Salaries Commission. He rang me up and said it was not worth my seeing them as they would not budge. However I insisted on seeing them and after an hour they saw sense and did change their minds, bless them, but it was an exhausting business.[14]

Compensation for expatriate officers had been worked out on a reasonably generous basis of a pension plus a lump sum, and many experienced officers realized that they would have to start a new career and the sooner they did it the better. Arden-Clarke was worried because so many officers were leaving that it was becoming increasingly difficult to keep the government machine running efficiently, and he saw clearly that if the Salaries Commission had been wound up, the situation would have been disastrous.

Having settled this crisis and launched the programme for the independence celebrations, he left to go on trek to the south west of the colony, through Sekondi, to the border of the Ivory Coast. In what had been a sadly neglected area he was glad to visit a number of projects bringing real benefits to the people—bridge construction works, new road works, water boring operations and new agricultural developments in the Axim and Half Assini area (he added he would like to have done something for the other half!). Finally, he inspected the operations where Gulf Oil were drilling for oil. As ever, he enjoyed being away from the office and trekking out in the bush.

Early in November 1956 Arden-Clarke left to spend his final leave visiting old friends in South Africa and in the High Commission Territories. He met Lady Arden-Clarke in Nairobi and they travelled on

[12] Letter to Lady Arden-Clarke 2.10.56.
[13] Letter to Lady Arden-Clarke 4.10.56.
[14] Letter to Lady Arden-Clarke 5.10.56.

to Johannesburg and Durban. From there they left on a leisurely fishing and walking holiday through Natal, the Drakensburg Mountains and at Maseru in Basutoland. While his wife stayed on in Basutoland, he returned to Accra on 18 December.

Arden-Clarke returned to Accra to face a major constitutional crisis which had been brewing since the date of independence had been announced. Busia who sought the Governor's advice on whether he should leave politics and pursue an academic career, accepted the leadership of the NLM and in September 1956 had written to *The Times* in a conciliatory vein, but had suggested that Lennox-Boyd should visit the Gold Coast to resolve the outstanding differences. As early as October Arden-Clarke had positively opposed this suggestion, taking the line that it must be settled locally, because at this stage of political development it would seriously detract from Nkrumah's government if the British government intervened. Although NLM spokesmen had already threatened secession, the two sides met in October, initially in a reasonable and friendly atmosphere. The conference dragged on into November with disputes over the flag, the coat of arms and even the name of the new state. The real point of dispute—a federal constitution—was never near to agreement, though the Opposition tried to get round the problem by proposing that the Police should be controlled by the Regions, and that there should only be four regions and not the five proposed by the CPP. The two sides were still far apart when in mid November the Assembly debated Independence—another debate boycotted by the Opposition. Almost immediately the NLM and its allies resolved to ask Britain to recognize Ashanti and the Northern Territories as separate independent states on 6 March 1957. They sent a ten-point plan to Lennox-Boyd asking for Ashanti and the Northern Territories to be recognized as a separate member of the Commonwalth and for the Queen to appoint a Governor-General. The plan suggested that existing members of the Assembly would form the new government, foreign investments and the tenure of expatriates would be safeguarded, and Britain would be asked to delineate the border with the Colony.[15] This document arrived in London just before the House of Commons debate on Ghana's Independence, but the debate showed that in spite of the vigorous lobbying of Busia and the NLM supporters there was little parliamentary support for their cause. For Arden-Clarke, the Commons debate was the culmination of seven years unstinted striving in which he had fought battles with politicians and civil servants, with Ashanti and the NLM—indeed with anyone who threatened the success of the great and challenging venture of bringing the first British territory in Africa along an orderly progress

[15] From *Ashanti Pioneer* 29.11.56.

to independence. An Under Secretary introduced the Bill, emphasizing that it was an historic day. James Griffiths who had done so much to liberalize British policy towards Africa, suggested that it would be wrong at Independence to cut off Ghana from the Colonial Development and Welfare Acts, because its economy—like many other colonies—had been shaped and patterned not by Ghana's needs but by British interests.[16] Winding up, Lennox-Boyd stated 'I am myself a believer in this great experiment. It is an experiment but it will be helped if we enter into it without shutting our eyes, but in high hopes that this great and romantic conception will justify the faith which so many people have put into bringing this about.'[17]

After the debate he replied to the NLM plan, 'Her Majesty's Government do not consider that partition of the Gold Coast is in the interests of the Gold Coast as a whole or of any of its component parts and cannot abandon their established policy which is directed towards the grant of Independence to the Gold Coast, as a whole. Her Majesty's Government are now proceeding with the preparation of the necessary constitutional instruments having regard to all the circumstances of the Gold Coast and the efforts that were made to reach agreement locally. The grant of independence to the Gold Coast is an act of good will which Her Majesty's Government trust will be received by the people of the Gold Coast in a spirit of responsibility which will command the respect of the world.'[18]

Although lacking support in Parliament the NLM through a flurry of letters to the Press, gained a little backing—notably from the *Daily Telegraph*. Their efforts both in London and in the Gold Coast continued through December, though by then the Northern Territories appeared to draw back from the more extreme measures proposed in Ashanti.

Arden-Clarke's firm opposition to the idea of a visit by Lennox-Boyd was gradually eroded. Just after Christmas the Asanteman Council renewed the invitation and Lennox-Boyd made it plain that he was prepared to make the visit. A key question facing the administration was how far Ashanti was, in practice, ready or prepared to secede. Arden-Clarke, already too familiar with the wilder outpourings of the *Ashanti Pioneer*, thought the threat was largely bluff, but Russell, the Chief Regional Officer in Ashanti, had given dire warnings about the security situation, though he was later to say that there was little evidence that the NLM had got beyond the planning stage. It appears that by the New Year both the Asantehene and Busia had drawn back from any decisive

---

[16] Hansard 11.12.57.
[17] Ibid.
[16] Quoted Rathbone Thesis p. 362.

move towards secession, while Arden-Clarke and Nkrumah began to see that the visit could serve a useful purpose, and had in fact become inevitable. After final discussions between them, Nkrumah issued a most cordial invitation to Lennox-Boyd to come to Accra, emphasizing that he wanted to help the Secretary of State finalize the detail of the White Paper on Ghana's Independence and that he wanted the new constitution to be launched in an atmosphere of the greatest goodwill. In another letter to *The Times*, Busia had pledged the fullest co-operation, and the NLM now publicly supported this.

Lennox-Boyd, whose trip was delayed by the resignation of Anthony Eden, arrived in Accra on 24 January 1957. Met by Arden-Clarke, the Government leaders and the Opposition, he announced that he had come to help iron out the difficulties, and hoped he would have their co-operation. On 26 he went to Kumasi where he was met by the Asantehene and A. C. Russell who had just received the CMG in the New Year's Honours. Ashanti gave a tumultuous welcome to Lennox-Boyd—partly because, significantly, he was not accompanied by Arden-Clarke. NLM spokesmen made the most of this situation. They started by claiming that since the Governor did not accompany the Secretary of State, that in itself was a great moral victory for the NLM. The purpose of Lennox-Boyd's visit was to make an impartial assessment and the fact that he came to Kumasi alone, proved that the Governor was no longer impartial.

> Why should Sir Charles be away when the Secretary of State with his multifarious duties has time to come in spite of Sir Charles? . . . At this critical moment in Ashanti history let it be noted that Sir Charles chose to stay away at Christiansborg Castle and left the Secretary of State to come to Ashanti alone.[19]

After visiting Tamale, Lennox-Boyd returned to Accra and in a final message stated that he had found a great deal of understandable anxiety among the Chiefs over their important office being lost sight of in the Ghana constitution. He was himself a strong believer in tradition, and Chiefs would have a big part to play for many years to come, and the Order in Council would protect the Chiefs' position. He had found an underlying unity more important than the matters which were dividing people and he appealed to both sides to move a little closer to each other, because the United Kingdom government had no intention whatsoever of changing the date of independence. Paying tribute to Arden-Clarke, he said that the Colonial Office was deeply indebted to Sir Charles for having done a brilliant job in the most difficult circumstances. Lennox-Boyd also deserves credit for he achieved the remarkable success of bringing together Nkrumah and Busia to discuss the proposed White

[19] *Ashanti Pioneer* 29.1.1957.

Paper—no mean achievement in the rancourous atmosphere of the time.

For Arden-Clarke, the Lennox-Boyd visit coincided with the long awaited announcement that the Duchess of Kent would represent the Queen at Independence, followed by the immediate visit of her Private Secretary to discuss details of the celebrations. It also had to fit in with his other commitments. One shrewdly timed event was a demonstration by the Army for all Members of the Assembly. It showed, with live ammunition, the fire power of an infantry company supported by a mortar platoon and a battery of 25 pounder guns. Arden-Clarke attended this and, in spite of the fierce political tensions at the time, noticed quite a lot of light hearted leg pulling and teasing of the Ashanti members who had threatened to go to war to gain their end. On another day he took Lady Patricia Lennox-Boyd to the formal opening of the Volta Bridge. This bridge was symbolic of the Union of Trans Volta Togoland and the independent Ghana, and an impressive short ceremony had been arranged. The Governor declared the bridge open, then got into the Rolls Royce with Lady Patricia, Nkrumah and Caseley-Hayford and drove slowly across the bridge to greet the Togoland Chiefs at the other end. Then, together, the party walked back to the middle of the bridge to greet the Gold Coast Chiefs.

When the last of Lennox-Boyd's delegation left on 1 February, Arden-Clarke wrote a detailed description of the previous day's negotiations which throws a fascinating light on both the personalities and the issues involved:

This week has been even madder than last. The Lennox-Boyd's got back here from Tamale on Monday (28th). They left again on Wednesday 30th but Eastwood[20] stayed on and we have been just as busy but I think more usefully and fruitfully engaged than when Lennox-Boyd was here. Eastwood left this morning (Friday 1st). I have been in the office every morning by 7.30 a.m. and have not managed to get to bed before 11.30 p.m. this week. Meals were merely an interlude in a series of engagements and even after dinner we were hammering away trying to find a compromise solution in which both sides would acquiesce to the many points of difference which divide them. The most hopeful sign is that both Nkrumah and Busia have been very reasonable and if it were left to the two of them there would be no difficulty in finding a workable solution. Unfortunately, neither of them is a strong man and they have unruly followers whom they cannot properly control. Each dog is all right but each has a tail that is likely to wag the dog.

Eastwood summed up the position by saying that while the Secretary of State had done his job splendidly, he felt it could have

[20] Mr C. G. Eastwood CMG.

been done by anyone else as he was pushing at a door already ajar. This is true up to a point—certainly it was no good asking him to come here to push against a door that was locked and triple barred and that was why I would not let him come before. But he was the ideal man for the job by virtue of his position, his strong personality and his charm. In addition he has been able to make some real contributions of his own towards the solution of one or two of our problems. The result of our efforts, which are not yet completed, will I think produce a weird and wonderful constitution which both sides will reluctantly agree to work and that is as much as anyone can expect at the present time. It has to deal with the political realities of the moment which are themselves pretty weird and wonderful. The shortest part of the constitution will deal with the fundamentals of parliamentary democracy and by far the longest part will be devoted to such details as how to change the boundaries of a region and how to create new ones, or how to arrange for the devolution of authority to Regional Assemblies which are not yet set up. Both sides I expect will say that the constitution is 'bogus and fradulent' but we have had quite a bit of experience in working such constitutions and I am hopeful that this will be yet another that will work and once it is working they will not find it too easy to change it.

The greater part of our time has been spent in talking with Nkrumah or with Busia or with the Cabinet as a whole, separately or together, but there have been other things to do. Lennox-Boyd and I attended the Assembly for half an hour to watch it working—not very interesting. He recorded a broadcast much of which was taken from an excellent draft by Peter Canham. He also gave a press conference which I attended, where I watched him give an outstanding exhibition of how to give the minimum of information with the maximum of words. His arrival had been informal but his departure was a formal affair with all the Ministers and other local VIPs drawn up to bid him farewell and a guard of honour. He confessed to me when he drove to the airport that inspecting guards of honour filled him with terror and one could see how nervous he was as he walked along the ranks—the only time during the whole course of his visit that I have seen him giving any sign that he is not completely master of himself and of the situation. I told him the secret was not to stop and try to talk but that, of course, is beyond the capacity of any politician.[21]

Lennox-Boyd had certainly enabled the NLM to retreat from their untenable position without any noticeable loss of face, but also made it clear to Nkrumah and the CPP that the White Paper must contain written guarantees of Regional Assemblies. The White Paper, published on 8 February 1957 and debated in the Commons, satisfied most of the demands of the NLM. It included establishment of a House of Chiefs to

[21] Letter to Lady Arden-Clarke 1.2.57.

which all disputes over tribal matters or the Chiefs' Stools would be referred, and it provided that Regional Assemblies would be established within three months of independence.[22] James Griffiths, for the Labour Opposition, welcomed the White Paper and paid tribute to Arden-Clarke for his outstanding work. Busia, Gbedemah and William Ofori Attah witnessed the debate from the Visitors' Gallery, and, soon afterwards the Asantehene gave the lead towards reconciliation by appealing to all parties to forgive and forget, and to work together for a better future. In the Assembly, Nkrumah announced that he and the Opposition were at one over the White Paper and he looked forward to a period of growing mutual confidence and co-operation. After the White Paper was published there remained only a few hectic weeks before the date of Independence—6 March 1957. In spite of the prominence and publicity, both in the Gold Coast and throughout the world, given to the political crisis in Ashanti, the real work of preparing the colony for independence had been proceeding virtually unchecked from 1951 when the great partnership between Arden-Clarke and Nkrumah began. Africans had been trained to fill all the necessary posts, and expatriates were given reasonable terms to encourage them to stay on after independence. British, European and American firms were actively operating throughout the country and showed little anxiety about their future. Above all, the economy had been wisely handled and the revenue from the buoyant cocoa market of the 1950s had been devoted to sane and practical schemes, which provided the infrastructure of a modern state, while at the same time leaving a huge credit balance to the new government. The civil service, the direct concern of Arden-Clarke, was manned by competent and dedicated men and women who were to serve their country loyally and steadfastly.

The world had witnessed the trauma of independence in the Indian sub-continent and now, ten years later, Ghana was to lead the way— poised to prove to a world, which generally gave positive support to its hopes and aspirations, that a former African colony could run its own affairs and take its place in the British Commonwealth of Nations as a stable and democratic country. The leaders of the Independence movements in every part of Africa—British, French, Belgian, Portuguese—took heart from Ghana's achievement and realized its direct significance for themselves. In the next ten years, following Ghana's lead, they were to achieve dramatic changes to the map of Africa that few anticipated in 1957.

Arden-Clarke had always had a deep sense of personal loyalty to the Sovereign, and this was paramount to his personal involvement in the

22 Hansard 7.2.1957.

arrangements for the celebration of Independence and for the visit of the Duchess of Kent. After the preliminary welcomes, receptions, and a State Banquet, the climax came on Wednesday 6 March with the State Opening of Parliament. It was carried out with all the pomp and panoply associated with Westminster but transposed to the more exuberant and colourful milieu of Accra. Early in the morning of 6 March, the Governor-General's swearing-in took place at Christiansborg Castle before the Chief Justice and a distinguished gathering of the country's leaders. The swearing-in was customarily a brief formality, but Arden-Clarke used the occasion to give it a personal touch which set the whole occasion in perspective:

I trust you will not consider it unconstitutional or inappropriate that my first words in the high office which I have been so greatly privileged to assume will be wholly of a personal nature.

It is now 37 years since I first joined the British Colonial Service— Her Majesty's Overseas Civil Service as it is now called. It is a very great Service to which I have always been deeply proud to belong. It was to West Africa that I was first appointed and it will be from West Africa that I shall shortly retire. Between my first service in Northern Nigeria and my last service in this country, I have had the privilege of serving the Queen in three other territories. The scene of my Colonial activities has thus changed from time to time over the past 37 years but the policy which it has been my privilege to try and execute has remained constant throughout.

The Colonial policy of Her Majesty's Government in the United Kingdom, so far as the man serving in the colonies is concerned, has not only been constant through the years: it has been quite simple and straightforward. These were the instructions I received when I arrived in Northern Nigeria as a young Administrative Officer:

'Your job is to teach the people committed to your care to stand on their own feet and to run their own show within the rule of law'. British colonial policy, as I have known it in the field for nearly 40 years, has been and still is to further by all available means the political, social and economic advancement of the dependent territories of the British connexion so that they may be brought, as quickly as possible, to the stage where they can take their place in the world as fully self-governing nations.

I will not pretend that when I first joined the Colonial Service the achievement of this aim of British policy seemed likely to be realized during my term of service, or even during my lifetime, but the world, particularly the colonial world, has moved far and fast since the first world war. Of the many forces that have been at work in this world, nationalism has been one of the most potent, though not always as happy in its effect on the contemporary scene as the outcome which we witness today. Here, thanks to the statesmanship of the political leaders, particularly the Prime Minister, and the good sense and good-will of the Chiefs and people, nationalism and colonialism have worked in partnership, a genuine partnership, animated by forbearance and mutual understanding, towards a common objective. Of her own free will, this country has chosen to remain within the British Commonwealth of Nations, and she has been welcomed as a member by all the other members. In so far as the birth of Ghana today is the natural outcome of British colonialism, I am proud to be a British Colonialist.

It is therefore with strong faith in the aims and ideals of the British Commonwealth of Nations and in the great qualities of the people of this country, the latest member of the Commonwealth family, that I, with all humility, assume my high office of Governor-General of Ghana.

In the days after all the excitement and euphoria of independence were over, and when the new state of Ghana had been royally launched, Arden-Clarke, as the new Governor-General, representing the Crown, and enjoying only the powers that the Crown had in England, felt rather deflated and forlorn. He commented 'At one stroke I have lost my two dearest enemies—Whitehall and my Ministers'. Referring to the visit of the Duchess of Kent he added 'The visit which we all looked forward to with some apprehension and expected to be an ordeal, turned out in fact to be a most friendly affair and will always be one of our pleasantest memories'. Having handed over power he was understandably eager to leave. He spent a few more weeks at the Castle and visited many parts of Ghana to attend farewell Durbars. He was sincerely touched by the tributes he received and by the generoisty of the people in their gifts to him. Finally on 11 May 1957 Nkrumah presided at a farewell banquet at the Ambassador Hotel when Sir Charles was presented with a gold coffee service. Along with the necessary political references to the CPP footsloggers of the national independence movement, and to the necessity of removing the last vestiges of colonialism and imperialism, Nkrumah paid handsome tributes to both Sir Charles and to Lady Arden-Clarke. In his reply Sir Charles went out of his way to compliment the members, both British and Ghanaian, of the Public Service, who had also played a key role in the march to Independence, and he expressed his sincere gratitude to the people of Ghana for making the past eight adventurous years the most stimulating and the most satisfying of his career.

His tragically short retirement—he died of cancer in 1962—was almost as active as when he had held office. In 1958 he was Chairman of a Commonwealth Commission on the West Indian Federation, and the following year, with Lady Arden-Clarke, he visited Canada on behalf of the Royal Commonwealth Society. When the Monckton Commission was set up in 1960 he was appointed as one of its most senior members. This involved him in a gruelling and demanding visit to the Central African Federation between February and May 1960, and with further meetings in London prior to the publication of the Monckton Report. He was in great demand as a lecturer for Colonial Office Courses at Oxford and for the Royal Commonwealth Society, and he carried out an energetic lecture tour to the United States, in the spring of 1961.

When Creech-Jones sent Arden-Clarke to the Gold Coast in 1949 he gave him a brief to take a tough and uncompromising line against what was considered a dangerous band of left wing rabble rousers. He had come directly from the Far East where communist insurgents were already penetrating Malaya and the islands, and he shared the concern of the Colonial Office that West Africa did not become another casualty of the Cold War. Soon after his arrival and still dependent on the defective security reports of his predecessor, he made his unguarded remark to the family about 'our local Hitler and his putsch'. At about the same time, talking to the veteran Colonel Bean, he said 'Can't you form a moderate party to keept these buggers out?' However poorly he had been briefed, there is little doubt that he expected to have to clamp down severely on the internal security situation and then to co-operate with Danquah and the more foreward looking and articulate Chiefs in leading the country slowly towards independence. He hardly expected this to happen in his lifetime, let alone while he held office.

The parameters of the situation in which he had to work had been laid down, before he arrived, in the Coussey Report, which set up the constitution which he and Nkrumah had to operate after the 1951 election. Obviously a fundamental change of attitude took place between 1949 and 1951, which was to change the face of Ghana and to have far reaching effects on the whole of Africa. Because he rapidly established an efficient security and information service, Arden-Clarke was one of the first to realize that the Burns and Coussey constitutions had totally changed the political situation, and that as Governor he now had a completely different role to play. He would be able to trim the ship, to guide and advise, and to use his strong personality and influence, but there was no way in the post-1951 political situation that he could arrest a process which others had begun. Many of the Europeans in Accra learned this lesson more slowly and initially were shrill in their criticism of him as one of the weakest governors there had been. His own trans- formation and that of his staff came in the two years of preparation for the 1951 election, when it rapidly emerged that the United Gold Coast Convention—the party of lawyers, merchants and chiefs—had totally failed to adapt to the modern democratic political situation which Coussey had created. They never adapted to the hurly-burly of the hustings and this failure virtually handed over power to the CPP, which was brilliantly led by Gbedemah, while Nkrumah was in prison. More than anyone else, Gbedemah appreciated the changed situation and organized an effective modern political party. Well before the election, the administration realized what had happened, and in many areas the preparations for the election were carried out jointly by the DCs and their staff working in co-operation with the CPP agents.

Arden-Clarke accepted this new situation readily and did not consider that it conflicted in any way with the policy he had tried to carry out since 1920, or with British policy, as it had emerged after the Durham Report of 1838: that we would not remain in a colony by force of arms if the people of the colony wished us to leave. He put this forcefully when addressing a gathering of Peers who suggested he should slow down or halt the move towards independence. 'Where is the Army, where is the Navy, where are the other forces with which we could hold the colony for a single day if the people did not wish us to be there?' To him the decision was clear-cut and obvious, but both in Britain and in the Gold Coast he had severe critics. Many of his older and more senior staff, who distrusted and disliked the type of man that the CPP threw up, felt that Arden-Clarke was letting down the chiefs and dishonouring pledges that Britain had made in good faith. Later, when this feeling was highlighted in the NLM movement, some of his field staff in Ashanti and the North were so offended by his policy that they came close to disloyalty. The NLM used their political contacts in Britain, and for a time made Arden-Clarke's policy into a political controversy at Westminster, but in the end they produced no viable alternative and could only dispute minor details of procedure. At the same time some of his fellow West African governors felt he was moving at too fast a pace and realized that what happened in Ghana would very quickly effect them.

Arden-Clarke obviously considered the international implications of his policy, but he tended not to see it in terms either of the Cold War and Russian infiltration, or of the struggle against colonialist exploitation. Instead he realized that the world was generally sympathetic to the exciting and challenging policy he was following, and he was determined, in spite of all obstacles, to show that with meticulous care and preparation, an African colony was able to take its place as a well ordered and democratic member of the British Commonwealth. In achieving this and handing over an independent Ghana in 1957 he did, as Malcolm MacDonald said, obtain his own niche in history, but his success also had a fundamental effect on the whole history of Africa after 1957. He had spent eight tempestuous years preparing Ghana for independence, and he felt only grief and shock when France and Belgium in 1960 abdicated their colonial responsibilities with indecent haste.

To achieve the orderly transfer of power Arden-Clarke would have taken on any opponent—the NLM, his own Ministers, his critics at home, or the Colonial Office. Throughout his service he was notorious for the belief that he, as the man on the spot, knew best, and his relations with the Colonial Office were not easy. He several times got his way by threatening resignation, and his instruction to his staff that correspondence with the Colonial Office was best conducted in the past tense was well known. Thus he did not endear himself to the Colonial Office who considered him to be a difficult customer, usually determined to get his own way. It is not known whether this affected his chances of gaining a peerage when he retired as Governor General, but, more than 20 years after his retirement, it was a matter that many Ghanaians spoke about vehemently. They felt that his outstanding contribution to Ghana, to Africa, and to the Commonwealth certainly merited such an honour.

While he had his critics in different places and at different times, it is from Ghana that he must be judged. Here, people who worked with him—or against him—revere his memory as a man of massive strength and integrity; a man of enormous tact and ability who, had he made a false step, could easily have wrecked the whole country—yet he never faltered. It is remembered that there were many occasions when he could have suspended the constitution and passed the buck to London—but he held firm. His staff remember him as a brilliant chairman of committee who compared favourably even with Mountbatten. He had a powerfully deep and resonant voice which he used effectively on all occasions, though, to the end, he hated the casual request 'to say a few words'. A cheerful man he liked relaxed and cheerful people round him. Komla Gbedemah remembers their first meeting after the desperate days of 1951 and the CPP election victory. From the moment when he cheerfully shook hands with them they trusted him and he gave an unwavering support to the aim of an orderly transfer of power to a democratic government. Gbedemah believes, as do most Ghanaians, that Arden-Clarke's toughness and integrity played a decisive role in that achievement.

Source Material

My main source has been the Arden-Clarke papers which were put at my disposal by Lady Arden-Clarke. They contain letters and documents spanning the years from 1918 when Sir Charles served in Germany and Russia, to the 1960s when he served on the Monckton Commission. From the end of 1920, when he arrived in Nigeria, he wrote regularly to his mother, and she meticulously kept every letter. These early letters give a fresh and vivid account of the life of a young District Officer. Later the papers include, as well as personal and family letters, voluminous documents and despatches he acquired as Resident Commissioner in Bechuanaland and Basutoland, and as Governor of Sarawak and Ghana.

In addition to these valuable papers I have had the privilege of interviewing or questioning many distinguished people both in Britain and Ghana, who knew Arden-Clarke, and who have been most helpful with their comments and advice, either to me direct or through Lady Arden-Clarke: Sir Edwin Arrowsmith, Professor Dennis Austin, Rev John Bardsley, Lord Boyd, Mr Peter Canham, Mr J. H. D. Dickson, Dr Cyril Griffith (USA), Sir Gordon Hadow, Lord Hemingford, Professor K. Ingham, Dr A. H. M. Kirk-Greene, Rt Hon Malcolm MacDonald, Miss Paddy Maguire, Mr Philip Mason, Mr T. A. Mead, Mr E. Norton-Jones, Professor Roland Oliver, Rev A. C. Russell, Mr W. E. F. Ward. Mr L. Frewer and the Rhodes House Library staff, Mr R. J. Townsend and staff of the Institute of Commonwealth Studies Oxford. In Ghana—Mr J. Aggrey-Orleans, George and Dorothy Amuah, Mr R. Baffuor, Neil and Margaret Bax, Colonel L. Bean, Mr Tom Boateng, Mr Kojo Botsio, Mr Daniel Chapman-Hyaho, Mr Robert Gardiner, Mr Komla Gbedemah, Mr K. Lamptey, Mr James Moxon, Dr Nkrumah (Jr), Jimmy and Rachel Phillips, Mr Sprigge, Mr Richard Taylor; the Staff of the State Archives Accra and the Balme Library at Legon.

Select Bibliography

ACHEBE, Chinua, 1958, *Things Fall Apart*. Heinemann

AGBODEKA, F., 1972, *Ghana in the Twentieth Century*. Ghana University Press

APTER, D., 1955, *The Gold Coast in Transition*, Princeton

ARMAH, K., 1965, *Africa's Golden Road*, Heinemann

——, 1974, *Nkrumah's Legacy*. Rex Collings

AUSTIN, Dennis, 1970, *Politics in Ghana*. O.U.P.

BENNION, F., 1962, *Constitutional Law of Ghana*. London

BENSON, M., 1960, *Tshekedi Khama*. Faber

BOAHEN, A., 1975, *Ghana: Evolution and Change*. Longman

BOATENG E. A., 1973, *Independence and Nation Building in Africa*. Ghana Publishing Co.

BOURRET, F. M., 1960, *Ghana*. OUP

BROOKS, S., 1970, *Queen of the Headhunters*. London

BING, G., 1968, *Reap the Whirlwind*. London

DAVIDSON, B., 1973, *Black Star*. Allen Lane

DIE ANANG, M. 1970, *Administration of Ghana's Foreign Relations*. Athlone Press

FITCH and OPPENHEIMER, 1966, *Ghana, End of an Illusion*. M.R. Press

GUTTERIDGE, W. F., 1970, *The Military in African Politics*. Methuen

HAILEY, Lord, 1973, *African Survey*. Allen Lane

HALL, D. G. E., 1955, *History of South East Asia*. Macmillan

JAMES, C. L. R., 1977, *Nkrumah and the Ghana Revolution*. Allison and Busby

JONES, Trevor, 1976, *Ghana's First Republic*. Methuen

KRASSOWSKI, A., 1970, *Development and the Debt Trap.* Croom Helm

LEE, J. M., 1969, *African Armies and Civil Order.* Chatto and Windus

LENIN, 1917, *Imperialism*, Progress Publishers

MACDONALD, M., 1956, *Borneo People.* Cape

METCALFE, G. E., 1964, *Great Britain and Ghana.* University of Ghana Press

NKRUMAH, K., 1957, *Autobiography.* Nelson
——, 1967, *Axioms.* Nelson
——, 1974, *Consciencism.* Panaf
——, 1975, *Some essential features of Nkrumaism.* Panaf

OCRAN, A. K., 1968, *A Myth is Broken.* Longman

OFOSU-APPIAH, 1974, *The Life and Times of J. B. Danquah.* Waterville

OLIVER and FAGE, 1962, *A Short History of Africa.* Penguin

OMARI, T. P., 1970, *Kwame Nkrumah.* Hurst

PADMORE, G., 1953, *The Gold Coast Revolution.* London

PERHAM, M., 1956, *Lugard.* Collins
——, 1966. *African Outline.* OUP

PINKNEY, R., 1972, *Ghana Under Military Rule.* Methuen

ROONEY, D. D., 1968. *The Story of the Commonwealth.* Pergamon
—— and HALLADAY, 1965, *The Building of Modern Africa.* Harrap

RUNCIMAN, Sir Steven, 1960, *The White Rajahs.* London

SYMONDS, R., 1966, *The British and their Successors.* Faber

WARD, W. E. F., 1945, *Short History of the Gold Coast.* Longman

WRAITH, R. E., 1967, *Guggisberg.* OUP

Manuscripts

The following were particularly valuable:

The Bardsley Diaries—Rhodes House Manuscripts.

'The Transfer of Power in Ghana 1945–57'. Ph.D. Thesis by Dr Richard Rathbone. London University, 1968.

Hugh Thomas Diaries, Rhodes House Manuscripts.

Index